Microsoft

Introducing Windows Server 2012 R2

Mitch Tulloch
with the Windows Server Team

PUBLISHED BY
Microsoft Press
A Division of Microsoft Corporation
One Microsoft Way
Redmond, Washington 98052-6399

Library of Congress Control Number: 2013945007
ISBN: 978-0-7356-8278-8

Microsoft Press books are available through booksellers and distributors worldwide. If you need support related to this book, email Microsoft Press Book Support at mspinput@microsoft.com. Please tell us what you think of this book at *http://www.microsoft.com/learning/booksurvey.*

Microsoft and the trademarks listed at *http://www.microsoft.com/about/legal/en/us/IntellectualProperty/ Trademarks/EN-US.aspx* are trademarks of the Microsoft group of companies. All other marks are property of their respective owners.

The example companies, organizations, products, domain names, email addresses, logos, people, places, and events depicted herein are fictitious. No association with any real company, organization, product, domain name, email address, logo, person, place, or event is intended or should be inferred.

This book expresses the author's views and opinions. The information contained in this book is provided without any express, statutory, or implied warranties. Neither the authors, Microsoft Corporation, nor its resellers, or distributors will be held liable for any damages caused or alleged to be caused either directly or indirectly by this book.

Acquisitions Editor: Anne Hamilton
Developmental Editor: Karen Szall
Project Editors: Valerie Woolley and Carol Dillingham
Editorial Production: Christian Holdener, S4Carlisle Publishing Services
Copyeditor: Andrew Jones
Indexer: Jean Skipp

Contents

What do you think of this book? We want to hear from you!

Microsoft is interested in hearing your feedback so we can continually improve our
books and learning resources for you. To participate in a brief online survey, please visit:

microsoft.com/learning/booksurvey

What do you think of this book? We want to hear from you!

Microsoft is interested in hearing your feedback so we can continually improve our
books and learning resources for you. To participate in a brief online survey, please visit:

microsoft.com/learning/booksurvey

Introduction

This book is intended to provide you with an overview of the new features and enhancements introduced in Windows Server 2012 R2. The intended audience for this book is IT pros who deploy, manage, and maintain Windows Server workloads in data center, private cloud, and hosting provider environments.

We assume that you are at least somewhat familiar with the features and capabilities of the previous platform Windows Server 2012. If you are not familiar with all the new features and enhancements Microsoft introduced previously in Windows Server 2012, we recommend that you first read *Introducing Windows Server 2012 RTM Edition* (Microsoft Press, 2012). This e-book is available as a free download from Microsoft in three formats:

- PDF from *http://aka.ms/682788pdf*
- EPUB from *http://aka.ms/682788epub*
- MOBI from *http://aka.ms/682788mobi*

A key feature of this book is the technical sidebars that have been contributed by Microsoft insiders. These sidebars were written by experts who have been closely involved in the Windows Server 2012 R2 development process and include Program Managers, Support Escalation Engineers, Technical Consultants, Data Center Specialists, and others who work at Microsoft in various capacities.

Acknowledgments

Three groups of people have helped make this book possible, and as the author I'd like to thank them all here. First, the following experts at Microsoft have contributed sidebars that explain and demonstrate different aspects of Windows Server 2012 R2:

- Deepak Srivastava
- Erez Benari
- Gene Chellis
- Jason M. Anderson
- Jeff Butte
- John Marlin
- Justin Turner
- Mark Gehazi
- Nir Ben Zvi

Second, the following Microsoft insiders have peer reviewed various portions of this book to help us ensure our content is as accurate as possible:

- Aanand Ramachandran
- Adam Carter
- Ben Armstrong
- Bryan Matthew
- CJ Williams
- Clinton Ho
- Deepak Srivastava
- Elden Christensen
- Erez Benari
- Gabriel Silva
- Guang Hu
- Jason Gerund
- Jeff Woolsey
- John Savill
- Jose Barreto
- Matthew John
- Raghavendran Gururajan
- Roiy Zysman
- Shivam Garg
- Symon Perriman
- Vijay Tandra Sistla
- Vijay Tewari
- Yang Cao Sun
- Yuheng Cai sun

Finally, I'd also like to thank Valerie Woolley, Content Project Manager at Microsoft Press; Christian Holdener at S4Carlisle Publishing Services; and copyeditor Andrew Jones.

Errata & book support

We've made every effort to ensure the accuracy of this content and its companion content. Any errors that have been reported since this content was published are listed on our Microsoft Press site:

http://aka.ms/introwinsrv2012R2/errata

If you find an error that is not already listed, you can report it to us through the same page.

If you need additional support, email Microsoft Press Book Support at *mspinput@microsoft.com*.

Please note that product support for Microsoft software is not offered through the addresses above.

We want to hear from you

At Microsoft Press, your satisfaction is our top priority, and your feedback our most valuable asset. Please tell us what you think of this book at:

http://aka.ms/tellpress

The survey is short, and we read every one of your comments and ideas. Thanks in advance for your input!

Stay in touch

Let's keep the conversation going! We're on Twitter: *http://twitter.com/MicrosoftPress*.

CHAPTER 1

Cloud OS

This chapter introduces Windows Server 2012 R2 which is at the heart of Microsoft's revolutionary new Cloud OS platform. The chapter describes five key areas Microsoft focused on when developing Windows Server 2012 R2 and sets the stage for the discussion of the new features and enhancements in Windows Server 2012 R2 that follow in the remaining chapters of this book.

The big picture

Information Technology (IT) is in the midst of a time of rapid change. More and more businesses are seeing cloud computing as a viable option for hosting their applications, services, and data. Some businesses have already implemented private clouds within their own data centers or have begun utilizing cloud services offered by hosting providers. Other businesses are in the process of evaluating the possible benefits they can reap from cloud availability, scalability, mobility, and agility. And for various reasons, some businesses are still skeptical of whether cloud computing is right for them.

But clearly, Microsoft isn't skeptical. In fact, Microsoft is fully committed to the cloud as the computing paradigm of the future. Nowhere is this more obvious than in this latest release of the Windows Server platform. Microsoft firmly believes that cloud computing isn't a trend but rather a golden opportunity for businesses. Why is that?

Because businesses need to become agile in order to survive in today's competitive landscape. And to have an agile business, you need to build your applications and services on a highly available and elastic development platform. Businesses need a uniform model for application lifecycle management with common frameworks across their physical infrastructure, virtual infrastructure, and the cloud. They need a highly scalable, secure identity solution they can use for managing their computing, networking, and storage assets, both on-premises and in the cloud. They need to be able to process, store, and transfer huge amounts of data and perform analytics quickly and easily. And businesses need to be able to do all this in a cost-effective manner.

In other words, what they need is a cloud-optimized business. And that's what Microsoft intends to deliver with their current product release cycle. Because for the first time in their history, Microsoft has synchronized the development cycles of three major platforms:

- **Windows Server**   A proven, enterprise-class platform that forms the foundation for building cloud solutions.

- **System Center**   An integrated platform that provides a common management experience across private, hosted, and public clouds.

- **Windows Azure**   An open and flexible cloud platform for building, deploying, and managing applications and workloads hosted on a global network of Microsoft-managed data centers.

Together, these three platforms comprise Microsoft's vision for a Cloud OS, as shown in Figure 1-1. This book only focuses on one portion of this Cloud OS, namely, Windows Server 2012 R2. It's a key portion, however, because it forms the foundation for businesses to be able to run their applications in private clouds, with service providers, or in the Windows Azure public cloud.

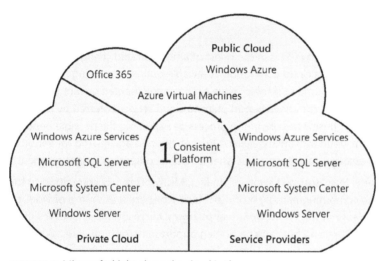

FIGURE 1-1 Microsoft thinks about the cloud in three parts.

Journey to the Cloud OS

To better understand Microsoft's vision for a Cloud OS, start by thinking about how IT has traditionally managed server workloads. In the early days of Windows Server, you deployed and managed lots of physical servers on-premises. Each server had to be individually managed, and this meant performing tasks like configuring storage for them, configuring networking, tuning performance, and so on. Lots of servers meant lots of tasks to perform, and although scripting could automate many of these tasks, such solutions were typically inflexible and difficult to maintain.

Then along came virtualization, and suddenly you saw that you could save money by retiring physical servers after migrating their workloads onto virtualization hosts. But the management paradigm stayed the same, for instead of managing lots of physical servers, you were now managing lots of virtual machines. But proliferation is proliferation whether it's in the physical or virtual realm, and managing thousands of individual virtual machines can be just as challenging as managing physical machines.

Then the concept of cloud computing arrived—with its promises of rapid elasticity, resource pooling, and on-demand self-service. Now, if a business wants to maintain control over its IT resources, it can implement a private cloud solution on-premises using Windows Server and System Center. If scalability is the issue, the business can opt for running its applications, services, or virtual machines in Windows Azure. And if reach and customization are important, the business can use the services of a cloud hosting service provider. Each of these approaches is equally valid, and it's up to the business to decide which to choose based on its needs and constraints.

From Microsoft's perspective, these three approaches (private cloud, service providers, and Windows Azure) are really one and comprise one consistent platform: the Cloud OS. Windows Server forms the foundation; System Center provides the management capability; and Windows Azure delivers the solutions. In other words, cloud is not just something that happens out there; it happens wherever and whenever you need it to optimize your business. That's what Microsoft means by cloud.

For example, do you need Active Directory? You can deploy it on-premises using Windows Server. But Active Directory is already waiting for you in Windows Azure. And with Windows Server 2012 R2 you can even virtualize domain controllers and host them in a service provider's cloud. The choice is yours.

Microsoft wants you to have the choice to implement the cloud computing model that best meets the needs of your business. And the Cloud OS—Windows Server, System Center, and Windows Azure—delivers that kind of choice to customers. Windows Server 2012 R2 is the foundation for all of this, and that's what this book is about.

Let's begin!

In the chapters that follow, we're going to examine what's new and enhanced in Windows Server 2012 R2. Because virtualization is at the heart of how cloud computing works, we're going to start by looking at Hyper-V first. Let's begin!

CHAPTER 2

Hyper-V

Hyper-V virtualization represents the foundation of Microsoft's vision for the cloud operating system. Storage and networking are the walls that help support your virtualization infrastructure. Then, on top of everything, comes management and automation. Together, these different functionalities enable a wide range of cloud solutions that can meet the needs of any business.

But the bottom line is that virtualization is at the core of everything in most IT shops nowadays. For example, when IT wants to deploy a new workload (such as a Microsoft SQL Server machine) the common way of doing this (and it's really a best practice) is to virtualize the workload first instead of deploying the workload on a physical server. As a second example, when IT wants to deploy a new desktop image, the common practice is to create the image in a Hyper-V virtual environment before deploying it onto physical desktop computers.

Windows Server 2012 R2 builds upon the improvements added earlier in Hyper-V on Windows Server 2012 and adds new features and functionality that can deliver greater gains in performance, availability, and agility. This chapter examines what's new in this latest version of Hyper-V, but first we'll briefly review what was previously introduced in Hyper-V on Windows Server 2012.

Previous enhancements to Hyper-V

A lot of powerful new features and capabilities were added to Hyper-V in the previous version of Windows Server, and space doesn't allow us to go into detail concerning each of them. As a quick summary, however, the following enhancements could be characterized as some of the more significant improvements in the platform:

- **Increased scalability and resiliency** Hyper-V hosts running Windows Server 2012 supported up to 320 logical processors and 4 terabytes (TB) of memory, and virtual machines running on these hosts could be configured with 64 virtual processors and 1 TB of memory.

- **New live migration options** Beginning with Windows Server 2012, you could perform a live migration in a nonclustered environment and could perform multiple live migrations simultaneously utilizing higher network bandwidths.

- **Storage migration**   Hyper-V in Windows Server 2012 allowed you to move the virtual hard disks used by a virtual machine to different physical storage while the virtual machine remained running.

- **Virtual machines on file shares**   Hyper-V in Windows Server 2012 supported using Server Message Block 3.0 (SMB 3.0) file shares as storage for virtual machines. This meant you could store your virtual machine files on a cost-efficient Scale-Out File Server running Windows Server 2012 instead of buying an expensive storage area network (SAN) for this purpose.

- **Extensible virtual switch**   Hyper-V on Windows Server 2012 included a new extensible virtual switch that provided an open framework to allow third parties to add new functionality such as packet monitoring, forwarding, and filtering into the virtual switch.

- **Windows PowerShell module**   Hyper-V in Windows Server 2012 included a Windows PowerShell module for Hyper-V that provided more than 160 cmdlets for automating Hyper-V management tasks.

- **VHDX format**   Hyper-V in Windows Server 2012 included a new virtual hard disk format called VHDX that supported up to 64 TB of storage. The VHDX format also provided built-in protection from corruption stemming from power failures and resisted performance degradation when using some large-sector physical disks.

- **Reclaiming snapshot storage**   With Hyper-V in Windows Server 2012, when a virtual machine snapshot was deleted, the storage space that the snapshot consumed before being deleted was made available while the virtual machine was running. This meant that you no longer needed to shut down, turn off, or put the virtual machine into a saved state to recover the storage space. And even more importantly for production environments, differencing disks are now merged with the parent while the virtual machine is running.

- **Improved virtual machine import**   The virtual machine import process in Hyper-V in Windows Server 2012 improved to help resolve configuration problems that might otherwise prevent a virtual machine from being imported. In addition, you could import a virtual machine by copying its files manually instead of having to export the virtual machine first.

- **Dynamic Memory improvements**   Dynamic Memory was improved in Hyper-V in Windows Server 2012 to include support for configuring minimum memory. In addition, Smart Paging, a new memory management mechanism, was introduced to provide a reliable restart experience for virtual machines configured with less minimum memory than startup memory.

- **Single-root I/O virtualization (SR-IOV)**   Hyper-V in Windows Server 2012 allowed you to assign network adapters that supported SR-IOV directly to virtual machines running on the host. SR-IOV maximized network throughput while minimizing network latency and CPU overhead needed for processing network traffic.

- **Virtual Fibre Channel**   Hyper-V in Windows Server 2012 allowed you to connect directly to Fibre Channel storage from within the guest operating system that runs in a virtual machine. This allowed you to virtualize workloads and applications that require direct access to Fibre Channel–based storage. It also made guest clustering (clustering directly within the guest operating system) possible when using Fibre Channel–based storage.

- **Hyper-V Replica**   Hyper-V in Windows Server 2012 allowed you to replicate virtual machines between storage systems, clusters, and data centers in two sites to provide business continuity and disaster recovery.

Now that we've reviewed the Hyper-V improvements introduced previously in Windows Server 2012, let's move on and examine some of the new capabilities added to Hyper-V in Windows Server 2012 R2.

Generation 2 virtual machines

One of the key ways that Windows Server 2012 R2 advances the Hyper-V virtualization platform is in its support for a new generation of virtual machines. Microsoft refers to these as "Generation 2" virtual machines, and they have the key following characteristics:

- **UEFI-based**   Beginning with Windows 8 and Windows Server 2012, Microsoft Windows now supports the Secure Boot feature of the Unified Extensible Firmware Interface (UEFI). This means that UEFI is now part of the Windows 8 and Windows Server 2012 boot architecture, and it replaces the Basic Input/Output System (BIOS) firmware interface used by previous versions of Windows for initiating the boot process. Generation 2 virtual machines comply with the UEFI Secure Boot standard and enable virtual machines to use Secure Boot.

- **Legacy free**   In previous versions of Hyper-V, virtual machines used a standard set of emulated hardware devices to ensure compatibility running all versions of Windows. These emulated devices include an AMI BIOS, Intel 440BX chipset motherboard, S3 Trio graphics display adapter, Intel/DEC 21140 network adapter, and so on. With Generation 2 virtual machines, many of these emulated devices have now been removed and replaced with synthetic drivers and software-based devices as summarized in Table 2-1.

- **SCSI boot**   Virtual machines in previous versions of Hyper-V needed to boot from integrated development environment (IDE) disks (virtual disks attached to the virtual machine using the IDE controller). Beginning with Windows Server 2012 R2, however, Generation 2 virtual machines can now boot directly from SCSI disks (virtual disks attached to the virtual machine using the SCSI controller). In fact, Generation 2 virtual machines don't even have an IDE controller! Generation 2 virtual machines can also boot from a SCSI virtual DVD.

- **Faster deployment**   Network-based installation of a guest operating system onto a Generation 2 virtual machine is significantly faster than for the previous generation of Hyper-V virtual machines for two reasons. First, the Legacy Network Adapter device is no longer required (or even supported) by Generation 2 virtual machines. Instead, you can PXE-boot a Generation 2 virtual machine using a standard network adapter. Second, the SCSI controller performs much better than the legacy IDE controller in the previous generation of virtual machines. The result is that installing a supported guest operating system in a Generation 2 virtual machine takes only about half the time as installing the same guest operating system in a previous generation virtual machine.

TABLE 2-1 Hardware Device Changes in Generation 2 Virtual Machines

Legacy Devices Removed	Replacement Devices	Enhancements
IDE controller	Virtual SCSI controller	Boot from VHDX (64 TB max size, online resize)
IDE CD-ROM	Virtual SCSI CD-ROM	Hot add/remove
Legacy BIOS	UEFI firmware	Secure Boot
Legacy NIC	Synthetic NIC	Network boot with IPv4 & IPv6
Floppy & DMA Controller	No floppy support	
UART (COM Ports)	Optional UART for debugging	Faster and more reliable
i8042 keyboard controller	Software-based input	No emulation—reduced resources
PS/2 keyboard	Software-based keyboard	No emulation—reduced resources
PS/2 mouse	Software-based mouse	No emulation—reduced resources
S3 video	Software-based video	No emulation—reduced resources
PCI Bus	VMBus	
Programmable Interrupt Controller (PIC)	No longer required	
Programmable Interrupt Timer (PIT)	No longer required	
Super I/O device	No longer required	

Because of all these hardware changes, Generation 2 virtual machines only support the following versions of Windows as guest operating systems:

- 64-bit versions of Windows 8 and Windows Server 2012
- 64-bit versions of Windows 8.1 and Windows Server 2012 R2

As Figure 2-1 shows, when you create a new virtual machine in Windows Server 2012 R2 using Hyper-V Manager, you now have the option of choosing whether to create a first-generation virtual machine or a Generation 2 virtual machine. You can also specify which type of virtual machine is to be created by using the New-Generation parameter of the New-VM Windows PowerShell cmdlet in Windows Server 2012 R2.

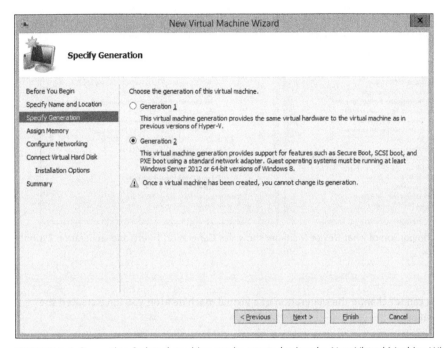

FIGURE 2-1 A Generation 2 virtual machine can be created using the New Virtual Machine Wizard.

Once the Generation 2 virtual machine has Windows Server 2012 R2 installed as the guest operating system, opening Device Manager reveals the various synthetic and software-based devices attached to the VMBus. Note that unlike first-generation virtual machines, there is no PCI-to-ISA bridge running in ISA mode, no PS/2 keyboard, no PS/2 mouse, no COM ports, and so on. Figure 2-2 compares Device Manager for Generation 1 virtual machines (left) with Device Manager for Generation 2 virtual machines (right).

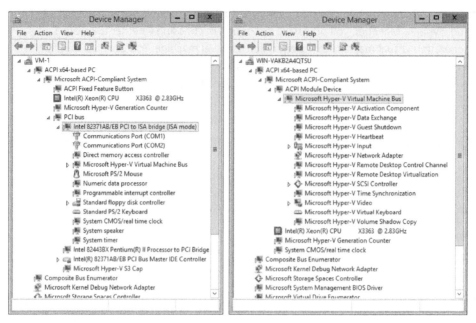

FIGURE 2-2 A comparison of what Device Manager shows for Generation 1 (left) and Generation 2 (right) virtual machines.

> **NOTE** You cannot change the generation of a virtual machine after you have created the virtual machine.

The key benefits of using Generation 2 virtual machines, as opposed to Generation 1 virtual machines, are twofold. First, as mentioned previously, new Generation 2 virtual machines can be quickly provisioned because they can boot from a SCSI device or a standard network adapter. This can be useful in scenarios where you need to quickly deploy new virtual machines in order to scale out a cloud-based application to meet rapidly increasing demand.

The second main benefit of Generation 2 virtual machines is in the area of security. Because Generation 2 virtual machines are UEFI-based and support Secure Boot, unauthorized operating systems, drivers, and firmware can be prevented from running when the virtual machine starts. In order for this to apply, however, Secure Boot must be enabled for the virtual machine. As Figure 2-3 shows, you can enable or disable Secure Boot on a Generation 2 virtual machine by opening the Settings of the virtual machine, selecting Firmware under Hardware, and selecting or clearing the Enable Secure Boot check box. By default, Secure Boot is enabled when you create a new Generation 2 virtual machine.

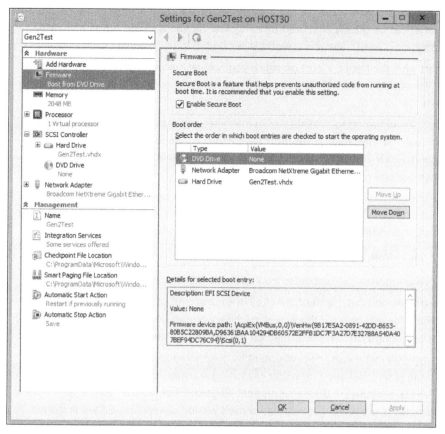

FIGURE 2-3 You can enable or disable Secure Boot in the virtual machine's Settings dialog.

MORE INFO   For a good explanation of UEFI Secure Boot, see the post titled "Protecting the pre-OS environment with UEFI" in the Building Windows 8 blog at *http://blogs.msdn .com/b/b8/archive/2011/09/22/protecting-the-pre-os-environment-with-uefi.aspx*.

Automatic Virtual Machine Activation

Starting way back with Windows Server 2003 R2 with Service Pack 2, the Datacenter edition of Windows Server has provided unlimited virtualization rights for servers to allow organizations to deploy as many virtual machines as they need in their environments. But until now this benefit has come with the cost of the administrative overhead of deploying a key management infrastructure for licensing and activating these virtual machines.

Beginning with Windows Server 2012 R2, however, the pain of managing product keys for virtual machines can be greatly alleviated by using new capability called Automatic Virtual Machine Activation (AVMA). The way it works is like this:

1. To start with, the Hyper-V host on which your virtual machines will be deployed must have Windows Server 2012 R2 Datacenter edition installed on it as the host operating system.

2. Next, to avoid having to activate virtual machines and manage their product keys, the virtual machines themselves must have either Windows Server 2012 R2 Standard, Windows Server 2012 R2 Datacenter, or Windows Server 2012 R2 Essentials installed on them as their guest operating system.

3. Once the guest operating system is installed in a virtual machine and the virtual machine is started, you can log on to the virtual machine, open an elevated command prompt, and install the AVMA key in the virtual machine by running this command:

```
slmgr /ipk <AVMA_key>
```

Doing this automatically activates the license for the virtual machine against the host.

4. Alternatively, you can use the AVMA key in an unattend.xml answer file and completely automate the activation of the virtual machine when an unattended installation of the guest operating system is performed on the virtual machine.

AVMA removes a major customer pain point by greatly reducing the time and effort needed by large enterprises and hosters for managing licensing and activation of large numbers of virtual machines in their environment. Regardless of whether your Hyper-V hosts are OEM machines or are running a volume-licensed version of Windows Server activated using Key Management Service (KMS) or Multiple Activation Key (MAK), if the host machine is running Datacenter edition and is activated, then all virtual machines running any Windows Server 2012 R2 edition as a guest operating system are automatically activated.

In addition, this is also completely secure with respect to your existing key management infrastructure since no keys are used to activate the virtual machines. So, if you should copy or move one of your virtual machines to someone else's environment, for example, as part of demonstration purposes, your keys won't be exposed. Of course, the other environment must also be using hosts running an activated copy of a Datacenter edition of Windows Server.

Remote access over VMBus

Virtual Machine Connection (VM Connect) is a tool that you use to connect to a virtual machine running on a Hyper-V host. VM Connect is installed on the host when you add the Hyper-V role to your server. Specifically, if the server is running Windows Server 2012, then the VM Connect is installed with the Hyper-V role provided that either the server with a GUI installation option has been selected or the Minimal Server Interface option has been configured. (VM Connect is not available on Windows Server Core installations of Windows Server.)

The purpose of VM Connect is to enable Hyper-V administrators to directly interact with the guest operating system in a virtual machine from the local console of the host. Although management of most virtual machines is typically performed remotely, using either Remote Desktop Connection (RDC) or Windows PowerShell, there are times when you might need to work with a virtual machine directly on the host, for example, when the virtual network adapter of a virtual machine stops functioning. In such cases, you can use Hyper-V Manager on the host and to connect to the virtual machine, and open its desktop within the VM Connect window to configure or troubleshoot the virtual machine and its guest operating system, even if the virtual machine has no connectivity with your network.

The way that VM Connect works in Windows Server 2012 and earlier is to present you with a bitmap image of the desktop of a virtual machine's guest operating system, which is generated by an emulated video card in the virtual machine. This bitmap image is updated in real time so you can see configuration changes as they happen. VM Connect also provides you with emulated keyboard and mouse devices in the virtual machine, so you can directly control the desktop of the guest operating system. Because VM Connect in Windows Server 2012 and earlier uses bitmap images, certain limitations exist in how you can use VM Connect to interact with the guest operating system. For example, you can copy and paste text between the host machine's desktop and the desktop of the guest operating system, but you can't copy/paste images or files between them.

Beginning with Windows Server 2012 R2, however, VM Connect no longer connects you to the guest operating system using an emulated video card, keyboard, and mouse in the virtual machine. Instead, VM Connect uses Remote Desktop Services (RDS) in the guest operating system of the virtual machine to provide the full RDS experience when you use it to connect to the virtual machine (see Figure 2-4). The result is an enhanced experience that enables you to:

- Copy/paste files between the desktop of the host and the desktop of the guest operating system by using a new Hyper-V integration service.
- Redirect audio on the virtual machine to the host.
- Enable the guest operating system to use smart cards attached to the host.
- Enable the guest operating system to access any USB device attached to the host.

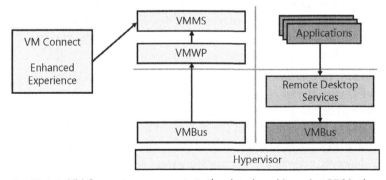

FIGURE 2-4 VM Connect now connects to the virtual machine using RDS in the guest operating system.

All of this is possible even if the virtual machine is not connected to the network. And you can do it with hosts you are managing remotely using Hyper-V Manager or Windows PowerShell. You don't have to be logged on interactively to the host to experience all this new VM Connect functionality.

Cross-version live migration

Windows Server 2012 R2 also includes several significant improvements to live migration that can benefit organizations deploying private cloud solutions built with Windows Server and Microsoft System Center. Live migration was introduced in Windows Server 2008 R2 to provide a high-availability solution for virtual machines running on Hyper-V hosts. Live migration uses the Failover Clustering feature to allow running virtual machines to be moved between cluster nodes without perceived downtime or loss of network connection.

Live migration provides the benefit of increased agility by allowing you to move running virtual machines to the best host for improving performance, achieving better scaling, or ensuring optimal workload consolidation. Live migration also helps increase productivity and reduce costs by allowing you to service your host machines without interruption or downtime for your virtualized workloads.

The ability to perform cross-version live migration between Hyper-V hosts running Windows Server 2012 and Windows Server 2012 R2 is new in Windows Server 2012 R2. Cross-version live migration can be performed using any of the live migration options supported by Windows Server 2012 including:

- Live migration on a failover cluster
- Live migration between failover clusters
- Live migration using a Scale-Out File Server that supports SMB 3.0
- Shared nothing live migration where no shared storage is used for the virtual machines

For organizations that have already begun deploying a private cloud solution based on Windows Server 2012, cross-version live migration means that you will be able to upgrade your private cloud solution from Windows Server 2012 to Windows Server 2012 R2 with zero downtime for the workloads running on your virtual machines. If you can tolerate a brief downtime window for your workloads, you can even choose to perform an in-place upgrade of your existing Hyper-V hosts from Windows Server 2012 to Windows Server 2012 R2.

And unlike previous versions of Windows Server, you don't have to perform a lot of preparatory actions before performing an in-place upgrade of your Hyper-V hosts. For example, you previously had to do things like turn off the virtual machines running on the host, and you also had to delete any snapshots and saved states of the virtual machines. When performing an in-place upgrade of a Hyper-V host from Windows Server 2012 to Windows Server 2012 R2, however, none of these preparatory steps are required, and all of the virtual machine's snapshots and saved states are preserved.

Let's now learn more about this new feature from one of our experts at Microsoft.

Benefits of cross-version live migration

Historically, every new version of Hyper-V has delivered very exciting and advanced features which added lots of value to customers' modern data centers and private/public clouds. In the past, migrating to the latest version of Hyper-V required more planning and some outage to the virtual environment while exporting and importing those virtual machines to the hosts running the latest version of Hyper-V.

With release of Windows Server 2012 R2 Hyper-V, administrators now can live migrate virtual machines from Windows Server 2012 Hyper-V to Windows Server 2012 R2 Hyper-V hosts. Microsoft private cloud administrators are very excited to be able to keep up with the latest innovations and feature improvements in Microsoft Hyper-V without negatively impacting their services and Service Level Agreements (SLAs).

In larger environments, private cloud fabric administrators can certainly take advantage of the Microsoft Hyper-V PowerShell module, and using the Move-VM cmdlet could help them create a sophisticated script and automate this migration according to their internal processes.

And last but not least, the majority of Microsoft Hyper-V environments are configured as Highly Available (HA) using Microsoft Failover Clustering and migrating to Windows Server 2012 R2 Hyper-V requires an administrator to remove each VM as an HA role, live migrate the Windows Server 2012 R2 host that is part of a new Server 2012 R2 Hyper-V cluster, and, preferably, place the VM files on the new Cluster Shared Volume (CSV), then add that VM as an HA role on the new cluster. This process should cause no outages to the virtual machine and of course, if it is needed, an administrator can use Microsoft Failover Cluster and Hyper-V PowerShell cmdlets to automate the entire process. This also could be even easier using Microsoft System Center Virtual Machine Manager (VMM) 2012 R2 as the centralized private cloud management solution.

Please note that this feature has been provided solely for upgrade purposes, and live migration of virtual machines to the previous version Hyper-V hosts will not be supported or possible.

Mark Gehazi
Data Center Specialist, US-SLG STU Infrastructure

Faster live migration

Live migration is also significantly faster in Windows Server 2012 R2 Hyper-V for two reasons. First, a new ability to compress live migration traffic can be used to reduce the amount of data that needs to be sent over the network during a live migration. This live migration compression capability is enabled by default for Hyper-V in Windows Server 2012 R2 and can often halve the time it takes to perform a live migration in a Windows Server 2012 R2 Hyper-V environment, depending on the processing resources available on the host machines for performing the compression operation.

Second, live migration can be faster in Windows Server 2012 R2 Hyper-V because of the ability to use network adapters that have Remote Direct Memory Access (RDMA) together with the SMB Direct and SMB Multichannel features of SMB 3.0. RDMA is a networking technology that enables high-throughput, low-latency communication that minimizes CPU usage on the computers using this technology. RDMA is an industry standard protocol defined in RFC 5040 that works by moving data directly between the memory of the computers involved, bypassing the operating systems on these machines. Examples of types of RDMA-capable network adapter hardware include Infiniband (IB), Internet Wide Area RDMA Protocol (iWARP), and RDMA over Converged Ethernet (RoCE).

SMB Direct, which is short for SMB over Remote Direct Memory Access (SMB over RDMA), is a feature of SMB 3.0 that supports the use of RDMA-capable network adapters. By using SMB Direct, for example, a Hyper-V host is able to access data on a remote SMB 3.0 file server (called a Scale-Out File Server) as quickly and easily as if the data was on local storage on the Hyper-V host. SMB Direct is available only on the Windows Server platform and was introduced in Windows Server 2012. SMB Direct requires that the SMB client and SMB server both support SMB 3.0.

SMB Multichannel is another feature of SMB 3.0 that enables the aggregation of network bandwidth and provides network fault tolerance whenever multiple paths are available between an SMB 3.0 client and an SMB 3.0 server. SMB Multichannel thus enables server applications to take full advantage of all available network bandwidth and be resilient to a network failure. SMB Multichannel is also the feature that is responsible for detecting the RDMA capabilities of network adapters to enable the use of SMB Direct. Once SMB Multichannel has determined that a network adapter is RDMA-capable, it creates multiple RDMA connections (two per interface) for that session. SMB Multichannel is also available only on the Windows Server platform and was introduced in Windows Server 2012, and it requires that the SMB client and SMB server both support SMB 3.0.

When a live migration is performed with virtual machines running on Hyper-V hosts that have RDMA-capable network adapters, SMB Direct and SMB Multichannel enable multiple network interfaces to be used for performing the live migration. This not only results in significantly faster live migrations, but also results in less use of processing resources on the hosts as well. This is different from live migration compression, which utilizes available processor resources on the host to reduce the network load involved in transferring the compressed virtual machine memory across the network.

When would you use live migration compression? A typical scenario would be when the primary constraining factor limiting the speed of live migration is your network bandwidth, but your Hyper-V hosts are not under heavy load as regards processing cycles. When would you use live migration using SMB Direct and SMB Multichannel? A scenario here would be when the primary constraining factor is high processor utilization on your host machines while you have lots of bandwidth available on your network. In general, if the network you are using for performing your live migration is 10 GbE or slower, you probably want to use the compression approach. If your network is faster than 10 GbE, then you should probably be using RDMA-capable network adapters so you can take advantage of the SMB Direct and SMB Multichannel capabilities of Windows Server 2012 and later.

Online VHDX resize

Another new capability of Hyper-V in Windows Server 2012 R2 is the ability to increase or decrease the size of a virtual hard disk attached to a virtual machine while that virtual machine is still running on the host. This means that if the workload running on a virtual machine should require more space, you can expand the virtual hard disk without interrupting any applications accessing the workload. And if you want to reallocate storage space from one virtual machine to another, you can shrink the virtual hard disk attached to the first virtual machine (provided that there is sufficient unpartitioned space on the disk) to free up space for expanding the disk on the second machine.

Online resizing of virtual hard disks requires that these disks be using the newer VHDX virtual hard disk format first introduced in Windows Server 2012. VHDX was designed to address the growing technological demands of today's enterprises and provides greater storage capacity, built-in data protection, and support for large-sector hard disk drives. In addition, online resizing requires that the virtual disk be attached to the virtual machine's SCSI bus.

For example, the following steps use Hyper-V Manager to expand the size of a running virtual machine:

1. In Hyper-V Manager, right-click the virtual machine and select Settings.

2. In the Settings dialog for the virtual machine, click the Hard Drive node under SCSI Controller for the virtual hard disk you want to expand, and then click the Edit button to launch the Edit Virtual Hard Disk Wizard.

3. Select the Expand option on the Choose Action page, click Next, type the new size you want the virtual hard disk to have (see Figure 2-5), and then click Next followed by Finish.

Once you've expanded a virtual hard disk, the option to shrink it will be displayed next time you use the Edit Virtual Hard Disk Wizard. Of course, you can also resize online virtual disks by using Windows PowerShell.

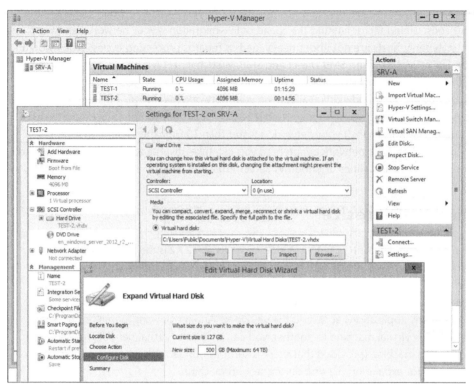

FIGURE 2-5 Virtual hard disks of running virtual machines can now be resized on Windows Server 2012 R2.

Live export

Not only can you now resize virtual hard disks attached to virtual machines while the virtual machines are running, you can also export a running virtual machine. You couldn't do this with virtual machines on Windows Server 2012 or earlier versions of Windows Server. However, with Windows Server 2012 R2 you can use Hyper-V Manager to export a complete copy of a running virtual machine or to export any snapshot of a running virtual machine. And you can use Virtual Machine Manager 2012 R2 to clone a running virtual machine, which basically involves exporting and then importing a virtual machine to create a new virtual machine that is based on the existing virtual machine. And you can even export snapshots (checkpoints) associated with a virtual machine while the virtual machine is running.

One scenario where live export can be helpful is when a running virtual machine in your environment begins to exhibit some instability but is still performing its expected workload. Previously, you had to choose between the lesser of two evils:

- Stop the virtual machine or take it offline and try to troubleshoot the problem. Unfortunately while the virtual machine is stopped or offline, its workload will no longer be available to users, and this can result in loss of either business or productivity.

- Let the virtual machine continue to run and hope it doesn't fail. This approach allows the virtual machine's workload to continue to be available, but instability often ends up with the application or guest operating system crashing, which means a probable interruption in workload will occur. Once again, this is likely to result in loss of either business or productivity.

With live export, however, you can now clone a copy of your unstable virtual machine without shutting the virtual machine down (see Figure 2-6). You can then let your production virtual machine continue to run while you perform troubleshooting steps on the cloned workload to try and see if you can resolve the issue causing the instability. Once you determine how to fix the problem by working with the cloned virtual machine, you might be able to repair your production virtual machine without needing to reboot the guest operating system or restart its running applications, depending on the issue causing the instability.

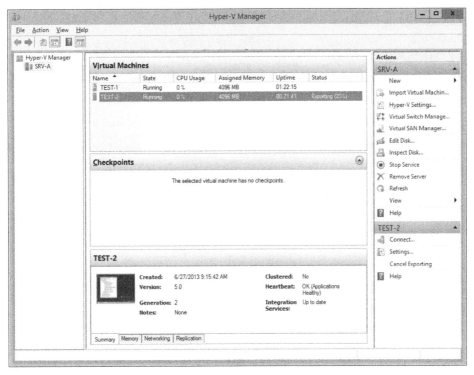

FIGURE 2-6 Running virtual machines can now be exported or cloned on Windows Server 2012 R2.

Some other scenarios where being able to export running virtual machines can be useful include troubleshooting problems with applications running in virtual machines, performing tests prior to moving a virtual machine from your private cloud to a hosted or public cloud environment (or vice versa), and when you want to duplicate your existing production environment to create a test lab.

More robust Linux support

Hyper-V has supported installing and running various Linux distros or "flavors" in virtual machines for some time now. Linux guest support in Hyper-V is especially desired by hosting providers who often like to provide their customers with a wide range of platform options for running their web applications and services. Linux (and UNIX) support in Hyper-V is also important in the enterprise space where heterogeneous IT solutions are generally the norm.

Because of the needs of these customer segments, Microsoft envisions Hyper-V virtualization as "cross-platform from the metal up" and supports a wide range of Linux distros, as shown in Table 2-2, by providing Linux Integration Services (LIS) for specific versions of popular distros. Microsoft also includes robust Linux/UNIX capabilities across the entire System Center family of products, and also in Windows Azure offerings as well. Linux/UNIX support is an integral part of all of these platforms and is not merely an extension of Windows-centric functionality.

TABLE 2-2 Current Availability of Linux Integration Services for Hyper-V in Windows Server 2012 R2

Distro	Version	LIS Availability
Red Hat Enterprise Linux	5.7, 5.8, 6.0-6.3	Download LIS from Microsoft
	5.9, 6.4	LIS built-in and certified by Red Hat
SUSE Linux Enterprise Server	11 SP2	LIS built-in
CentOS	5.7, 5.8, 6.0-6.3	Download LIS from Microsoft
	5.9, 6.4	LIS built-in
Ubuntu Server	12.04, 12.10, 13.04	LIS built-in
Debian	7.0	LIS built-in

As part of Microsoft's continuing commitment to making Hyper-V the best all-around virtual platform for hosting providers, Linux support for Hyper-V in Windows Server 2012 R2 has now been enhanced in the following ways:

- **Improved video**   A virtualized video driver is now included for Linux virtual machines to provide an enhanced video experience with better mouse support.

- **Dynamic Memory**   Dynamic Memory is now fully supported for Linux virtual machines, including both hot-add and remove functionality. This means you can now run Windows and Linux virtual machines side-by-side on the same host machine while using Dynamic Memory to ensure fair allocation of memory resources to each virtual machine on the host.

- **Online VHDX resize**   Virtual hard disks attached to Linux virtual machines can be resized while the virtual machine is running.

- **Online backup**   You can now back up running Linux virtual machines to Windows Azure using the Windows Azure Online Backup capabilities of the in-box Windows

Server Backup utility, System Center Data Protection Manager, or any third-party backup solution that supports backing up Hyper-V virtual machines.

Managing Hyper-V hosts running previous versions of Windows Server

Previously with Hyper-V in Windows Server 2012, if you wanted to manage a previous version Hyper-V host running Windows Server 2008 R2 or Windows Server 2008, you couldn't use the Windows Server 2012 version of Hyper-V Manager to do this. Instead, you would typically establish a Remote Desktop connection from the Windows Server 2012 host to the previous version host to run the previous version of Hyper-V Manager remotely on the previous version host.

Now, however, you can use Hyper-V Manager running on a Windows Server 2012 R2 Hyper-V host to manage hosts running either Windows Server 2012 R2 or Windows Server 2012. This means that you can now deploy the latest version of Hyper-V in your environment without needing to upgrade your Hyper-V management workstation immediately. Alternatively, you can upgrade your management station from Windows 8 to Windows 8.1, install the Remote Server Administration Tools (RSAT) for Windows 8.1, and use your upgraded management workstation to manage both hosts running Windows Server 2012 R2 and hosts running Windows Server 2012.

Note, however, that when you connect to a Windows Server 2012 R2 host from a host running Windows Server 2012 (or a management workstation running Windows 8 with RSAT installed) you will only be able to perform those actions that are supported by Hyper-V in Windows Server 2012.

Hyper-V Replica enhancements

In the short time that Windows Server 2012 has been released, Hyper-V Replica has proven to be one of its most popular features. Hyper-V Replica provides asynchronous replication of virtual machines between two Hyper-V hosts. It's easy to configure and doesn't need either shared storage or any particular storage hardware. Any server workload that you can virtualize on Hyper-V can be replicated using this capability, and replication is encrypted during transmission and works over any IP-based network.

You can use Hyper-V Replica with standalone Hyper-V hosts, failover clusters of hosts, or a mixture of these environments. The host machines can either be physically co-located or widely separated geographically. And they don't need to be in the same domain or even domain-joined at all.

Hyper-V Replica is an ideal technology for organizations that want to add support for disaster recovery to their Hyper-V environment to ensure business continuity. For example, you could use it to provide disaster recovery support for the branch offices by replicating their virtual machines to hosts at the head office. Another possible scenario would be to have a hosting provider set up a Replica server at their data center to receive replication data from a number of Hyper-V hosts running virtualized workloads on the premises of customers.

In Hyper-V Replica in Windows Server 2012 R2, greater control over the frequency at which data is replicated between hosts is a new feature. In Windows Server 2012, the replication frequency was fixed at every five minutes. Some customers provided feedback that this was not frequent enough for their environment, while others requested the option of performing replication less frequently. So now, as Figure 2-7 shows, there are two new replication frequencies you can choose from besides the default one of five minutes when you enable replication for a server:

- **30 seconds** Choosing this option means that the host in the replica site will never be more than a minute behind the host in the primary site. This option was provided in Windows Server 2012 R2 so that Hyper-V Replica could be used as an alternative to more expensive SAN solutions that have a similar low latency. Organizations that simply need to replicate data as quickly as possible, for example between two data centers in the same metropolitan area, might choose this option.

- **15 minutes** This option was provided especially for organizations that wanted to replicate data over networks that had very high latency or low reliability, for example over a satellite link. To ensure that replication would tolerate network outages and succeed in such scenarios, a long replication window like this can now be chosen when you enable replication on a host in Windows Server 2012 R2, and choosing this option means that the host in the replica site will never be more than an hour behind the host in the primary site.

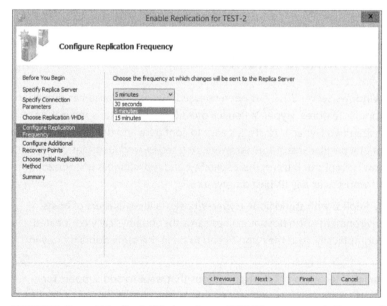

FIGURE 2-7 Hyper-V Replica in Windows Server 2012 R2 now supports three possible replication frequencies.

A second new capability for Hyper-V Replica in Windows Server 2012 R2 is the introduction of extended replication. This allows a chain of replication to be configured between hosts so that, for example, HOSTA automatically replicates to HOSTB, which automatically replicates to HOSTC. As Figure 2-8 shows, you configure extended replication when you enable replication on a host.

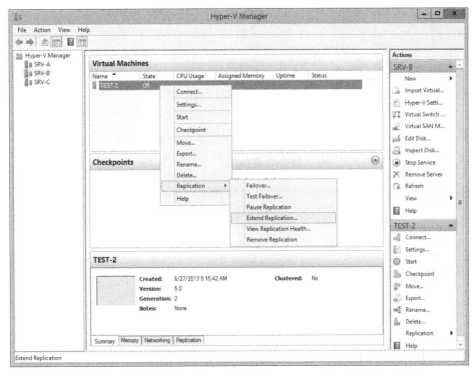

FIGURE 2-8 Hyper-V Replica in Windows Server 2012 R2 now supports extended replication.

One possible use for this new feature would be enterprises that want to do replication both on-premises and to a local hoster. With extended replication, enterprises can do a first-hop replication on-premises and then a second hop offsite, like this:

On-premises host A → On-premises host B → Hosting provider

Another usage scenario might be for hosting providers that provide Hyper-V Replica services to their customers and also want to replicate customer virtual machines to the hoster's backup data center. Extended replication in this scenario would thus be:

Customer site → Primary data center → Secondary data center

These enhancements to Hyper-V Replica in Windows Server 2012 R2 don't just represent new features added to the platform in response to customer requests; they also represent the next steps in Microsoft's vision of offering cloud-scale disaster recoverability solutions based on the Windows Server platform, System Center, and Windows Azure. As Figure 2-9 shows, another key part of this vision is Windows Azure Hyper-V Recovery Manager, a Windows Azure service that provides orchestration of the replication of private clouds managed using System Center Virtual Machine Manager 2012 R2.

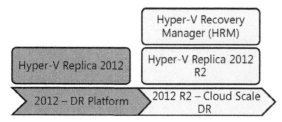

FIGURE 2-9 Hyper-V Replica and Hyper-V Recovery Manager (HRM) are part of Microsoft's vision for cloud-scale disaster recoverability.

For example, by using Hyper-V Recovery Manager together with VMM 2012 R2, you can replicate your organization's primary data center to your disaster recovery site as shown in Figure 2-10. Using Hyper-V Recovery Manager, you can enhance your organization's disaster recovery preparedness by performing failovers of selected virtual machine workloads in your environment to replicate them to your backup site. And the best thing about it is that you can do this at a fraction of the cost of using traditional SAN replication.

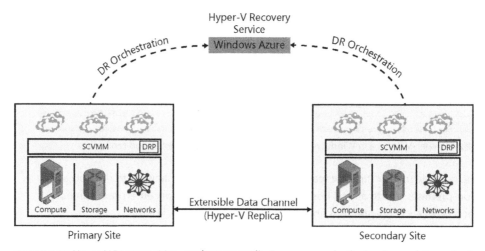

FIGURE 2-10 Hyper-V Recovery Manager lets you replicate your organization's primary data center to your disaster recovery site using Windows Azure.

Additional Hyper-V improvements

Hyper-V in Windows Server 2012 R2 also includes support for Quality of Service (QoS) management for virtual hard disks, which allows you to monitor and restrict the Input/Output Operations Per Second (IOPS) for a virtual hard disk attached to a virtual machine. We'll talk about this in Chapter 3, "Storage," since it fits well into the theme of that chapter.

Hyper-V in Windows Server 2012 R2 also now allows guest clustering using shared VHDX files. This new capability is going to be a game changer, especially for hosters who want to maintain separation between their own storage infrastructure and that of their tenants. Since this is related to the topic of clustering, we'll defer discussion of this until we get to Chapter 4, "Failover Clustering" later in this book.

Finally, the Hyper-V Virtual Switch and Hyper-V Network Virtualization have also been enhanced in Windows Server 2012 R2 in a number of important ways. Since this is related to the topic of networking, we'll defer discussion of this to Chapter 5, "Networking" later in this book.

Learn more

You can learn more about the new Hyper-V features and enhancements in Windows Server 2012 R2 by checking out the following topics on Microsoft TechNet:

- "What's New in Hyper-V in Windows Server 2012 R2" at *http://technet.microsoft.com/en-us/library/dn282278.aspx.*
- "Generation 2 Virtual Machine Overview" at *http://technet.microsoft.com/en-us/library/dn282285.aspx.*
- "Automatic Virtual Machine Activation" at *http://technet.microsoft.com/en-us/library/dn303421.aspx.*
- "Online Virtual Hard Disk Resizing Overview" *at http://technet.microsoft.com/en-us/library/dn282286.aspx.*

Be sure also to check out the following videos from TechEd 2013 on Channel 9:

- "Overview of Windows Server 2012 Hyper-V" at *http://channel9.msdn.com/Events/TechEd/NorthAmerica/2013/MDC-B338.*
- "Understanding Hyper-V Replica: Performance, Networking and Automation" at *http://channel9.msdn.com/Events/TechEd/NorthAmerica/2013/MDC-B373.*
- "Comparing Windows Server Hyper-V and VMware vSphere" at *http://channel9.msdn.com/Events/TechEd/NorthAmerica/2013/MDC-B353.*

CHAPTER 3

Storage

Storage is a key part of any IT infrastructure. For many organizations, storage is also a major cost center that consumes a large portion of the budget of the IT department. Maximizing the performance and efficiency of storage while helping to reduce costs was a major goal of Windows Server 2012, and the numerous new features and capabilities introduced in that platform now provide enterprises with new ways of squeezing the most out of shrinking IT budgets when it comes to storage.

Windows Server 2012 R2 takes these previous enhancements a step further and enables organizations to re-envision how storage infrastructure can be built and managed. This chapter examines the new storage features in Windows Server 2012 R2, focusing mainly on improvements to file- and block-based storage in the platform. The next chapter will build on this one by examining how failover clustering has been enhanced in Windows Server 2012 R2 and how Hyper-V virtualization can benefit from the improvements to storage and failover clustering. But first we'll briefly review some of the storage enhancements that were previously introduced in Windows Server 2012.

Previous enhancements to storage

A number of new storage capabilities were introduced in the previous version of Windows Server, and space doesn't allow us to describe each of them in detail. But as a quick summary, the following might be characterized as some of the more significant storage improvements in the platform:

Storage Spaces   Storage Spaces provided storage virtualization capabilities that allow you to group industry-standard disks (such as Serial ATA or Serial Attached SCSI disks) into storage pools. You could then create virtual disks called "storage spaces" or "spaces" from the available capacity in the pools and provision resilient storage volumes as they were needed. This allowed you to make more efficient use of disk capacity, provision storage quickly and easily without impacting users, delegate the administration of storage, and provide cost-effective storage for business-critical applications that make use of low-cost, commodity-based just-a-bunch-of-disks (JBODs).

SMB 3.0   A new version of the Server Message Block (SMB) protocol, a network file sharing protocol that enables applications on a computer to read and write to files and to request services from server programs on a network, was introduced in

Windows Server 2012. These improvements included SMB Direct, SMB Multichannel, SMB Transparent Failover, and other enhancements that enabled new scenarios such as storing Hyper-V virtual machine files and Microsoft SQL Server database files on file shares on an SMB 3.0 file server (called a Scale-out File Server) instead of having to store these files on local storage, Direct Attached Storage (DAS), or a Storage Area Network (SAN) array.

ReFS The new Resilient File System (ReFS) introduced in Windows Server 2012 provided enhanced integrity, availability, scalability, and error protection for file-based data storage. ReFS supported volume sizes up to 18 exabytes and could be especially useful on file servers storing large amounts of data or running disk-intensive applications that require high levels of performance. ReFS in Windows Server 2012 did not support certain NTFS features, however, such as disk quotas.

Data deduplication Data deduplication allowed more data to be stored in less space without compromising the integrity or fidelity of the data stored on the volume. It accomplished this by segmenting files into small, variable-sized chunks, identifying any duplicate chunks present, and maintaining only a single copy of each unique chunk of data. One scenario where this was useful was when data was transferred over the WAN to a branch office using the BranchCache feature of Windows Server 2012.

iSCSI Target Server The iSCSI Target Server provides block storage to servers and applications on the network using the Internet SCSI (iSCSI) standard. When combined with other availability technologies in Windows Server 2012, iSCSI Target Server provided continuously available storage that previously required organizations to purchase expensive, high-end SAN arrays.

ODX Offloaded Data Transfer (ODX) functionality in Windows Server 2012 enabled ODX-capable storage arrays to bypass the host computer and directly transfer data within or between compatible storage devices. The result was to minimize latency, maximize array throughput, and reduce resource usage, such as CPU and network consumption on the host computer. For example, by using ODX-capable storage arrays accessed via iSCSI, Fibre Channel, or SMB 3.0 file shares, virtual machines stored on the array could be imported and exported much more rapidly than they could without ODX capability being present.

Chkdsk Windows Server 2012 introduced a new Chkdsk model that allowed organizations to confidently deploy large, multiterabyte NTFS file system volumes without worrying about their availability being compromised should file system corruption be detected on them. The new version of Chkdsk ran automatically in the background and actively monitored the health state of the file system volume. Should file system corruption be detected, NTFS now instantaneously self-healed most issues online without requiring Chkdsk to run offline. This means that the amount of time needed for running Chkdsk on multiterabyte data volumes can be reduced from hours to only a few seconds, plus in many scenarios you won't even need to take the disk offline and run Chkdsk on it at all.

Storage management improvements Beginning with Windows Server 2012, you could now use the File and Storage Services role in Server Manager to remotely manage multiple file servers running Windows Server 2012, including their storage pools, volumes, shares, and iSCSI virtual disks, all from a single user interface. You could also use the new Windows PowerShell cmdlets in Windows Server 2012 to automate the same storage management tasks.

Now that we've reviewed the storage improvements introduced previously in Windows Server 2012, let's move on and look at some of the new storage capabilities and enhancements added in Windows Server 2012 R2.

Microsoft's vision for storage

As you can see from the previous section, Windows Server 2012 introduced a lot of new storage features and capabilities to the Windows Server platform. Together with System Center 2012 SP1, Windows Server 2012 provided organizations with a cost-effective solution for building and deploying private clouds using file-based storage access composed of low-cost commodity storage accessed over a standard Ethernet network.

Although the R2 release of Windows Server 2012 adds a number of incremental improvements to both file- and block-based storage and to how storage is managed on the Windows Server platform, it also represents something more. Microsoft's vision and goals with respect to storage for this new release are threefold:

- To greatly reduce the capital and operational storage and available costs for organizations deploying Infrastructure-as-a-Service (IaaS) services for private clouds, hosted clouds, and cloud service providers.

- To disaggregate compute and storage resources so they can be independently managed and scaled at each layer of cloud infrastructure.

- To allow enterprises to build software-defined storage solutions using inexpensive, industry-standard servers, networks, and shared JBOD storage.

With this focus in mind, the incremental improvements to storage capabilities in Windows Server 2012 R2 are designed to specifically target the above three goals.

Building the solution using Windows Server 2012 R2

To understand how Windows Server 2012 R2 can be used to implement the above vision for cloud computing, let's look at an example. Figure 3-1 shows the compute, networking, and storage components of a simple private cloud solution built using the Windows Server platform. You can think of this solution as having four layers as follows:

- **Compute layer**   At the top are several Hyper-V hosts joined together in a failover cluster. These hosts use commodity server hardware to provide cost-efficient scale-out capabilities. For example, if the solution needs more processing power to run more workloads running in virtual machines, you can add another commodity server to the Hyper-V cluster. Utilizing the scale-out approach like this is often a more cost-effective solution for organizations than using a scale-up solution that involves only two expensive high-end host machines, where you need to add another processor to each host if you want to run more workloads.

- **Network layer** A low-cost industry-standard Ethernet network is used to connect the Hyper-V cluster that provides compute resources for the solution with the Scale-out File Servers (SoFS) that provide virtualized storage resources for the cloud. This kind of approach can be a lot more cost-effective for many organizations than utilizing a proprietary SAN for their storage layer. That's because you don't need to install expensive host bus adapters (HBAs) in the Hyper-V hosts to enable them to connect to storage volumes (logical unit numbers, or LUNs) provisioned on the SAN. This approach is only possible, however, because of new capabilities in version 3.0 of the SMB protocol that was first introduced in Windows Server 2012.

- **Virtualized storage layer** The virtual machines running on the clustered Hyper-V hosts have their virtual machine files (virtual hard disks, configuration files, snapshots, and so on) stored on SoFS. SoFS was first introduced in Windows Server 2012 and represented clustered file servers that allow you to store server application data, such as Hyper-V virtual machine files or SQL Server database files, on file shares while maintaining a similar level of reliability, availability, manageability, and high performance as using a SAN for storing such files. With a SoFS, all file shares are online on all nodes simultaneously in an active-active cluster configuration. Again, this kind of approach can be much more cost-effective for organizations than using a SAN for storing the virtual machine files for a Hyper-V cluster. And again, using a scale-out approach instead of scale-up can be a more cost-effective solution, and as we'll see in the next chapter, Windows Server 2012 R2 increases the scale-out capabilities of the SoFS role service.

  To enable the virtualization of storage resources, Storage Spaces can be used on SoFS. This allows the physical storage resources for the solution to be pooled together to provide resiliency in case of failure of a storage device. Storage Spaces was also introduced in Windows Server 2012 and provides two types of resiliency—mirroring and parity. Storage devices can be selectively reserved as hot spares so they can automatically replace devices that fail, thus ensuring that the integrity of data is preserved in the event of a power interruption or hardware failure. The storage pools you create using Storage Spaces can be used to provision virtual disks (virtualized storage) on which you can create new volumes and shares for your solution.

- **Physical storage layer** Depending on the performance needs of the workloads running in the solution, the virtual machine files for the Hyper-V clusters can be stored on different types of storage devices. Supported drives include Serial ATA (SATA) and Serial Attached SCSI (SAS) disks, which can be either hard disk drives (HDDs) or solid-state drives (SSDs). These disks can either be internal to the SoFS, directly connected as DAS, or within JBOD enclosures.

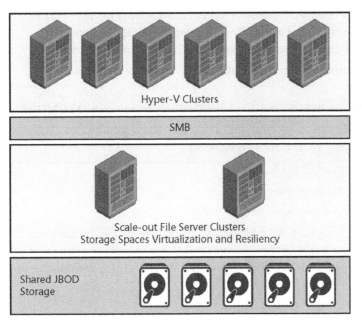

FIGURE 3-1 Microsoft's vision for storage can implemented by using Windows Server 2012 Hyper-V, SoFS clusters, and shared JBOD storage.

Although this kind of cloud solution is already possible using Windows Server 2012, the enhancements to virtualization, storage, and networking in Windows Server 2012 R2 now make it possible to optimize such solutions to achieve enterprise-quality levels of performance, reliability, and availability. That's why Windows Server 2012 R2 is being positioned by Microsoft as a cloud-optimized server operating system.

Enabling the solution using System Center 2012 R2

Windows Server 2012 R2 only represents the foundation for a cloud solution. To manage the cloud solution and the workloads running on it, you also need System Center, and in particular you need System Center Virtual Machine Manager (VMM). What truly makes this new release of Windows Server a cloud-optimized operating system is that it represents the first time that Microsoft has synchronized the product release cycles of Windows Server and System Center. The goal of doing this is to ensure that Microsoft can deliver to both its enterprise and service provider customers a completely integrated solution for building and deploying both private and hosted clouds.

To achieve this goal, the R2 release of System Center 2012 (particularly in VMM 2012 R2) also includes numerous enhancements, particularly in the areas of storage performance, provisioning, and management. For example, System Center 2012 R2 now supports:

- Faster enumerations through its Storage Management Initiative - Specification (SMI-S) storage service
- Real-time updates for out-of-band changes using Common Information Model (CIM) indications
- Fibre Channel fabric discovery and zone provisioning
- Support for Hyper-V Virtual Fibre Channel
- ODX optimized virtual machine deployments
- Rapid provisioning using differencing disks

Although the focus of this book is on Windows Server 2012 R2 and its new features and enhancements, System Center 2012 R2 (and particularly VMM) should really be considered the default platform going forward for managing a cloud solution built using Windows Server 2012 R2 as its foundation.

Storage Management API

One of the key storage management improvements introduced in Window Server 2012 and System Center 2012 was the Storage Management application programming interface (SM-API). SM-API is a Windows Management Infrastructure (WMI)–based programming interface that provides a standards-based way of managing storage on the Windows Server platform, and it supersedes the Virtual Disk Service (VDS) API used in previous versions of Windows Server. And in VMM 2012, the new Windows Standards–Based Storage Management service—which utilizes SM-API—replaces the Microsoft Storage Management Service used in previous versions of VMM.

Figure 3-2 shows how SM-API can be used to manage different kinds of storage providers, arrays, and devices by using Server Manager, VMM, or a third-party storage management tool. (You can also use Windows PowerShell to manage storage on Windows Server 2012.) Some examples of different types of storage providers and arrays you can manage using SM-API include:

- Older symmetric multiprocessing (SMP) based internal storage subsystems
- Newer SMI-S-based internal storage subsystems
- SMI-S-based network attached storage (NAS) devices
- SMI-S-compliant Fibre Channel switches on SAN arrays using CIM pass through
- JBODs that are compatible with Storage Spaces using CIM pass through

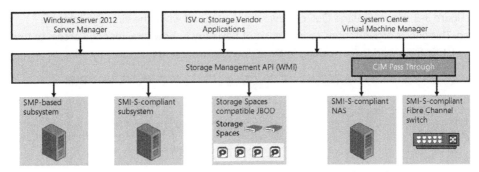

FIGURE 3-2 SM-API can be used to manage a wide range of storage providers and arrays.

Although SM-API isn't new in this R2 release of Windows Server 2012, it has been enhanced in several ways, and especially in the area of performance. Specifically, the new version of SM-API includes:

- A new architecture that performs enumerations of storage resources 10 times faster than previously
- The addition of remoting and cluster-awareness when managing Storage Spaces
- Support for new Storage Spaces features like write-back caching and storage tiering which are described later in this chapter
- The ability to use VMM to manage Storage Spaces and SoFS using SM-API

Storage QoS

Storage Quality of Service (QoS) is another new feature of file-based storage introduced in Windows Server 2012 R2. Storage QoS is enabled at the VHDX layer and allows you to limit the maximum IOPS allowed to a virtual disk on a Hyper-V host. It can also allow you to set triggers to send notifications when a specified minimum IOPS is not met for a virtual disk. Possible usage scenarios for this feature include:

- Configuring different service-level agreements (SLAs) for different types of storage operations within your infrastructure. For example, a hoster might use this feature to configure Bronze, Silver, and Gold SLAs for storage performance available for different classes of tenants. You can even set alerts that trigger when virtual machines are not getting enough IOPS for storage access.
- Restricting the disk throughput for overactive or disruptive virtual machines within your environment that are saturating the storage array. Hosting providers will especially love this capability since it means they won't have to worry about one tenant consuming excessive storage fabric resources at the expense of other tenants.

As Figure 3-3 shows, Storage QoS can even be configured while the virtual machine is running. This allows organizations to have a lot of flexibility in how they manage access to the storage fabric from workloads running in their cloud environments.

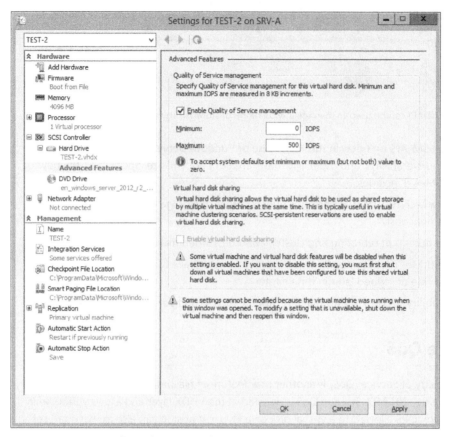

FIGURE 3-3 You can configure Storage QoS for a virtual machine using Hyper-V Manager.

iSCSI Target Server enhancements

Internet Small Computer System Interface (iSCSI) is an industry-standard protocol that allows sharing of block-level storage over a TCP/IP network. Block-level storage is typically used in SANs and is supported by the iSCSI, Fibre Channel, and SAS connection mechanisms. File-level storage involves using network shares on volumes that have been formatted using a file system like NTFS or ReFS.

iSCSI is designed to transmit and receive Small Computer System Interface (SCSI) commands and data encapsulated as TCP packets. This enables servers to utilize storage on an iSCSI-based storage device, such as an iSCSI SAN, even when the servers and SAN are in different locations.

Fibre Channel SANs can be prohibitively expensive for a small or midsized business because they require specialized connection hardware such as HBAs and cabling. By contrast, iSCSI needs no specialized connection hardware or special-purpose cabling because it can use a standard Ethernet network for connecting servers with the storage array. This means that iSCSI storage can be deployed using an organization's existing network infrastructure, which helps keep the cost of the iSCSI approach low.

Beginning with Windows Server 2012, a built-in role service (iSCSI Target Server) and client component (iSCSI Initiator) are included and can be used to implement an iSCSI-based storage solution without the need of purchasing a third-party iSCSI SAN. Using these new features, organizations can deploy iSCSI storage without the need of purchasing any additional storage hardware or software.

Some of the usage scenarios for iSCSI storage include:

- Deploying diskless servers that boot from iSCSI virtual disks over the network
- Providing block storage to applications that require or can benefit from it
- Creating iSCSI storage test environments where you can validate applications before deploying them onto a third-party iSCSI SAN

Because Microsoft iSCSI technologies are based on industry standards, you can also deploy Windows Server–based iSCSI storage solutions together with third-party solutions.

One of the key components of the iSCSI implementation in Windows Server 2012 is iSCSI Target Server, a role service under the File and Storage Services role. In a typical iSCSI storage scenario, an iSCSI initiator (a service running on the server consuming the storage) establishes a session (consisting of one or more TCP connections) with an iSCSI target (an object on the target server that allows an iSCSI initiator to establish a connection with the target server) in order to access an iSCSI virtual disk (storage backed by a virtual hard disk file) on the iSCSI Target Server (the server or device, such as a SAN, that shares storage so that users or applications running on a different server can consume the storage). Figure 3-4 shows how these different iSCSI components work together on the Windows Server platform.

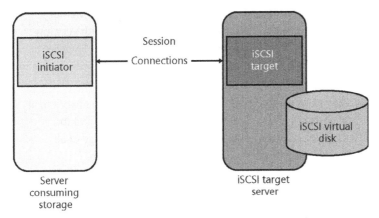

FIGURE 3-4 The basic iSCSI components work together on Windows Server.

In the R2 release of Windows Server 2012, the iSCSI Target Server role service has been enhanced in a couple of important ways:

- VHDX support is now included, which enables the provisioning of larger LUNs up to 64 TB in size. VHDX support also means you can now expand or shrink iSCSI LUNs while they are online (see the section "Online VHDX resize" in Chapter 2, "Hyper-V") and dynamically grow them for greater scalability and flexibility. And VHDX is now the default virtual disk format when creating new iSCSI LUNs.

- iSCSI Target Server can now be fully managed using SMS-S. This means that you can now perform end-to-end management of your iSCSI storage system using VMM.

SMB 3.0 enhancements

SMB 3.0 is at the core of the new SoFS functionality introduced previously in Windows Server 2012 and enables file-based storage solutions (file servers) to provide network storage for servers that have similar performance to expensive, proprietary SAN solutions. Using SMB 3.0 and the Windows Server 2012 platform, organizations can build low-cost scale-out storage fabrics that can meet the needs of a broad range of private and hosted cloud solutions.

Some of the key features of SMB 3.0 include:

- **SMB Scale Out**   Allows you to create file shares using Cluster Shared Volumes (CSV) to provide simultaneous access to data files, with direct I/O, through all nodes in a file server cluster. This results in improved utilization of network bandwidth, load balancing of SMB 3.0 clients, and optimized performance for server applications.

- **SMB Transparent Failover**   Allows you to perform hardware or software maintenance of nodes in a clustered SMB 3.0 file server (an SoFS) without interruption to server applications storing data on the file shares. If a hardware or software failure occurs on a cluster node, SMB 3.0 clients can transparently reconnect to another cluster node without interruption as well.

- **SMB Direct**   Supports using network adapters that have Remote Direct Memory Access (RDMA) capability, which allows them to function at full speed with very low latency and very low CPU utilization. When used with workloads, such as Hyper-V or SQL Server, the result is that a remote SMB 3.0 file server can resemble local storage in its performance.

- **SMB Multichannel**   Provides aggregation of network bandwidth and network fault tolerance when multiple paths are available between the SMB 3.0 client and the SMB 3.0 file server. This results in server applications taking full advantage of all available network bandwidth and being more resilient to network failure.

- **SMB Encryption**   Provides end-to-end encryption of SMB data to protect data from eavesdropping without the need for configuring Internet Protocol security (IPsec), deploying specialized hardware, or utilizing WAN accelerators. Encryption can be configured on a per share basis or for the entire SMB 3.0 file server.

With the release of version 3.0 of SMB, the SMB protocol has become more than just a network file sharing protocol used for copying files over a network. Some of the additional uses for SMB now include:

- A protocol transport for CSV that enables I/O forwarding between the nodes of a failover cluster.
- A storage protocol that enables Hyper-V hosts to access and run virtual machine files stored on file servers on the network.
- A protocol transport for performing live migrations of virtual machines between clustered and nonclustered Hyper-V hosts.

A number of improvements have been made to SMB 3.0 in Windows Server 2012 R2. For example, the performance of SMB Direct has been enhanced to provide a 50 percent improvement for small IO workloads when used with RDMA-capable network adapters. For example, 8KB data transfers have now increased from about 300K I/O operations per second (IOPS) to about 450K IOPS per interface.

A second improvement is the increased efficiency and density of hosting workloads with small I/Os, for example, when running an online transaction processing (OLTP) database workload inside a virtual machine. SMB Direct in Windows Server 2012 R2 also includes optimizations for using 40 Gbps Ethernet and 56 Gbps InfiniBand for network transport.

SMB connections can also now be managed per share on SoFS instead of per file server as in Windows Server 2012. But we'll defer further discussion of this until we reexamine SoFS in Chapter 4, "Failover Clustering."

Another new feature of SMB 3.0 in Windows Server 2012 R2 is SMB Bandwidth Management. Because SMB now has so many different functions in a network and storage infrastructure built using Windows Server 2012, it now represents a common infrastructure component in many environments. That means it's important to be able to control how much bandwidth SMB uses when it's performing many different tasks within an infrastructure. As Figure 3-5 shows, you can now configure bandwidth limits for different categories of SMB usage. For example, the figure shows that three categories of bandwidth limits have been configured to ensure optimal performance of the various infrastructure components present in this infrastructure:

- **Default**   A limit of 100 MB/s has been configured for Hyper-V host 1 to use SMB when performing file copies from the file server used for library storage by VMM 2012 R2.
- **VirtualMachine**   No limit has been set for the amount of bandwidth that Hyper-V host 1 can utilize when using SMB to access virtual machine files stored on the SoFS.
- **LiveMigration**   A limit of 500 MB/s has been set for SMB to use when performing live migrations of virtual machines from Hyper-V host 1 to Hyper-V host 2.

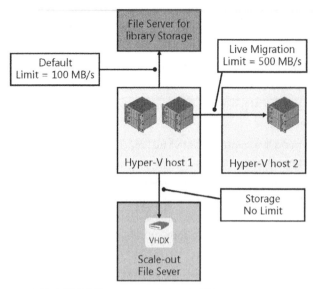

FIGURE 3-5 SMB 3.0 now supports bandwidth management.

Data deduplication enhancements

Data deduplication was introduced in Windows Server 2012 to help enterprises cope with exponentially increasing growth of data storage in their environments. Data deduplication allows Windows Server 2012 to store more data in less physical space to optimize the capacity of their storage fabric. Data deduplication is highly scalable, resource efficient, and nonintrusive in Windows Server 2012 and can run on multiple volumes simultaneously without affecting other workloads running on the server. Checksums, consistency, and identity validation are used to ensure data integrity, and redundant copies of file system metadata are maintained to ensure data is recoverable in the event of corruption.

Windows Server 2012 R2 includes several important improvements to the way data deduplication works. For example, in the previous version deduplication could only be used with files that are closed, such as virtual machine files stored in the VMM library. With this new release, however, deduplication can now be used even with open virtual hard disk files (both VHD and VHDX) for virtual desktop infrastructure (VDI) scenarios using SMB 3.0 remote storage.

Deduplication in Windows Server 2012 was also incompatible with CSVs. This meant that deduplication couldn't be used to optimize storage of virtual machine files stored on SoFS. This limitation has now been removed in the R2 release of Windows Server 2012 with support for deduplication of data stored on CSVs used by SoFS. For example, Figure 3-6 shows a failover cluster of Hyper-V hosts with the virtual machine files being stored on CSVs used by a two-node SoFS. In order for this scenario to work, SMB 3.0 must be used as the network storage protocol. Although SoFS running Windows Server 2012 can provide this functionality, using SoFS running Windows Server 2012 R2 enables deduplication to be turned on for the CSVs, which enables space savings as high as 90 percent on the CSVs. This type of space savings can be especially beneficial for Windows Server 2012 or Windows Server 2012 R2 Hyper-V or VDI deployments using remote storage on the Windows Server 2012 R2 SoFS.

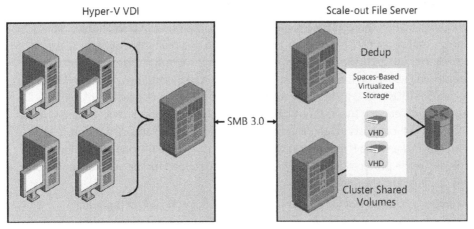

FIGURE 3-6 Windows Server 2012 R2 now supports data deduplication on CSV volumes and live VDI image files on SMB 3.0 storage.

Other improvements to data deduplication in Windows Server 2012 R2 include performance enhancements resulting from faster read/write of optimized files and improved optimization speed. Deduplication is supported only for data volumes, however, and not for boot or system volumes. In addition, ReFS volumes do not support using deduplication.

Storage Spaces enhancements

Until Windows Server 2012 was released, implementing storage virtualization required purchasing proprietary third-party SAN solutions that were expensive and required using their own set of management tools. Such solutions also required special training to implement, manage, and maintain them effectively. Storage Spaces, first introduced in Windows Server 2012, was designed to make storage virtualization affordable even for small businesses. Storage Spaces is simple to deploy and manage, and it can provide businesses with shared storage that can grow on demand to meet an organization's changing needs.

Some of the benefits of using Storage Spaces include:

- **Increased scalability** Additional physical storage can easily be added and used to meet increasing business demands.

- **Increased flexibility** New storage pools can be created and existing ones expanded as the need arises.

- **Increased efficiency** Unused storage capacity can be reclaimed to enable more efficient use of existing physical storage resources.

- **Increased elasticity** Storage capacity can be preallocated by using thin provisioning to meet growing demand even when the underlying physical storage is insufficient.

- **Lower cost** Low-cost, commodity-based storage devices can be used to save IT departments money that can be better allocated elsewhere.

To understand how Storage Spaces might be used for private cloud solutions, Figure 3-7 compares a traditional SAN-based storage solution with one built using Storage Spaces in Windows Server 2012. On the left side is a cluster of Hyper-V hosts whose virtual machine files are stored in LUNs on the SAN. These LUNs are backed by enterprise-class SAS disks (which can be HDDs or SSDs) mounted in disk shelves in the SAN chassis. Establishing connectivity between the Hyper-V host cluster and the SAN requires installing Fibre Channel or iSCSI HBAs in these hosts (depending on type of SAN involved) and data is transferred between the SAN and the Hyper-V host cluster using either Fibre Channel or iSCSI as a block-level storage protocol. Proprietary technology is required for this solution in the form of HBAs, cabling, and the SAN chassis.

By comparison, using Storage Spaces on the right requires no use of proprietary technology. Instead, all of the components of this solution can use off-the-shelf commodity-based server hardware. The SAN chassis is replaced with a cluster of file servers running Windows Server 2012 on enterprise-level server system hardware and rack-based JBOD enclosures containing the same kind of enterprise-class SAS disks (HDDs or SSDs) that might be used in the traditional SAN approach. Connectivity between the Hyper-V host cluster requires only a standard Ethernet network (typically 10 GbE) and high-performance network interface cards installed in the Hyper-V hosts and uses SMB 3.0 as a file-based storage protocol. Everything is commodity hardware here, and there's no vendor lock-in as there is with the traditional SAN approach.

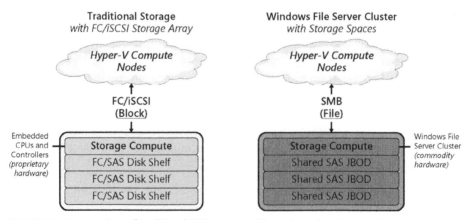

FIGURE 3-7 A comparison of traditional SAN storage with one based on Storage Spaces.

Storage Spaces in Windows Server 2012

The reaction when Storage Spaces was announced was somewhat qualified, especially by large enterprises that run workloads requiring the highest levels of performance involving millions of IOPS and massive throughput. The reason for this was because it was initially assumed that the performance of a virtualized storage solution based on Storage Spaces would fall short of what a typical SAN array can deliver. However, Microsoft soon proved its critics wrong with a demonstration performed at TechEd 2012, where a three-node high-performance server cluster was connected to a 24-bay JBOD filled with enterprise-grade SSDs. When Storage Spaces was used to present storage from the JBOD to the cluster nodes, the performance resulted in an aggregate sequential throughput of 12 GB/s and 1.45 million IOPS. When a second JBOD was added to the environment, the IOPS were increased to 2.7 million! Clearly, Storage Spaces is an enterprise-ready storage virtualization technology and its usage scenarios are not limited only to smaller deployments.

The challenge, however, with the Windows Server 2012 version of Storage Spaces is deciding whether you want to optimize performance or storage capacity when building your storage virtualization solution. For example, if you use Storage Spaces to create storage pools backed by low-cost, large-capacity commodity HDDs, you get a capacity-optimized storage solution, but the performance might not be at the level that some of your applications require. This is typically because large-capacity HDDs are optimized for sequential data access, whereas many server applications perform best with random data access. On the other hand, if you create pools using more expensive SSDs, you can easily achieve the kind of random I/O performance your applications require, but you probably won't have enough room in your budget to meet your capacity requirements for storage.

The logical solution is to use a mix of low-cost, large-capacity commodity HDDs together with expensive, high-performance enterprise-class SSDs. Building a Storage Spaces solution along these lines can provide you with the best of both worlds and deliver high levels of IOPS at a relatively low cost compared to using a SAN. This means that there are three ways you can build a virtualized storage solution using Storage Spaces in Windows Server 2012:

- **Capacity-optimized approach**   Uses only low-cost, large-capacity commodity HDDs to provide high capacity while minimizing cost per terabyte
- **Performance-optimized approach**   Uses only expensive, high-performance enterprise-class SSDs to provide extreme performance, high throughput, and the largest number of IOPS per dollar
- **Balanced approach**   Uses a mix of HDDs and SDDs to achieve good performance and reasonable capacity at an acceptable cost

Unfortunately, there's a problem with the balanced approach. This is because although most enterprise workloads have a relatively large data set, the majority of data in this working set is often cold (seldom-accessed) data. Only a minority of data is typically in active use at a given time, and this hot data can be considered the working set for such workloads. Naturally, this working set also changes over time for the typical server workload. Since the working set is small, it would seem natural to place the hot data (the working set) on high-performance

SSDs while keeping the majority of the data (which is cold data) on high-capacity HDDs. But the working set changes over time, so how do you seamlessly ensure that hot data is placed on SSDs and cold data on HDDs when you use Storage Spaces to create pools containing both SSDs and HDDs?

The answer is you couldn't do that with Storage Spaces—until now.

Storage Spaces in Windows Server 2012 R2

As Figure 3-8 shows, the Windows Server 2012 R2 version of Storage Spaces now allows you to create a tiered storage solution that transparently delivers an appropriate balance between capacity and performance that can meet the needs of enterprise workloads. The result is that the workload's most frequently accessed data (the working set) will automatically be stored on the SSD tier while the rest of the workload's data is stored on the HDD tier.

How does Storage Spaces accomplish this? By having the file system actively measure the activity of the workload in the background and then automatically and transparently move data to the appropriate tier (SSD or HDD) depending on how hot or cold the data is determined to be. Storage Spaces in Windows Server 2012 R2 can thus ensure that the workload's hot data is always stored on the SSD tier to take advantage of the high performance of this tier, and its cold data on the HDD tier to make use of the high capacity of this tier. If a portion of the data for a particular file becomes hotter (is accessed more frequently), then it gets moved from the HDD tier to the SSD tier. And if the portion of data becomes cooler (is accessed less frequently), then it gets moved from the SSD tier to the HDD tier.

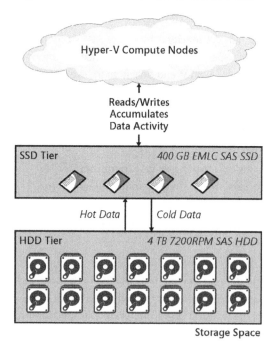

FIGURE 3-8 Storage Spaces in Windows Server 2012 R2 now supports data tiering.

This seamless movement of data between tiers is configured by default to happen daily in 1 MB chunks, but you also have the option of configuring the scheduled task for this operation to run as frequently as you want. Data moves between tiers in the background and has minimal impact on the performance of the storage space. If needed, you can use Windows PowerShell to assign certain files to a specific tier, thereby overriding the automatic placement of data based on heat. For example, the parent virtual hard disk file for a collection of pooled virtual machines in a VDI environment might be assigned to the SSD tier to ensure the file always remains pinned to this tier. The result of doing this can be to achieve significant improvements in the boot times of the hundreds or thousands of virtual desktops derived from this parent virtual hard disk.

Tiered Storage Spaces is an exciting new capability in Windows Server 2012 R2, and when this book is revised and enlarged in the RTM timeframe, we'll take a closer look at how it can be implemented. But there's one additional new feature of Storage Spaces that we'll briefly describe here, and it's called write-back caching. Whereas the goal of tiering is to balance capacity against performance, the purpose of write-back caching is to smooth out short-term bursts of random writes. Write-back caching integrates seamlessly into tiered volumes and is enabled by default. The write-back cache is located on the SSD tier of a storage space and services smaller, random writes; larger, sequential writes are serviced by the HDD tier. You can also enable write-back caching on non-tiered volumes.

Now let's hear from one of our insiders at Microsoft to learn more about the Storage Spaces enhancements in Windows Server 2012 R2 and watch these new features in action.

Storage Spaces in action

Let's examine the new features of Storage Spaces in Windows Server 2012 R2 and see some of them in action.

Storage tiering

It has been observed that SSDs with 15k speed are expensive and low capacity, but with some good performance and poor $/GB rate. On the other hand, 7.5K drives can give much better capacity at a great $/GB rate, but they're slow. We wanted to give our customers a new way to balance scalability and performance, and we have added tiered storage functionality in Windows Server 2012 R2 Storage Spaces.

Using storage tiering, the most active data (hot data) can be placed on SSD and less active data (cold data) will be placed on normal HDD, and hence it provides great throughput for I/O operations.

Tiered storage helps maximize IOPS/$ because it:

- Utilizes best characteristics of SSDs and HDDs in single storage
- Provides balance between capacity and performance
- Allows admins to assign files to specific storage

When creating a virtual disk, we can assign some capacity from the fast tier and slow tier as well. Windows will automatically analyze the data on your virtual disk to identify hot spots (Most Active Data) and cold spots (Less Active Data) and move them into fast and slow tiers, respectively. This capability is very useful in multiple scenarios and provides maximum throughput. For example:

- Assume we are using Storage Spaces for storing VDI virtual machines. The parent VHDX will be pinned to the fast tier, while the child differential disks live in the slow tier.

- During the boot process, SSD provides the good IOPS bandwidth to reduce logon time.

Write-back cache

The write-back caching feature creates a separate write-back cache for each accelerated volume from available SSDs in the Storage Spaces pool. There are many scenarios when we observe spikes in disk I/O and these can reduce write performance. To overcome this, a virtual disk leverages tiered storage to absorb the spike in write activity. Whenever a spike is detected, the SSDs in the fast tier are used, which offers greater IOPS and can take the pressure that the normal HDD tier cannot.

Dual parity and parity space support for failover clusters

This provides resiliency to **two-disk** failures for archival workloads, while minimizing $/TB and space utilization for resiliency. It also provides:

- Efficient rebuild times
- Windows Clustering support
- Integrated journaling for power fault resiliency

Faster storage space rebuild

A storage space and a RAID array can be configured with the traditional hot spare (one or more). When a disk fails, the other available disk is used to replace it. This will offer more IOPS to normal production storage activity and leave your business less vulnerable during a repair process.

Let's watch this in action. The following is a demo showcasing the dual parity capability and the disk repair process for maximizing uptime. We'll start with a Windows Server 2012 R2 that has seven SSDs of different capacities totaling 230 GB that is direct-attached via SAS to the server:

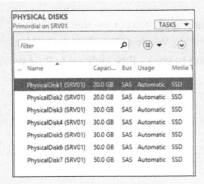

As you can see, there is only the primordial storage pool:

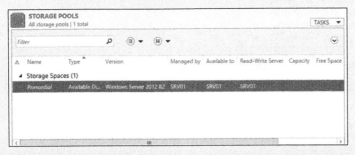

Now let's use all seven physical disks in the primordial pool to create a new storage pool named StoragePool01:

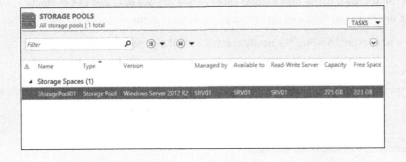

Note that the total capacity of the StoragePool01 is 225 GB but the free space is only 223 GB because some disk space is reserved by Windows for internal purposes. The capacity of the seven physical disks changes to reflect their addition to the new pool:

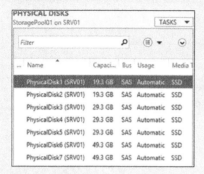

Now let's create a new virtual disk with dual parity mode:

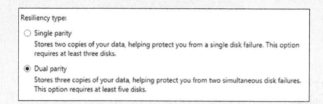

As you can see, dual parity mode stores three copies of your data and can protect against simultaneous failure of up to two physical disks in the underlying pool.

Here's a screenshot showing the newly created virtual disk named vdisk01:

The Health Status of the new virtual disk is Healthy while its Operational Status is OK. All seven disks are in use:

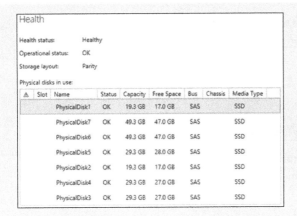

After we created the new virtual disk, we created a new volume E: on it as shown here:

Now let's check out the dual parity capability. First, let's detach two physical disks (disks 1 and 2) from the server to simulate the simultaneous failure of two physical disks. When we do this, Storage Spaces shows a warning message for the pool:

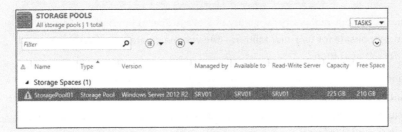

In addition, the two detached physical disks display Unknown for their Bus type:

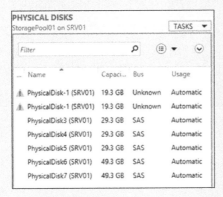

The virtual disk also shows a warning message:

The Health Status of the virtual disk has changed from Healthy to Warning, and the Operational Status has changed from OK to Degraded:

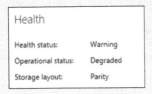

However, the volume E: that we created from the virtual disk is still accessible:

As you can see, the dual parity capability of Storage Spaces in Windows Server 2012 R2 can compensate for two-disk failures—the volume created previously is in good status for I/O operations.

Now let's see what happens when we remove a third physical disk from the server to simulate the simultaneous failure of three physical disks. When this is done, the virtual disk is now in a failed state since dual parity only tolerates up to two simultaneous disk failures:

The Health Status for the virtual disk now changes to Unhealthy, and its Operational Status becomes Detached:

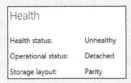

Health	
Health status:	Unhealthy
Operational status:	Detached
Storage layout:	Parity

If we had additional disks in the pool and wanted Storage Spaces to automatically compensate for disk failures, these additional disks could be configured in Hot Spare mode as per recommended practices. When this is done, a spare disk will switch to Automatic mode whenever a disk failure is detected to ensure maximum uptime. You can change the existing usage mode of a physical disk to Hot Spare mode either using the Storage Spaces canvas of Server Manager or by using Windows PowerShell as shown here:

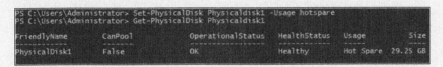

```
PS C:\Users\Administrator> Set-PhysicalDisk Physicaldisk1 -Usage hotspare
PS C:\Users\Administrator> Get-PhysicalDisk Physicaldisk1

FriendlyName     CanPool          OperationalStatus     HealthStatus     Usage          Size
------------     -------          -----------------     ------------     -----          ----
PhysicalDisk1    False            OK                    Healthy          Hot Spare   29.25 GB
```

Conclusion

Storage Spaces in Windows Server 2012 supports mirrored storage and single parity, which allows single disk failure, but with Windows Server 2012 R2 two disk failures are supported if you configure the inbuilt dual parity mechanism. Additionally, Windows Server 2012 R2 introduces a parallelized repair process, where the remaining healthy disks move around and take responsibility of data that was stored on the failed disk. It is extremely quick because all disks in the storage space are involved. Hence, Storage Spaces delivers sophisticated storage virtualization capabilities, which empower customers to use industry-standard storage for single computer and scalable multinode deployment.

Deepak Srivastava
Partner Consultant, Microsoft

Work Folders

Work Folders is another new File and Storage Services feature introduced in Windows Server 2012 R2 that can help organizations address the bring your own device (BYOD) scenario that so many of them are currently facing as the modern workplace evolves. Work Folders provides a consistent way for users to access their work files from their personal computers and devices anywhere from centrally managed file servers on the corporate network. Work Folders can also be deployed alongside existing deployments of other Microsoft data synchronization solutions such as Folder Redirection (FR), Offline Files (also known as client-side caching, or CSC), and even home folders.

To learn more about how Work Folders works, how you set it up, and how you use it, let's now hear from some insiders on the team who developed this exciting new feature.

Understanding and implementing Work Folders

During Windows Server 2012 R2 planning, we noticed two converging trends around managing and protecting corporate data:

- Users "I need to work from anywhere on my different devices"
- IT "I'd like to empower my information workers (users) while reducing information leakage and keeping control of the corporate data that is sprawled across devices"

Work Folders is a new file server-based sync solution in Windows Server 2012 R2 and Windows 8.1 that is designed to address these two trends. Work Folders enables IT administrators to provide information workers the ability to sync their work data on all their devices wherever they are while remaining in compliance with company policies. This is done by syncing user data from devices to on-premises file servers, which are now extended to include a new sync protocol.

Work Folders as experienced by an information worker

To show how this works, here's an example of how an information worker, Joe, might use Work Folders to separate his work data from his personal data while having the ability to work from any device. When Joe saves a document on his work computer in the Work Folders directory, the document is synced to an IT-controlled file server. When Joe returns home, he can pick up his Surface RT (where the document is already synced) and head to the beach. He can work on the document offline, and when he returns home the document is synced back with the file server and all of the changes are available to him the next day when he returns to the office.

Look familiar? Indeed, this is how consumer storage services such as SkyDrive and business collaboration services such as SkyDrive Pro work. We kept the user interaction simple and familiar so that there is little user education required. The biggest difference from SkyDrive or SkyDrive Pro is that the centralized storage for Work Folders is an on-premises file server running Windows Server 2012 R2, but we'll get to that a little later in this post.

Work Folders as experienced by an administrator

IT administrators can use Work Folders to gain more control over corporate data and user devices and centralize user work data so that they can apply the appropriate processes and tools to keep their company in compliance. This can range from simply having a copy of the data if the user leaves the company to a wide range of capabilities such as backup, retention, classification, and automated encryption.

For example, when a user authors a sensitive document in Work Folders on his or her work PC, it gets synced to the file server. The file server then can automatically classify the document based on content, if configured using File Server Resource Manager, and encrypt the document using Windows Rights Management Services before syncing the document back to all the user's devices. This allows a seamless experience for the user while keeping the organization in compliance and preventing leakage of sensitive information.

Capabilities of Work Folders

Our main design focus around Work Folders was to keep it simple for the information workers while allowing IT administrators to use the familiar **low-cost, high-scale** Windows file server with all the rich functionality available on the back end from high availability to comprehensive data management. Some of the functionality provided by Work Folders includes the following:

- It provides a single point of access to work files on a user's work and personal PCs and devices (Windows 8.1 and Windows RT 8.1, with immediate plans to follow up with Windows 7 and iPad support and other devices likely in the future).

- It enables users to access work files while offline and sync with the central file server when the PC or device next has Internet or network connectivity.

- It helps maintain data encryption in transit, as well as at rest, on devices and allow corporate data wipe through device management services such as Windows Intune.

- It uses existing file server management technologies, such as file classification and folder quotas, to manage user data.

- You can configure security policies to instruct user PCs and devices to encrypt Work Folders and use a lock screen password, for example.

- You can implement Failover Clustering together with Work Folders to provide a high-availability solution.

Considerations for Work Folders

When planning for the implementation of Work Folders, you need to be aware of the following considerations:

- Backend storage is provided by on-premises file servers and Work Folders must be stored in local storage on the file server (for example, data can be on local shares on a Windows Server 2012 R2).
- Users sync to their own folder on the file server—there is no support for syncing arbitrary file shares (for example, sync the sales demos share to my device).
- Work Folders doesn't provide collaboration functionality such as sharing sync files or folders with other users (we recommend using SkyDrive Pro if you need document collaboration features).

Comparison between Work Folders and other data sync solutions

The table below compares the different underlying technologies used and intended usage scenarios for Work Folders, FR/CSC, Microsoft SkyDrive, and Microsoft SkyDrive Pro.

Sync solution	Data location	Access protocol	Intended usage scenarios	Support for personal devices
Work Folders	File server	HTTPS	The user's work data	Yes
FR/CSC	File server	SMB (on-premises or VPN)	The user's work data	No
SkyDrive	Public cloud	HTTPS	The user's personal data	Yes
SkyDrive Pro	SharePoint Online in Office 365 or on-premises SharePoint 2013	HTTPS	The user's work data and team work data	Yes

Setting up Work Folders

The following is a brief overview of how to set up and use Work Folders. Note that additional steps are required to enable the client computer to be able to retrieve Work Folders settings and connect to the server across the Internet. For more detailed information see the Work Folders Test Lab Deployment Guide referenced in the Learn More section at the end of this chapter.

Work Folders requires an Active Directory environment. Start by installing the Work Folders role service on a file server running Windows Server 2012 R2. The Work Folders role service is part of the File and iSCSI Services role service for the file and Storage Services role:

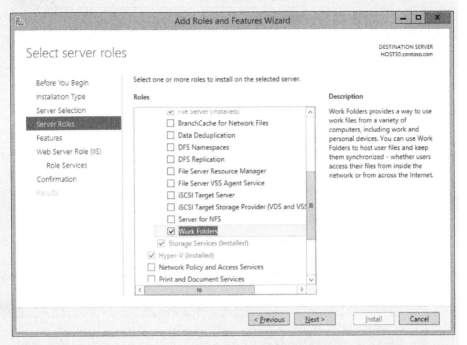

Installing the Work Folders role service will also install some components of the IIS (Web Server) role.

A new Work Folders page will be added to the File and Storage Services canvas in Server Manager. To configure Work Folders, you first need to create a sync share, which maps to a local path where all the user folders will be hosted under and to the group of users who can access the sync share:

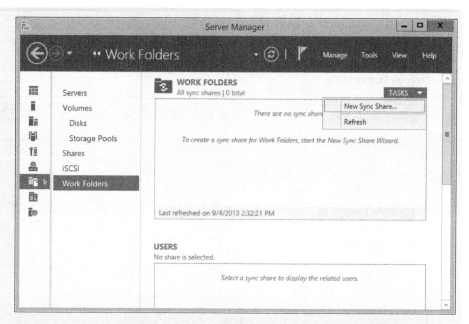

Creating a sync share simply allows the user to access the data hosted on the file
server through the Sync protocol. Selecting the New Sync Share task, as shown
previously, launches the New Sync Share Wizard:

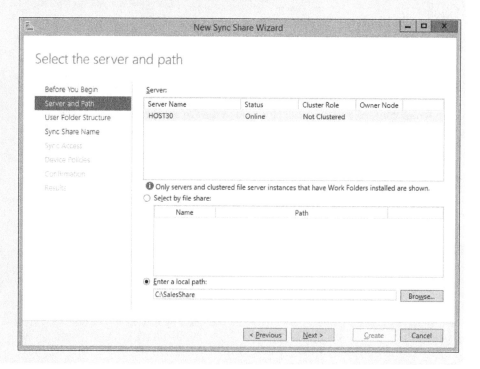

If you already have a local path that has been configured as an SMB share, such as a Folder Redirection share, you can simply select the first option, Select By File Share. In this walkthrough, we have selected the Enter A Local Path option to create a new SMB share for the folder C:\SalesShare on the file server.

The next page of the wizard allows us to specify the structure for user folders. There are two options here:

- **Using user alias**   This option is selected by default and is compatible with other technologies such as Folder Redirection or home folders. For example, the folder for Karen Berg will be named after her alias kberg.

- **Using a combination of user alias and domain information**   This option ensures the uniqueness of the folder name for users across domains. For example, let's say your organization has two users named Karen Berg, one in the hq.contoso.com domain and the other in the research.contoso.com domain. The folder for the first Karen will be named kberg@hq.contoso.com and the folder for the second Karen will be named kberg@research.contoso.com, thus ensuring each Karen has her own unique folder.

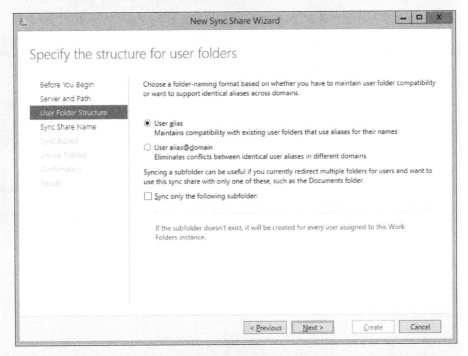

By default, all the folders/files under the user folder will be synced to the devices. The **check box** allows the admin to specify a single subfolder to be synced to the devices.

The next page allows you to specify the sync share name and an optional description:

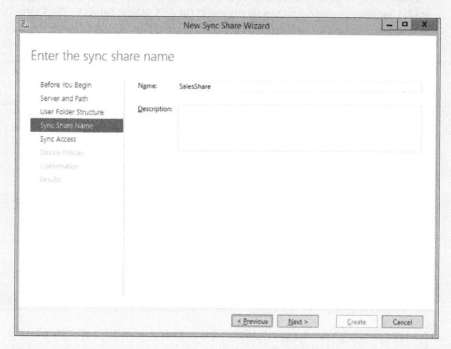

The next page is where you can assign specific security groups for sync share access:

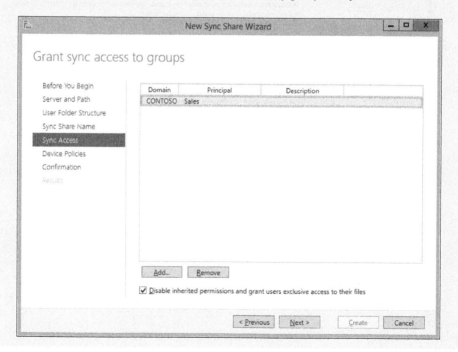

Note that, by default, administrators will not be able to access user data on the file server. If you want to enable administrator access to user data, clear Disable Inherited Permissions And Grant Users Exclusive Access To Their Files.

The next page is where you can configure device policies:

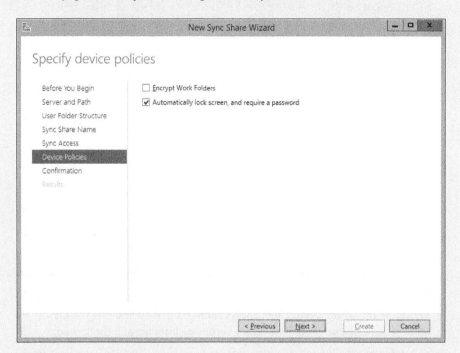

Selecting the Encrypt Work Folders Policy will ensure the document under the work folders on the client devices is encrypted with the Enterprise ID. By default, the Enterprise ID is the user primary SMTP email address (which is also the proxyAddresses attribute of the user object in Active Directory). Encryption using a different key ensures that deleting the user's Work Folder documents will not delete the user's personal documents on the same device.

Selecting the Automatically Lock Screen And Require A Password Policy (this is selected by default) enforces the following policy on the user's device:

- Minimum password length of 6
- Autolock screen set to be 15 minutes or less
- Maximum password retry of 10 or less

If the user's device doesn't meet the configured policies, the user will not be able to set up Work Folders.

Once you've completed the wizard, we can enable the sync share for SMB access by right-clicking the SalesShare folder in Windows Explorer and selecting Share With, and then Specific People. Then in the File Sharing dialog, add the Sales group and give it Read\Write access, as shown here, and then click Share:

All of the above can also be done of course with Windows PowerShell commands, if desired.

By default, the Work Folders client always **connects** to the file server using SSL, which requires the server to have an SSL certificate installed and configured.

Once Work Folders has been set up on the file server, the user can now set up Work Folders on client computers and devices. For example, on a computer running Windows 8.1 the user would open Control Panel, select System and Security, and then select Work Folders. Doing this displays the Manage Work Folders item as shown here:

The user then provides his or her email address and domain credentials, accepts or changes where the Work Folders will be stored (by default in the user profile), and consents to the configured Work Folders policies being applied.

At this point a new icon labeled Work Folders will be displayed under This PC in Windows Explorer on the user's computer:

At this point Work Folders has been configured on both the server and client sides and is ready for use. To test Work Folders, the user could use two client PCs running Windows 8.1. The user begins by using Notepad to create a new text file named "test" on the first PC and saves the file to the Work Folders location (which, as the previous screenshot shows, has been added under Favorites in Windows Explorer). When the file is saved, Work Folders automatically syncs the file to the Work Folders location on the second PC as shown here:

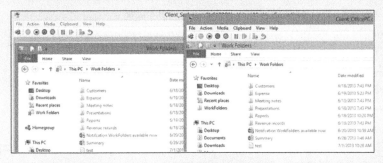

For a more detailed demonstration of how to configure Work Folders on both the server and client sides, and of how the user can store and access data using Work Folders, see the Work Folders Test Lab Deployment guide, which is referenced in the "Learn more" section at the end of this chapter.

Nir Ben Zvi
Principal Program Manager, WSSC WS PM USA

Learn more

You can learn more about the new storage features and enhancements in Windows Server 2012 R2 by checking out the following topics on Microsoft TechNet:

- "New and changed functionality in File and Storage Services" at *http://technet .microsoft.com/en-us/library/4cb00829-8d05-4499-8adc-7506e159f857#BKMK_NEW*.

- "What's New for iSCSI Target Server in Windows Server 2012 R2" at *http://technet .microsoft.com/en-us/library/dn305893.aspx*.

- "What's New for SMB in Windows Server 2012 R2" at *http://technet.microsoft.com/ en-us/library/hh831474.aspx*.

- "Storage Quality of Service for Hyper-V" at *http://technet.microsoft.com/en-us/library/ dn282281.aspx*.

- "Storage Spaces Overview" at *http://technet.microsoft.com/en-us/library/hh831739 .aspx*.

- "Work Folders Overview" at *http://technet.microsoft.com/en-us/library/dn265974.aspx*.

The following Microsoft TechNet and MSDN blog posts also have lots of information about the new storage features and enhancements in Windows Server 2012 R2:

- "Storage Transformation for your Datacenter" at *http://blogs.technet.com/b/ windowsserver/archive/2013/06/26/storage-transformation-for-your-datacenter.aspx*.

- "What's New for SMI-S in Windows Server 2012 R2" at *http://blogs.technet.com/b/ filecab/archive/2013/07/31/what-s-new-for-smi-s-in-windows-server-2012-r2.aspx*.

- "Introducing Work Folders on Windows Server 2012 R2" at *http://blogs.technet.com/b/ filecab/archive/2013/07/09/introducing-work-folders-on-windows-server-2012-r2.aspx*.

- "Work Folders Test Lab Deployment" at *http://blogs.technet.com/b/filecab/ archive/2013/07/10/work-folders-test-lab-deployment.aspx*.

- "Work Folders Certificate Management" at *http://blogs.technet.com/b/filecab/ archive/2013/08/09/work-folders-certificate-management.aspx*.

- "Extending Data Deduplication to New Workloads in Windows Server 2012 R2" at *http://blogs.technet.com/b/filecab/archive/2013/07/31/extending-data-deduplication- to-new-workloads-in-windows-server-2012-r2.aspx*.

- "Deploying Data Deduplication for VDI storage in Windows Server 2012 R2" at *http://blogs.technet.com/b/filecab/archive/2013/07/31/deploying-data-deduplication- for-vdi-storage-in-windows-server-2012-r2.aspx*.

- "Storage and File Services PowerShell Cmdlets Quick Reference Card for Windows Server 2012 R2 [Preview Edition]" at *http://blogs.technet.com/b/filecab/ archive/2013/07/30/storage-and-file-services-powershell-cmdlets-quick-reference- card-for-windows-server-2012-r2-preview-edition.aspx*.

- "Windows Server 2012 R2 Storage: Step-by-step with Storage Spaces, SMB Scale-Out and Shared VHDX (Physical)" at *http://blogs.technet.com/b/josebda/ archive/2013/07/31/windows-server-2012-r2-storage-step-by-step-with-storage- spaces-smb-scale-out-and-shared-vhdx-physical.aspx.*

- "Step-by-step for Storage Spaces Tiering in Windows Server 2012 R2" at *http://blogs .technet.com/b/josebda/archive/2013/08/28/step-by-step-for-storage-spaces-tiering- in-windows-server-2012-r2.aspx.*

- "iSCSI Target Server in Windows Server 2012 R2" at *http://blogs.technet.com/b/filecab/ archive/2013/07/31/iscsi-target-server-in-windows-server-2012-r2.aspx.*

Be sure also to check out the following videos from TechEd 2013 on Channel 9:

- "Storage Changes in Windows Server 2012 R2" at *http://channel9.msdn.com/Events/ TechEd/NorthAmerica/2013/C9-14.*

- "Reduce Storage Costs with Data Deduplication" at *http://channel9.msdn.com/Events/ TechEd/NorthAmerica/2013/MDC-B342.*

- "Storage Spaces: What's New in Windows Server 2012 R2" at *http://channel9.msdn .com/Events/TechEd/NorthAmerica/2013/MDC-B218.*

- "Storage and Availability Improvements in Windows Server 2012 R2" at *http://channel9 .msdn.com/Events/TechEd/NorthAmerica/2013/MDC-B333.*

CHAPTER 4

Failover Clustering

B oth virtualization and storage can only take you so far unless you also add high
availability into the mix. Failover Clustering, a key feature of the Windows Server
platform, is designed to do just that by providing high availability and scalability to many
types of server workloads including Hyper-V hosts, file servers, and different server
applications such as Microsoft SQL Server and Microsoft Exchange Server that can run on
both physical servers and virtual machines.

Whereas Windows Server 2012 included a number of important enhancements to
the Failover Clustering feature, Windows Server 2012 R2 adds even more. This chapter
continues the discussion of what's new in Windows Server 2012 R2 by describing several
of the key improvements to Failover Clustering functionality in the new platform.

But first let's start by reviewing the Failover Clustering enhancements that were
previously introduced in Windows Server 2012.

Previous enhancements to Failover Clustering

Some of the many ways that Failover Clustering was enhanced in Windows Server 2012
include:

- **Improved scalability**   Compared with Failover Clustering in Windows Server
  2008 R2, the number of cluster nodes supported increased from 16 to 64 in
  Windows Server 2012. The number of clustered roles or virtual machines also
  increased from 1,000 to 8,000 (up to 1,024 per node) in the new platform.
  This increased scalability enabled new scenarios and efficiencies to help IT
  departments deliver more for the dollar.

- **Cluster Shared Volumes enhancements**   Cluster Shared Volumes (CSV) were
  introduced in Windows Server 2008 R2 to provide common storage for clustered
  virtual machines. CSV was enhanced in Windows Server 2012 and enabled to
  provide storage for additional clustered roles such as the new Scale-out File Server
  (SoFS) feature, which can provide continuously available and scalable file-based
  (SMB 3.0) server storage for Hyper-V and applications such as SQL Server. CSV
  could also be integrated with the new Storage Spaces feature of Windows Server
  2012 to enable scale-out access to data by virtualizing cluster storage on groups
  of inexpensive disks (JBODs). CSV in Windows Server 2012 was also integrated

with new SMB 3.0 features like SMB Multichannel and SMB Direct, which allow CSV traffic to stream across multiple networks in the cluster and leverage network adapters that support Remote Direct Memory Access (RDMA). Other CSV improvements in Windows Server 2012 included support for BitLocker Drive Encryption, removal of external authentication dependencies, and improved file backup.

- **Updating failover cluster nodes**   Cluster-Aware Updating (CAU) was introduced in Windows Server 2012 to enable software updates to be applied automatically to the host operating system or other system components on the nodes of a failover cluster while maintaining availability during the update process. CAU reduced maintenance time by automating what was previously a very repetitive task.

- **Quorum improvements**   New features of the cluster quorum feature in Windows Server 2012 included simplified quorum configuration, support for specifying which cluster nodes had votes in determining quorum, and dynamic quorum, which provides the administrator the ability to automatically manage the quorum vote assignment for a node based on the state of the node.

- **Other enhancements**   Some of the many other enhancements to Failover Clustering in Windows Server 2012 included simplified migration of the configuration settings of clustered roles, more robust integration with Active Directory Domain Services, improved cluster validation tests, improved Windows PowerShell support, Node Maintenance Mode, clustered tasks, new clustered roles like iSCSI Target, guest clusters using virtual Fibre Channel, and more. Many of the Hyper-V enhancements in Windows Server 2012 are also relevant to Failover Clustering, for example, virtual machine prioritization, pre-emption to shut down low-priority virtual machines, virtual machine health monitoring, Hyper-V Replica Broker, and so on.

Guest clustering using shared virtual disks

As we mentioned briefly at the end of Chapter 2, Hyper-V in Windows Server 2012 R2 now allows guest clustering using shared VHDX files. This new exciting capability will be especially appreciated by hosters who want to maintain separation between their own storage infrastructure and that of their tenants. Why is that?

Hosting highly available workloads

Consider your typical hoster for a moment. A hoster provides its customer with services that allow them to run their virtual machines in the cloud instead of on location at their company premises. These virtual machines are pretty important to the customers too, since they are typically running server workloads—like SQL Server—that are critical to the operation of the customer's business. In fact, they're so important to the customer that they want the hoster to make sure these workloads are highly available. And since the hoster says it has the infrastructure to do this and wants the customer's business, it agrees.

Now let's say that until today, the customer has been running their virtualized workloads on-premises. To ensure high availability for their workloads, they've been using two types of failover clustering, namely, guest host clustering and guest clustering. First, the customer has been using host clustering, which means running the Failover Clustering feature in the parent partition of two or more Hyper-V hosts. (To understand host clustering, think of making a single virtual machine highly available.) Using host clustering helps you ensure continuous availability in the event of a hardware failure on a host, when you need to apply software updates to the parent partition resulting in a reboot being required, and similar scenarios.

Second, the customer has been using guest clustering, which means running the Failover Clustering feature in the guest operating system of two or more virtual machines. (To understand guest clustering, think of multiple virtual machines in a failover cluster.) Using guest clustering helps you proactively monitor application health and mobility within the guest operating system and protect against application failures, guest operating system problems, host and guest networking issues, and other problem scenarios.

By combining both types of failover clustering like this, the customer has the best of both worlds. In other words, having a cluster of clusters (guest clustering on top of host clustering) gives you the highest level of availability for your virtualized workloads.

But now let's say that the customer wants to move their virtualized workloads into a hosted cloud. So, the customer asks the hoster to provide them with high availability similar to what they've been using on-premises. The hoster agrees but wants to maintain complete separation between the tenant's virtual workloads and the hoster's own physical storage infrastructure.

Separating virtual resources from physical infrastructure

The new guest clustering using shared virtual disks capability of Windows Server 2012 R2 now makes such a scenario possible for hosters. As you'll see in a moment, what this new capability enables you to do is to keep your physical infrastructure layer (computer, storage, and network) and your virtualized resources (tenant virtual machines and the workloads running on them) separate from one another.

This approach can benefit hosters since it allows them to maintain strict control over the physical infrastructure of their cloud while providing great flexibility in how they deliver virtual resources to customers. Specifically, it allows them to provision virtual machines, services, and applications to customers (together with the virtual compute, storage, and network resources needed) while keeping the underlying physical resources opaque to them.

For example, when a customer spins up a new virtual machine, the customer doesn't care which Hyper-V host it's running on, which physical network that host is sitting on, or which logical unit number (LUN) its virtual machine files are stored on. All the customer cares about is that they get the necessary virtualized compute, storage, and network resources they need to run their workload with the performance they desire. The hoster should be able to reallocate, reconfigure, and upgrade their physical infrastructure without interrupting customer workloads or even the customers being aware of it.

With guest clustering in the previous versions of Windows Server, maintaining strict separation of tenant virtual machines and the hoster's physical infrastructure just wasn't possible. That's because in order to implement guest clustering you had to present a LUN to your virtual machines so they could use it as shared storage for the Failover Clustering feature running in the guest operating system of the virtual machines. In Windows Server 2008 R2, you would generally do this by having iSCSI initiators running in the guest operating system to enable connectivity with an iSCSI-based storage device. (You could also use Fibre Channel over Ethernet, or FCoE, for this purpose as well, but the point is that you were still restricted to using NICs to transport the data.) Typically you would host the LUN on an iSCSI SAN, but you could also download and install the free Microsoft iSCSI Target Software from the Microsoft Download Center, install it on a server running Windows Server 2012 R2, and use that server as shared storage for the guest cluster.

Windows Server 2012 made guest clustering easier in two ways. First, the iSCSI Software Target is now an in-box feature integrated into the Failover Clustering feature, and this makes it easier to implement guest clustering using shared iSCSI storage. Second, Windows Server 2012 also includes an in-box Hyper-V Virtual Fibre Channel adapter that allows you to connect directly from within the guest operating system of a virtual machine to LUNs on a Fibre Channel SAN. This means that in Windows Server 2012 you have three choices for the shared storage you'll need if you want to implement guest clustering, namely, iSCSI storage, Fibre Channel storage, or Hyper-V over SMB 3.0.

But the problem with guest clustering in Windows Server 2012 is that it still requires that something in your virtual infrastructure (the guest operating system of the clustered virtual machines) needs to be able to directly connect to something in your physical infrastructure (a LUN on your iSCSI or Fibre Channel SAN). What this effectively does when guest clustering is implemented is to open a hole between the physical infrastructure and the clustered virtual machines as shown in Figure 4-1.

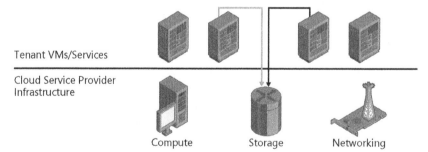

Tenant VMs/Services

Cloud Service Provider Infrastructure

Compute   Storage   Networking

FIGURE 4-1 Hosters like to keep their customers' virtual machines and their own supporting infrastructure separate, but until now guest clustering has required establishing a connection between them.

What's the problem with opening such a hole? For hosters, it basically ties their hands because they can't make changes to their physical storage infrastructure without having it potentially impact the virtualized workloads of the customers that they're hosting. Because of this, hosters usually decline to implement guest clustering because it limits their ability to separate their physical infrastructure from the tenant's workloads. Customers that want to move workloads into the cloud and have high availability ensured by both host and guest clustering are unable to do this, and this makes them unhappy because they are unable to migrate their workloads into the hoster's cloud to simplify the operations and management of their workloads. So, hosters who want to offer both host and guest clustering to customers can't do this, and they lose out on potential business opportunities.

But now with the new guest clustering using shared VHDX capability of Windows Server 2012 R2, hosters can provide guest clustering to customers without the need of providing direct access by the clustered virtual machines to an iSCSI target or a LUN on a Fibre Channel storage array. This means you can now implement guest clustering for tenant virtual machines running in a hoster's cloud while maintaining complete separation between the hoster's physical storage infrastructure and the virtualized storage resources consumed by the virtual machines (see Figure 4-2). This is an important issue for most hosters because they usually utilize separate networks for providing tenant virtual machine connectivity and storage infrastructure connectivity and, for security and reliability reasons, they want to keep these networks completely separate.

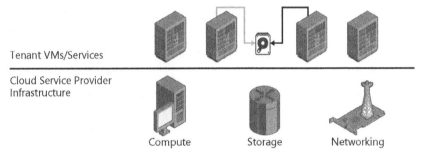

FIGURE 4-2 Guest clustering using shared virtual disks in Windows Server 2012 R2 enables hosters to keep their customers' virtual machines and their own supporting infrastructure separate.

Understanding shared virtual disks

The key to being able to implement guest clustering for tenant virtual machines running in a hoster's cloud is a new capability in Windows Server 2012 R2 that allows a VHDX file (the new virtual hard disk format introduced earlier in Windows Server 2012) to be shared by multiple virtual machines running on one or more Hyper-V hosts. To the hosts, these shared virtual disks look like simple VHDX files attached to multiple virtual machines (each virtual machine already has at least one other virtual hard disk for the guest operating system). To the virtual machines themselves, however, the shared virtual disks appear to be (and behave as if they are) virtual Serial Attached SCSI (SAS) disks that can be used as shared storage for a failover cluster. The virtual machines in a guest cluster can share one or more virtual SAS disks depending on how the cluster is configured. Figure 4-3 shows how the hosts and virtual machines view the shared VHDX files in a guest cluster.

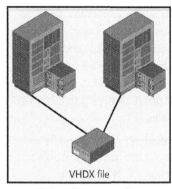 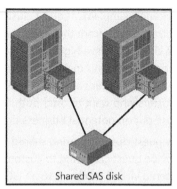

VHDX file	Shared SAS disk
Hyper-V hosts see only a simple VHDX file	Virtual machines see a shared SAS disk

FIGURE 4-3 Hyper-V hosts see shared virtual disks as simple VHDX files, but the guest cluster of virtual machines running on these hosts sees the virtual disks as shared SAS disks.

As in Windows Server 2012, the actual physical storage backing the shared storage volume(s) used by the failover cluster can be implemented using one of two approaches as shown in Figure 4-4:

- Using CSV disks for block storage, for example, by placing the shared VHDX file on a CSV disk provisioned from a virtual disk using Storage Spaces

- Using a SoFS for file storage, which allows the shared VHDX file to be stored on an SMB 3.0 shared folder

Both of these approaches allow the use of low-cost commodity storage instead of more expensive SAN solutions for the shared storage used by the guest cluster. They also allow you to deliver guest clustering using exactly the same infrastructure you use to deliver standalone virtual machines. In other words, you don't need to have specialized storage such as an iSCSI or Fibre Channel SAN or a Windows Server system with the Microsoft iSCSI Target Software installed in order to implement guest clustering.

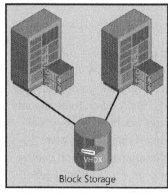 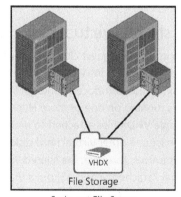

Block Storage	File Storage
Cluster Shared Volumes (CSV) for block storage	Scale-out File Server for file storage

FIGURE 4-4 Guest clusters using shared virtual disks can use either CSV disks for block storage or SoFS for file storage.

Using shared virtual disks

Implementing guest clustering using shared virtual disks on Windows Server 2012 R2 is easy:

1. Create a new VHDX file on the volume you will use for shared storage for the cluster.

2. Open the Settings dialog for a virtual machine in Hyper-V Manager.

3. Click the SCSI Controller option under the Hardware category, select Hard Drive, and click Add to add a new hard drive to the controller.

4. Browse to select the VDHX file you created earlier, and then expand the new hard drive under the SCSI Controller to expose the Advanced Features option.

5. Click the Advanced Features option and select the Enable Virtual Hard Disk Sharing check box as shown in Figure 4-5, and then click OK (or Apply) to apply all the changes.

6. Repeat steps 2 through 5 of the above procedure for each virtual machine in the guest cluster.

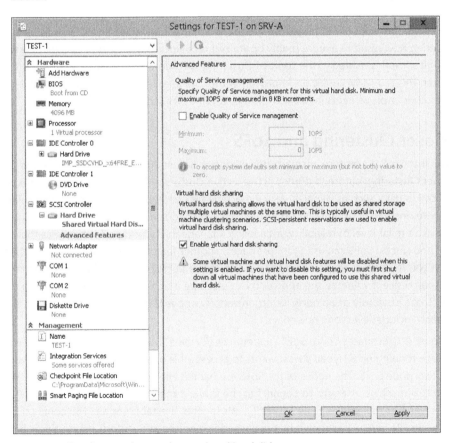

FIGURE 4-5 Use these settings to share a virtual hard disk.

A few things to consider:

- The shared virtual disk must be a data disk; guest operating system disks cannot be shared.
- The shared virtual disk must use the newer VHDX format; it cannot use the older VHD format.
- The shared virtual disk must be attached to the virtual machine's SCSI controller; it cannot be attached to the IDE controller.
- When performing the above procedure, don't click Apply until you have selected the Enable Virtual Hard Disk Sharing check box. If you do this, you will have to remove the disk from the controller and reselect it in order to share it.

Of course, all this can be done using Windows PowerShell as well.

CSV and SoFS enhancements

At the end of Chapter 3, "Storage," we mentioned that enhancements to CSV in Failover Clustering now result in a more highly optimized rebalancing of how the SoFS feature works, but that since this related to the topic of clustering we'd defer discussing it until this present chapter. This is a fairly significant improvement for SoFS, so let's look at it now together with some other improvements in how CSV works in Windows Server 2012 R2.

Failover Clustering and SoFS

Recall that SoFS is a feature introduced in Windows Server 2012 that allows you to use the Failover Clustering feature to deploy active-active clusters of file servers that can store server application data, such as Hyper-V virtual machine files or SQL Server database files, using file shares instead of using LUNs on a SAN. The key of course is that a SoFS allows you to achieve a similar level of reliability, availability, manageability, and performance as that of a SAN. And since a SoFS can use Storage Spaces, another feature of Windows Server 2012 that allows you to use low-cost commodity disks to create pools of storage from which you can provision resilient volumes, the approach can often be much more cost-effective than using a SAN. That's obviously good news for organizations whose IT budgets are constrained, which probably includes everyone nowadays.

Figure 4-6 illustrates how a SoFS can redirect I/O over SMB to the optimal node. A virtual machine running on a Hyper-V host wants to access a file in a shared folder named Share2 on a two-node SoFS. The nodes of the SoFS are named File Server 1 and File Server 2. When the virtual machine attempts to connect to the share, it might connect to either Share2 on File Server 1 or to Share2 on File Server 2. Let's say that it establishes an SMB connection to Share2 on File Server 1 as shown by the dashed line on the left. Unfortunately, this is not an optimal connection because the file it wants to access is actually located on storage attached to File Server 2. The SoFS detects this situation, however, and it automatically and seamlessly transitions the SMB connection from Share2 on File Server 1 to Share2 on File Server 2 as shown by the dashed arrow at the bottom. From this point until the end of the SMB session, to provide optimal I/O and throughput, the SMB connection between the virtual machine and Share2 on File Server 2 can use direct I/O as shown by the solid line.

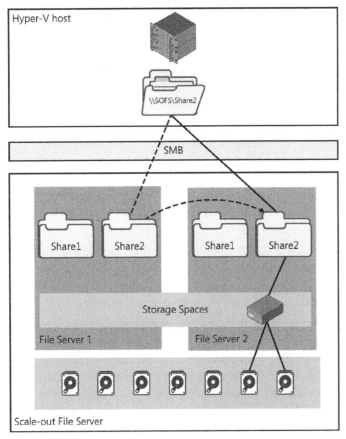

FIGURE 4-6 A SoFS can redirect I/O over SMB to the optimal node.

Optimized ownership of CSV disks

To ensure that a SoFS can deliver SAN-quality throughput and IOPS, Microsoft has made a couple of optimizations in how a SoFS works in Windows Server 2012 R2. We'll begin by considering things from the perspective of CSV. Recall that CSV allow multiple nodes in a failover cluster to simultaneously have read-write access to the same LUN (disk) provisioned as an NTFS volume. This enables clustered roles to fail over quickly from one node to another node without requiring a change in drive ownership or dismounting/remounting a volume. CSV also help simplify managing a large number of LUNs in a large failover cluster. CSV work by providing a general-purpose, clustered file system layered on top of NTFS. Examples of CSV applications can include clustered virtual hard disk (VHD or VHDX) files for clustered Hyper-V virtual machines and scale-out file shares to store application data for the SoFS role.

Consider a failover cluster with a bunch of nodes with a bunch CSV disks, and each CSV disk is backed by a shared LUN exposed through Storage Spaces on a SoFS. Applications running on any node have simultaneous read/write access to the shared LUN even if it is only mounted on one of the cluster nodes. The coordinator node, one of the cluster nodes, handles all synchronization of metadata for file system I/O on the shared LUN and is the only node where NTFS is mounted. An example of such metadata would be the file system changes that occur when a virtual machine running on a Hyper-V cluster is turned off. Such metadata changes are routed over the SMB path to the coordinator node. By contrast, file system I/O that is not metadata is sent directly down the stack to the storage to provide direct I/O performance.

In Windows Server 2012, the Failover Clustering feature handles orchestration of file system changes on CSV disks by performing orchestration separately for each LUN. This meant that if you had eight cluster nodes using four LUNs for shared storage, you had to manually spread the CSV disks across the cluster. Also, Failover Clustering in Windows Server 2012 had no built-in mechanism for ensuring that they stayed spread out. In fact, all of the CSV disks could be owned by a single node.

Failover Clustering in Windows Server 2012 R2, however, now includes a mechanism for fairly distributing the ownership of CSV disks across all cluster nodes based on the number of CSV disks each node owns. Rebalancing ownership of CSV disks happens automatically whenever a new node is added to the cluster, a node is restarted, or a failover occurs.

Another enhancement in Windows Server 2012 R2 is when a workload, such as a virtual machine running on a Hyper-V host, attempts to establish an SMB 3.0 connection with a SoFS, the SoFS will try to determine whether the workload has an optimized I/O path it can use to access the CSV disk using direct I/O. One of the key improvements with Failover Clustering in Windows Server 2012 was that CSV disks could perform more operations in direct I/O mode than occurred in Windows Server 2008 R2. Direct I/O can be used with storage that has Fibre Channel, iSCSI, or SAS connectivity and involves writing directly to a CSV disk. Drivers for devices that can transfer large amounts of data at a time can use direct I/O for those transfers, and using direct I/O for such transfers improves a driver's performance, both by reducing its interrupt overhead and by eliminating the memory allocation and copying operations inherent in buffered I/O.

Increased CSV resiliency

CSV in Windows Server 2012 R2 now has health monitoring of the Server service to help increase the resilience of your Failover Clustering solution. This is important because if the Server service becomes unhealthy on a failover cluster, it can impact the ability of the CSV coordinator node to orchestrate metadata updates and accept I/O requests from other nodes. To protect against this, when the Server service is detected as being unhealthy in a Windows Server 2012 R2 failover cluster, ownership of the CSV is automatically transitioned to another node in the cluster.

Another improvement is that multiple Server service instances are now allowed per failover cluster node. Specifically, you can now have:

- The default instance, which handles incoming traffic from SMB clients that access ordinary file shares.
- A second CSV instance that handles only inter-node CSV traffic such as metadata access and redirected I/O traffic.

Improved CSV cache allocation

The CSV cache enables the server to use system memory as a write-through cache to increase the performance of a Failover Clustering solution. In Windows Server 2012, you could only allocate up to 20 percent of the total physical memory on the server for use by the CSV cache. Now, in Windows Server 2012 R2, you can allocate up to 80 percent of the total physical memory of the server to the CSV cache. This can result in huge performance gains in certain scenarios such as failover clusters of Hyper-V hosts and Scale-out File Server deployments.

Another change with the CSV cache is that it is now enabled by default. Previously in Windows Server 2012, the CSV cache was disabled by default and had to be manually enabled. However, you still need to allocate the size of the block cache you want to reserve. You can do this by using Windows PowerShell. For example, the following command will configure a cache of 512 MB to be reserved on each node of a failover cluster:

```
(Get-Cluster).SharedVolumeBlockCacheSizeInMB = 512
```

After you have modified the amount of memory allocated to the CSV cache, you need to restart each node in the cluster.

CSV and other storage features

CSV in Windows Server 2012 R2 now supports the Resilient File System (ReFS), data deduplication, and parity Storage Spaces. ReFS is a new file system introduced previously in Windows Server 2012 that is designed to maximize the integrity and availability of data by safeguarding against common errors that cause data loss. ReFS can scale to very large volumes and is designed to handle the very large data sets of the future.

Data deduplication and Storage Spaces have been discussed previously in Chapter 2, "Storage," of this book. By supporting ReFS, data deduplication, and parity Storage Spaces, greater flexibility has been added in Windows Server 2012 R2 in how organizations can implement Failover Clustering solutions.

Changes to heartbeat threshold

Although the goal of failover clustering is to deliver high availability for server workloads, beneath the hood, failover clustering is simply a health detection model. Each and every second, a heartbeat connection is tested between nodes in the cluster. If no heartbeat is heard from a node one second, nothing happens. No heartbeat for two seconds? Nothing happens. Three seconds? Nothing. Four seconds? Nothing. Five seconds?

Five seconds is the default heartbeat threshold for all cluster roles in the Windows Server 2012 version of Failover Clustering. That means if the coordinator node doesn't hear from one of the other cluster nodes in five seconds, it assumes that the other node has failed or is partitioned, so it takes corrective action to remedy the situation and ensure continued availability of the workloads currently running on the failed node.

As an example, let's say you have a single-subnet failover cluster of Hyper-V hosts with virtual machines running on them. VM-A is currently running on HOST-1 and everything is working fine until an unexpected network interruption occurs on the network connecting the nodes. A transient issue with the network switch could be the cause, perhaps because someone tripped over the switch's power cable in the server room and plugged it back in immediately, but the switch took a few seconds to reboot. Whatever the cause of the network interruption, Failover Clustering decides that since the heartbeat threshold had been exceeded for HOST-1, that node must be down, so it assumes that VM-A has become unavailable even though clients are still able to access the workload running on the virtual machine. Since HOST-1 has been determined to have failed, Failover Clustering begins taking remedial action on that node, which terminates any active client connections to the workload. Meanwhile, it starts booting up VM-A on a different node so clients will be able to access the workload again.

What has actually happened here, unfortunately, is that Failover Clustering could be said to have triggered a false failover. Of course, that's not really true—it's the network interruption that caused the problem. The best action in this case would be to ensure that all network cables are physically secured. But what if your network experiences more mysterious transient failures? And what if you, as cluster administrator, can't identify or address these network failures because another section of the IT department oversees the network infrastructure and they aren't cooperative or helpful? For one reason or another, transient network interruptions are sometimes unavoidable for some customers. Yet network interruptions that exceed the heartbeat threshold can cause a cluster to fail over when such action is neither necessary nor desired. What's to be done?

To address this issue, the Windows Server team made a change in Failover Clustering in Windows Server 2012 R2. Instead of the five-second heartbeat threshold used for all clustered roles in Windows Server 2012, the heartbeat threshold has been increased, but only for the Hyper-V clustered role. For Hyper-V cluster nodes on the same subnet, the threshold is now 10 seconds. And for Hyper-V cluster nodes on different subnets, the threshold is now 20 seconds. This reduction of cluster sensitivity to health problems was specifically made to enable Hyper-V clusters to provide increased resiliency to packet loss on unreliable networks. However, increasing the heartbeat threshold like this can have the negative result of greater downtime when a real failure does happen, so administrators also have the option of configuring a lower threshold if they want to. But you shouldn't raise the threshold any higher than 20 seconds or it can cause TCP sessions to unexpectedly terminate. And remember, increasing the heartbeat threshold doesn't fix the underlying network problems you're experiencing—it only masks them.

Detecting the health of virtual machines

Interruptions in the physical network infrastructure of a failover cluster aren't the only types of network problems that can cause problems for clusters. Network disconnections can also occur at the virtual machine level on the clustered Hyper-V hosts. If this happens in Windows Server 2012, the virtual machine continues to run on the cluster node even though the workload on the virtual machine is no longer available to clients.

A new setting called Protected Network in Windows Server 2012 R2 can resolve this kind of problem by automatically moving the virtual machine to a different cluster node if the virtual machine's network becomes disconnected. To enable this capability for a virtual machine running on a Hyper-V host cluster, simply do the following:

1. Open the Settings dialog for a virtual machine in Hyper-V Manager.

2. Expand the Network Adapter node under Hardware, and select the Advanced Features option.

3. Select the Protected Network check box, as shown in Figure 4-7.

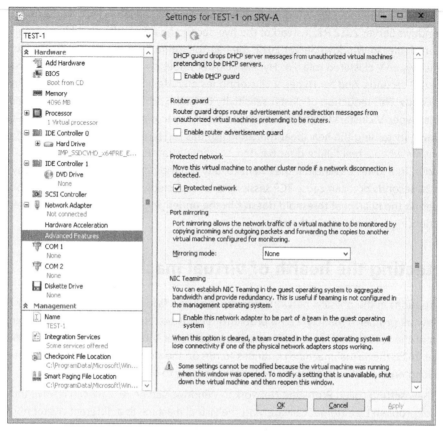

FIGURE 4-7 You can now enable the Protected Network setting.

For more information on this new capability and how to configure it using Windows PowerShell, let's now hear from one of our experts at Microsoft.

Configuring virtual machine health protection

n Windows Server 2008 R2 Failover Clustering, we had our first health type check, wherein, if the virtual machine hangs, we would restart it. In Windows Server 2012, we introduced Virtual Machine Monitoring. This monitoring could be set up to monitor specific services running inside of the virtual machine and restart them if necessary.

However, there was still one scenario where Failover Clustering would not react—that was the disconnect of a network. If a network disconnected in previous versions of Failover Clustering, it would remain on the current node and not do anything. There really was nothing that could be done—from a cluster standpoint—to have it automatically move unless there was an IP address resource also in the group. This was ugly and meant you had IP addresses on the network that would never be utilized.

This has been addressed in Windows Server 2012 R2 Failover Clustering. Now, a component level virtual machine health detector is included. With highly available virtual machines, there is a new thorough (IsAlive) health check that implements checks to the external connectivity of a VM switch to that virtual machine.

This is not something that is enabled as a default and is not for all networks or virtual machines. To configure this, you must first identify which network is your "protected" network. The "protected" network could be the network that the clients will access for their virtual machines.

So let's take this example: I have a highly available virtual machine called Bob and a Hyper-V network called Public that will be my protected network. I would bring up the settings of the virtual machine in Failover Cluster Manager, expand my Network Adapter identified as Public, and go to the Advanced Features. Here is where I can select it to be the Protected Network.

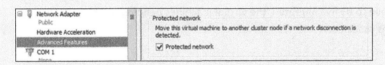

This will also verify that the destination node has the network available. You can configure this for any virtual machine and any network. If you had a virtual machine that you wanted to protect multiple networks, you can. Simply select all the networks that you want. You may not always want to do this on all networks that the virtual machine has.

You can also set this using Windows PowerShell and we'll examine that now.

For example, if I just wanted to turn this off for a specific virtual machine called Acct, the command would be:

```
PS C:\>Get-VMNetworkAdapter -VMName Acct | Where-Object {$_.SwitchName
-eq "Public"} | Set-VmNetworkAdapter -NotMonitoredInCluster False
```

If I wanted to turn it off for all virtual machines that use Public as the network switch, the command would be:

```
PS C:\>Get-VMNetworkAdapter * | Where-Object {$_.SwitchName -eq
"Public"} | Set-VmNetworkAdapter -NotMonitoredInCluster False
```

Keep in mind that the previous commands are only going to work for the highly available virtual machines currently running on the node you run the commands on. If you wanted to execute this against the Acct virtual machine running on a different node, the command would be:

```
PS C:\>Get-ClusterGroup Acct | Get-VM | Get-VMNetworkAdapter |
Where-Object {$_.SwitchName -eq "Private"} | Set-VMNetworkAdapter -
NotMonitoredInCluster False
```

Now that we have the protected network, we are monitoring the health of that network and the connectivity to the machine.

If we lose network connectivity on this network from this node, the cluster is going to check all remaining nodes to see if this network is up. If it is, it is going to do a live migration of the virtual machine to that node. If all other nodes do not have access to the network either, the virtual machine will remain in the current state it is in until the network is reconnected.

The virtual machine live migrations will be queued if there are more VMs affected by a network issue on a host than can be concurrently live migrated. If the disconnected network becomes available again and there are VMs virtual machines in the queue to be live migrated, the virtual machines pending will have the live migrations canceled.

John Marlin
Senior Support Escalation Engineer, Windows CORE TX

Virtual machine drain on shutdown

Previously in Windows Server 2012, if you shut down a node on a failover cluster of Hyper-V hosts running virtual machines without first draining the node, the virtual machines on the node were put into a saved state, moved to other nodes in the cluster, and then resumed. The result was an interruption in the availability of the virtual machines. In addition, if Failover Clustering determined that it was taking too long to save the state of the virtual machines on the node shutting down, the virtual machines might be turned off and then restarted on other nodes. This can not only cause an interruption in the availability of the virtual machines but might also result in data loss for business applications running in the virtual machines.

Failover Clustering in Windows Server 2012 R2 now solves this problem by automatically live migrating all running virtual machines from the node being shut down to other nodes in the cluster. The result of this change is to significantly improve the availability of applications and virtual machines running on failover clusters of Hyper-V hosts.

Let's learn more about this exciting new capability by listening again to one of our experts at Microsoft.

Ensuring virtual machine availability

Windows Server 2012 Failover Clustering introduced the ability to drain resources off of a node. This process was used in cases where a node was to be patched or shut down. When a node is drained, the Cluster service will pause the node, which prevents any new virtual machines (or other workload) from coming to it. It would also automatically move all the virtual machines off to another node.

When these virtual machines moved off, the type of move would depend on the priority setting. Virtual machines that are set as high or medium are live migrated, whereas low priority machines are quick migrated.

These moves are primarily based on preferred owners that may be set on the virtual machine resource as well as to random nodes. The problem with this is that you could run into an issue in which you overload one of the nodes and cause other virtual machines or the virtual machine you moved to fail.

In Windows Server 2012 R2, things were changed for the better with this process.

The first change is with the low priority machines. When a virtual machine is quick migrated, it does go down as it is put in a saved state. Once over on the other machine, it comes out of this saved state. Because it is down, any user(s) connected to it also loses connectivity and must re-establish the connectivity. In Failover Clustering with Windows Server 2012, this has been changed to have the low priority also live migrated.

Since we are now moving all virtual machines using live migration, this allows for the next item that was updated in regard to the virtual machine mobility. As mentioned previously:

"You could run into an issue in which you overload one of the nodes and cause other virtual machines or the virtual machine you moved to fail."

Now, we are being smarter with how things are moved. Before the virtual machines are moved, we will detect resources on the other nodes to better determine where virtual machines are placed. This will provide a better way of preventing failures of virtual machines for the moves and it truly moves the virtual machines to the "best available node."

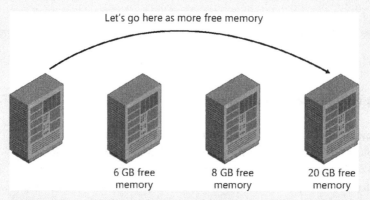

Let's go here as more free memory

6 GB free memory   8 GB free memory   20 GB free memory

This change allows for all virtual machines to remain up and connected to users. However, what happens if you were to forget to move virtual machines off or drain a node when the node is to be shut down? When a group is moved by means other than by the administrator, it falls back to the "cluster-controlled action" because the cluster must move it.

The recommendation has always been to move all workloads off of a node before it is shut down. When it is inadvertently forgotten, then connectivity is lost to the virtual machine due to the way the quick migration process works. Once the process starts, there is no stopping it.

So, in the thoughts of virtual machine availability, the next new change for the better was done. When a node is now shut down, it will issue a drain of the node first. The same draining process as described above is what occurs here.

This change is controlled by the cluster common property DrainOnShutdown, which is enabled (1) as a default. This can be changed to being disabled (0), but really, why would you when the name of the game is availability?

John Marlin
Senior Support Escalation Engineer, Windows CORE TX

Dynamic witness

In Failover Clustering, the quorum configuration determines the maximum number of failures that the cluster can sustain and still keep running. In Windows Server 2012, you had to determine when to configure a witness. In addition, you had to manually adjust the quorum configuration if the node membership changed. You needed to do this to keep the total number of votes at an odd number. And you had to do this every time you added or evicted cluster nodes. For example, if you added another node to your cluster, you had to manually adjust the quorum configuration. This is important because if there is an odd number of votes, then the quorum witness doesn't get to vote. But if the witness should have been able to vote and wasn't able to because of misconfiguration, then the possibility exists of the cluster going down because of witness failure.

With Failover Clustering in Windows Server 2012 R2, however, a new feature called dynamic witness allows the quorum witness vote to be dynamically adjusted based on the state of the witness resource. For example, if the witness resource is offline or failed, the cluster sets the witness vote to zero. The cluster thus decides whether to use the witness vote based on the number of voting nodes that are available in the cluster. As a result, Microsoft now recommends that you always configure a quorum witness when implementing a Failover Clustering solution using Windows Server 2012 R2.

A related enhancement to this dynamic quorum functionality is that a failover cluster can now dynamically adjust a running node's vote in order to keep the total number of votes at an odd number. To accomplish this, the cluster first tries to adjust the quorum witness vote through dynamic witness. But if a quorum witness is not available, the cluster can adjust a node's vote directly.

You can also now configure a cluster property that will determine which side of the cluster continues running in the event of a 50 percent node split where neither side would normally have a quorum. Previously, when this happened to a failover cluster running Windows Server 2012, both sides of the cluster would go down. Now, however, one side of the cluster can continue to run in the event of a tie like this.

You can configure this behavior by assigning the LowerQuorumPriorityNodeID cluster common property to a cluster node in your secondary site so that your primary site will continue to run in the event of a tie. You can configure this property using Windows PowerShell as follows:

```
(Get-Cluster).LowerQuorumPriorityNodeID = <node_ID_of_secondary_site>
```

You can determine the node IDs, node names, and node state using this command:

```
Get-ClusterNode | ft
```

Active Directory–detached clustering

One more (and potentially very useful for many customers) new feature of Failover Clustering in Windows Server 2012 R2 is the ability to deploy a failover cluster without any dependencies in Active Directory Domain Services (AD DS) for network names. What this means is that you can now register the cluster network name together with the network names of clustered roles that have client access points on your DNS servers without the need of creating corresponding computer objects in AD DS. This new capability is called Active Directory–detached clustering.

The main benefit of this new option for implementing Failover Clustering is that it can simplify the process of deploying, managing, and maintaining your failover clusters. For example, if you use Active Directory–detached clustering, then you will no longer need permissions to create these computer objects in AD DS or ask your Active Directory administrator to pre-stage the computer objects in AD DS. In addition, you will no longer need to manage and maintain the cluster computer objects for the cluster.

The chance of an administrative error causing your failover cluster to go down can also be reduced if you implement Active Directory–detached clustering in your environment. For example, it has been known to happen in the past that an administrator accidentally deletes a cluster object in Active Directory. Such mistakes, of course, can have disastrous consequences not only for your failover cluster and the workloads running on it, but for your business operations as well.

Note that Active Directory–detached clustering does not mean you don't need Active Directory for your Failover Clustering solution. The nodes in a failover cluster must still be joined to an Active Directory domain. Windows Server does not support deploying failover clusters in a workgroup environment using standalone servers.

Note also that you must use Windows PowerShell to implement Active Directory–detached clustering. For more information on how to do this, see the link on this topic in the "Learn more" section at the end of this chapter.

> **IMPORTANT**   Microsoft does not recommend implementing Active Directory–detached clustering for any scenario that requires Kerberos authentication.

Learn more

You can learn more about the new Failover Clustering features and enhancements in Windows Server 2012 R2 by checking out the following topics on Microsoft TechNet:

- "What's New in Failover Clustering in Windows Server 2012 R2" at *http://technet.microsoft.com/en-us/library/dn265972.aspx.*
- "Virtual Hard Disk Sharing Overview" at *http://technet.microsoft.com/en-us/library/dn281956.aspx.*

- "Deploy a Guest Cluster Using a Shared Virtual Hard Disk" at *http://technet.microsoft .com/en-us/library/dn265980.aspx.*

- "Deploy an Active Directory-Detached Cluster" at *http://technet.microsoft.com/en-us/ library/dn265970.aspx.*

The following Microsoft TechNet and MSDN blog posts also have lots of information about the new Failover Clustering features and enhancements in Windows Server 2012 R2:

- "How to Enable CSV Cache" at *http://blogs.msdn.com/b/clustering/ archive/2013/07/19/10286676.aspx.*

- "How to Properly Shutdown a Failover Cluster or a Node" at *http://blogs.msdn.com/b/ clustering/archive/2013/08/23/10443912.aspx.*

- "Windows Server 2012 R2 Virtual Machine Recovery from Network Disconnects" at *http://blogs.msdn.com/b/clustering/archive/2013/09/04/10446482.aspx.*

Be sure also to check out the following videos from TechEd 2013 on Channel 9:

- "Continuous Availability: Deploying and Managing Clusters Using Windows Server 2012 R2" at *http://channel9.msdn.com/Events/TechEd/NorthAmerica/2013/MDC-B305.*

- "Failover Cluster Networking Essentials" at *http://channel9.msdn.com/Events/TechEd/ NorthAmerica/2013/MDC-B337.*

- "Upgrading Your Private Cloud with Windows Server 2012 R2" at *http://channel9.msdn .com/Events/TechEd/NorthAmerica/2013/MDC-B331.*

- "Application Availability Strategies for the Private Cloud" at *http://channel9.msdn.com/ Events/TechEd/NorthAmerica/2013/MDC-B311.*

- "Storage and Availability Improvements in Windows Server 2012 R2" at *http://channel9 .msdn.com/Events/TechEd/NorthAmerica/2013/MDC-B333.*

- "Understanding the Hyper-V over SMB Scenario, Configurations, and End-to-End Performance" at *http://channel9.msdn.com/Events/TechEd/NorthAmerica/2013/ MDC-B335.*

CHAPTER 5

Networking

Currently, IT is all about the cloud, and the foundation of cloud computing is infrastructure. If you're an enterprise that's going to build and manage a private cloud, then you'll be dealing with three main kinds of infrastructure: compute, storage, and network. And if you're a hoster creating a cloud for selling services to customers, then you'll be working with the same three building blocks but on a much larger scale and with additional features that are essential for hosting environments such as multitenant isolation, IP address management, and Network Virtualization.

In Chapter 2, "Hyper-V," we looked at Hyper-V improvements in Windows Server 2012 R2. Hyper-V hosts provide the compute infrastructure needed for running virtualized workloads in a cloud infrastructure. In Chapter 3, "Storage," we examined storage improvements in the new platform. Storage Spaces and the Scale-out File Server (SoFS) are two storage technologies that can enable new scenarios and help lower costs when deploying the storage infrastructure for a cloud solution. In Chapter 4, "Failover Clustering," we looked at how the Failover Clustering feature has been enhanced in the platform. Failover clustering enables your compute and storage resources to be highly available, which is essential for today's always-on businesses.

In this chapter, we'll now examine the networking improvements in Windows Server 2012 R2. Networking is the underlying glue that holds your infrastructure together, makes possible the delivery of services, makes remote management a reality, and more.

But first let's begin by reviewing the networking enhancements introduced earlier in Windows Server 2012.

Previous enhancements to networking

Some of the many networking improvements introduced previously in Windows Server 2012 included the following:

- **Dynamic VMQ** Virtual Machine Queue (VMQ) allows a host's network adapter to pass DMA packets directly into the memory stacks of individual virtual machines. The net effect of doing this is to allow the host's single network adapter to appear to the virtual machines as multiple network interface cards (NICs) which then allows each virtual machine to have its own dedicated NIC. Windows Server 2012 improved this by introducing Dynamic VMQ, which dynamically distributed incoming network traffic processing to host processors, based on processor use and network load. The earlier implementation, which was also called Static VMQ, was removed in Windows Server 2012.

- **Receive Side Scaling**   Receive Side Scaling (RSS) allows network adapters to distribute kernel-mode network processing across multiple processor cores in multicore systems. Such distribution of processing enables support of higher network traffic loads than are possible if only a single core is used. RSS was enhanced in Windows Server 2012 to support systems with up to 64 processors, improved scalability across Non-Uniform Memory Access (NUMA) nodes, improved management and diagnostics, and automatic load balancing capabilities for non-TCP traffic such as UDP unicast, multicast, and IP-forwarded traffic.

- **Windows NIC Teaming**   Also known as load balancing and failover (LBFO), Windows NIC Teaming enables multiple NICs on a server to be grouped together into a team. This has two purposes: to help ensure availability by providing traffic failover in the event of a network component failure and to enable aggregation of network bandwidth across multiple NICs. Previously, implementing NIC teaming required using third-party solutions from independent hardware vendors (IHVs). Beginning with Windows Server 2012, however, NIC teaming was now an in-box solution that worked across different NIC hardware types and manufacturers.

- **Quality of Service enhancements**   Quality of Service (QoS) refers to technologies used for managing network traffic in ways that can meet service level agreements (SLAs) and/or enhance user experiences in a cost-effective manner. For example, by using QoS to prioritize different types of network traffic, you can ensure that mission-critical applications and services are delivered according to SLAs and to optimize user productivity. Windows Server 2012 introduced a number of new QoS capabilities including Hyper-V QoS, which allows you to specify upper and lower bounds for network bandwidth used by a virtual machine, and new Group Policy settings to implement policy-based QoS by tagging packets with an 802.1p value to prioritize different kinds of network traffic.

- **Data Center Bridging**   Data Center Bridging (DCB) is an IEEE standard that allows for hardware-based bandwidth allocation for specific types of network traffic, which means that DCB is yet another QoS technology. DCB-capable network adapter hardware can be useful in cloud environments where it can enable storage, data management, and other kinds of traffic all to be carried on the same underlying physical network in a way that guarantees each type of traffic its fair share of bandwidth. Windows Server 2012 supported DCB, provided that you had both DCB-capable Ethernet NICs and DCB-capable Ethernet switches on your network.

- **Dynamic Host Configuration Protocol enhancements**   Dynamic Host Configuration Protocol (DHCP) functionality was enhanced in several ways in Windows Server 2012. DHCP Server Failover was introduced as a new approach for ensuring DHCP availability by enabling two DHCP servers to replicate lease information between them. That way, one of the DHCP servers could assume responsibility for providing addresses to all the clients on a subnet when the other DHCP server became unavailable. Policy-based assignment allowed a DHCP server to evaluate DHCP requests against policies you defined for a specific scope and in a defined processing order.

- **Domain Name System enhancements**   Domain Name System (DNS) functionality was also enhanced in several ways in Windows Server 2012. The DNS Server component included improved support for DNS Security Extensions (DNSSEC) including support for DNS dynamic updates in DNSSEC signed zones, automated trust anchor distribution through Active Directory, automated trust anchor rollover, and support for updated DNSSEC standards. The DNS Client component included improved support for Network basic input/output system (NETBIOS) and Link-local multicast name resolution (LLMNR), binding order optimization, and asynchronous DNS caching.

- **IP Address Management**   IP Address Management (IPAM) is a new built-in framework introduced in Windows Server 2012 for discovering, monitoring, auditing, and managing the IP address space used on a corporate network. IPAM provided a central and integrated experience for managing IP addresses that could replace manual, work-intensive tools such as spreadsheets and custom scripts that can be tedious, unreliable, and scale poorly.

- **Network virtualization**   Network virtualization was introduced in Windows Server 2012 as a way for organizations to keep their own internal IP addresses when moving their servers into a hoster's cloud. Network virtualization works by allowing you to assign two different IP addresses to each virtual machine running on a Windows Server 2012 Hyper-V host: the customer address, which is the IP address that the server had when it resided on the customer's premises before it was migrated into the cloud; and the provider address, which is the IP address assigned by the cloud provider to the server once the server has been migrated to the provider's data center. Network virtualization thus lets the cloud provider run multiple virtual networks on top of a single physical network in much the same way as server virtualization lets you run multiple virtual servers on a single physical server. Network virtualization also isolates each virtual network from every other virtual network, with the result that each virtual network has the illusion that it is a separate physical network. This means that two or more virtual networks can have the exact same addressing scheme, yet the networks will be fully isolated from one another and each will function as if it is the only network with that scheme.

- **BranchCache enhancements**   BranchCache allows organizations to increase the network responsiveness of centralized applications that are being accessed from remote offices, with the result that branch office users have an experience similar to being directly connected to the central office. BranchCache was first introduced in Windows Server 2008 R2 and was enhanced in Windows Server 2012 with improved performance and reduced bandwidth usage, default encryption of cached content, new tools that allowed you to preload cachable content onto your hosted cache servers even before the content was first requested by clients, single instance storage and downloading of duplicated content, and tighter integration with the File Server role.

There were also other networking technologies introduced or improved in Windows Server 2012 that closely relate to other infrastructure components like compute and storage. For example, there was the Hyper-V Extensible Switch, which added new virtual networking functionality to the Hyper-V server role. There was version 3.0 of the Server Message Block (SMB) file-sharing protocol, which enabled new network storage scenarios such as the SoFS. There was single-root I/O virtualization (SR-IOV), which enabled a network adapter to divide access to its resources across various PCIe hardware functions and reduced processing overhead on the host, which can make the network performance of a virtual machine nearly as good as that of a physical computer. And there was a lot more new networking features and capabilities introduced previously in Windows Server 2012.

Many of the above networking features and technologies have now been improved even more in Windows Server 2012 R2. Let's examine some of these enhancements now.

Virtual RSS

Today, enterprise-grade NICs can be extremely fast—so fast in fact that a single processor core of the server won't be able to make full use of the NIC's throughput capability. RSS in Windows Server 2012 helps you get around that by allowing kernel-mode network processing to be spread across multiple cores in a multicore server system. In Windows Server 2012, however, virtual machines were limited to using only one virtual processor for processing network traffic. As a result, virtual machines running on Hyper-V hosts were unable to make use of RSS to utilize the highest possible network traffic loads. To compound the problem, VMQ would affinitize all traffic destined for a virtual machine to one core inside the host for access control list (ACL) and vmSwitch extension processing.

With Windows Server 2012 R2, however, this is no longer a limitation. That's because a new feature called virtual RSS (vRSS) maximizes network utilization for a virtual machine by spreading the processing of the traffic across multiple virtual processors inside the virtual machine and also inside the host. This is demonstrated by Figure 5-1, which shows a virtual machine that has four virtual processors assigned to it. The physical NIC can now spread traffic among available cores inside the host, while the virtual NIC distributes the processing load across the virtual processors inside the virtual machine.

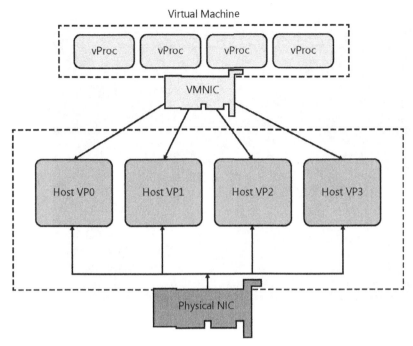

FIGURE 5-1 Virtual Receive Side Scaling (vRSS) is available in Windows Server 2012 R2.

The result of using vRSS is that it is now possible to virtualize network-intensive physical workloads that were traditionally run on bare-metal machines. A typical usage scenario might be a Hyper-V host that has a small number or only one virtual machine running on it, but the applications running in that virtual machine generate a large amount of network traffic. For example, vRSS can be especially useful for virtual network appliances, virtual gateways, file servers, and similar network-intensive applications, because you'll now be able to virtualize them without any network throughput degradation.

A nice thing about vRSS is that it will work on existing network hardware that is VMQ-capable. This means you don't have to upgrade your hardware in order to take advantage of this new capability.

RSS (and vRSS) is disabled by default in Windows Server 2012 and should only be enabled on network-intensive virtual machines. This is because extra processing is required for vRSS to spread the incoming network traffic inside the host. In other words, enabling vRSS trades CPU cycles for network throughput.

You can configure and manage vRSS by using Windows PowerShell commands and scripts. Figure 5-2 shows how to use the Get-NetAdapterRss cmdlet to get all RSS-capable network adapters on a system that have RSS enabled and display their names, interface description, and state. The figure also shows how to use the Get-Command cmdlet to display a list of all cmdlets available for managing RSS and vRSS.

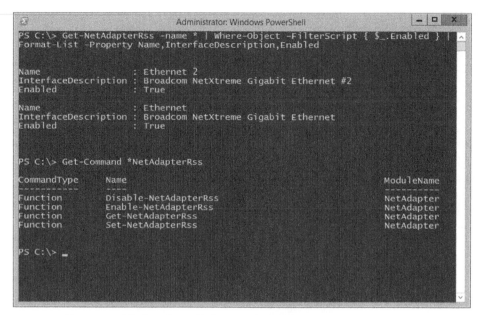

FIGURE 5-2 You can use Windows PowerShell to manage vRSS.

Windows NIC Teaming enhancements

Windows servers today are often huge beasts with tons of processing power to handle the biggest business workloads. Getting data in and out of such servers requires fat pipes—lots of network bandwidth—and for some environments even a single 10 GbE Ethernet network interface card (NIC) is insufficient and becomes a bottleneck. And what if that NIC fails for some reason? Your enterprise-class server suddenly becomes an expensive paperweight!

NIC teaming can address such problems. Also known as Load Balancing/Failover (LBFO), NIC teaming refers to any technological approach that enables two or more NICs to be linked together to form a team of some kind. Until recently, if you wanted to use NIC teaming, you had to implement a proprietary solution provided by your NIC hardware vendor. But beginning with Windows Server 2012, you now have an in-box solution called Windows NIC Teaming that you can use for implementing NIC teaming on your Windows servers.

NIC teaming can provide two types of benefits for enterprise networks. First, it allows you to aggregate the throughput from multiple network adapters. For example, let's say you have a server system that has two 1 gigabit network adapters configured as a team. The result is that the total throughput of the team is 1 + 1 = 2 gigabits, so teaming network adapters together basically gives your server a bigger "pipe" for sending and receiving traffic over the network the server is connected to.

The second benefit of NIC teaming is that it helps ensure continuous availability of the server's connection to the network by providing fault tolerance. For example, let's say that one of the NICs in the above team fails. If this happens, the throughput drops from 2 gigabits to 1 gigabit, and although such a 50 percent drop in network traffic handling capability could affect the performance of applications running on the server, the good thing is that the server still has some connectivity with the network. Without NIC teaming, failure of a single NIC would have caused the throughput to drop from 1 gigabit to zero, which is probably much worse from a business point of view.

Before Windows Server 2012, if you wanted to make use of NIC teaming, then you had to use third-party NIC teaming software from your network adapter vendor. With the release of Windows Server 2012, however, NIC teaming became a built-in feature called Windows NIC Teaming that makes it possible to team together even commodity network adapters to aggregate throughput and enable fault tolerance.

NIC Teaming in Windows Server 2012

Let's begin with a quick overview of what Windows NIC Teaming is, what kinds of scenarios it can address, and what types of configuration modes it supports. The following short description is excerpted from the free e-book *Introducing Windows Server 2012 RTM Edition* (Microsoft Press, 2012) which has been downloaded over 650,000 times since it was released just over a year ago.

Windows NIC Teaming is the name for the new network adapter teaming functionality included in Windows Server 2012. Network adapter teaming is also known as LBFO and enables multiple network adapters on a server to be grouped together into a team. This has two purposes:

- To help ensure availability by providing traffic failover in the event of a network component failure
- To enable aggregation of network bandwidth across multiple network adapters

Previously, implementing network adapter teaming required using third-party solutions from independent hardware vendors (IHVs). Beginning with Windows Server 2012, however, network adapter teaming is now an in-box solution that works across different NIC hardware types and manufacturers.

Windows NIC Teaming supports up to 32 network adapters in a team in three teaming modes:

- **Static Teaming**   Also called Generic Teaming and based on IEEE 802.3ad draft v1, this mode is typically supported by server-class Ethernet switches and requires manual configuration of the switch and the server to identify which links form the team.
- **Switch Independent**   This mode doesn't require that the team members connect to different switches; it merely makes it possible.

- **LACP**   Also called Dynamic Teaming and based on IEEE 802.1ax, this mode is
  supported by most enterprise-class switches and allows automatic creation of a team
  using the Link Aggregation Control Protocol (LACP), which dynamically identifies links
  between the server and a specific switch. To use this mode, you generally need to
  enable LACP manually on the port of the switch.

Since a picture is worth a thousand words, Figure 5-3 shows the three teaming modes you
can choose from when creating a new team in Windows Server 2012:

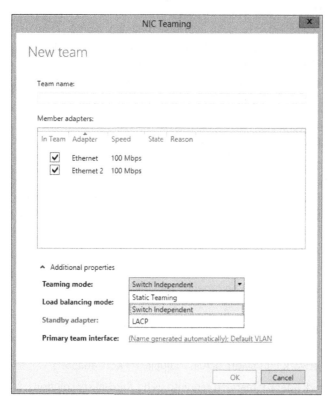

FIGURE 5-3 Configuring NIC Teaming in Windows Server 2012.

NIC Teaming in Windows Server 2012 R2

Although NIC Teaming in Windows Server 2012 provided both distribution of network load
across NICs in a team and failover support for teamed NICs, network traffic was not distributed
across teamed NICs in a balanced fashion. Beginning with Windows Server 2012 R2, however,
a new feature called dynamic load balancing automatically and continuously balances traffic
across teamed NICs in an equitable fashion.

Figure 5-4 is another thousand-word picture that illustrates this new functionality for NIC Teaming in Windows Server 2012 R2. Previously in Windows Server 2012, you only had two load-balancing modes you could choose from:

- **Address Hash** This algorithm distributes traffic among the teamed NICs by creating a hash from the address components of the packets that comprised a single stream of TCP traffic. The algorithm then assigns packets that have that particular hash value to one of the NICs in the team.

- **Hyper-V Port** This approach distributes traffic among the teamed NICs on the basis of the Mac address or port that a virtual machine uses to connect to the virtual switch on a Hyper-V host.

As you can see from the figure, however, a third load-balancing mode called Dynamic has now been added to NIC Teaming in Windows Server 2012 R2. Not only that, but this new mode is now the default load-balancing mode when you create a new team on the new platform. By using dynamic load balancing, you can now use all members of a NIC team even when the team is in Switch Independent mode.

FIGURE 5-4 Configuring NIC Teaming in Windows Server 2012 R2.

Choosing the right teaming mode

We saw from Figure 5-4 that when you use the UI to create a new NIC team in Windows Server 2012 R2 you have a choice of three teaming modes to choose from:

- Static Teaming
- Switch Independent
- LACP

This is actually a bit confusing because there are really only two types of teaming modes available:

- Switch Independent
- Switch Dependent

The UI doesn't display a mode called Switch Dependent but instead displays two types of switch dependent modes:

- Static Teaming
- LACP

So your choices for teaming mode really look like this:

- Switch Independent
- Switch Dependent
    - Static Teaming
    - LACP

When should you use Switch Independent teaming mode?

Switch Independent is the default teaming mode when you create a new team. This mode assumes that you don't need your Ethernet switches to participate in making NIC teaming happen for your server. In other words, this mode assumes the Ethernet switch isn't even aware that the NICs connected to it are teamed.

Because of this, selecting Switch Independent mode allows you to connect each NIC in a team to a different Ethernet switch on your backbone. However, you can also use this mode when all the NICs in the team are connected to the same Ethernet switch.

One scenario where you could use this functionality is to provide fault tolerance in the case of one of the teamed NICs failing. For example, you could create a team from two NICs (NIC1 and NIC2) on your server and then connect NIC1 to SWITCH1 and NIC2 to SWITCH2. You could then configure NIC1 as the active adapter for the team, and NIC2 as the standby adapter for the team. Then if NIC1 fails, NIC2 will automatically become active and your server won't lose its connectivity with your backbone.

Note that the above approach, which is variously called Active/Passive Teaming or Active/Standby Teaming, provides fault tolerance but not bandwidth aggregation for your server's connection to the network. You can just as easily leave both NICs configured as active and get both fault tolerance and bandwidth aggregation if you prefer, but the choice is up to you.

And when should you use Switch Dependent teaming mode?

You can only use one of the Switch Dependent modes (Static Teaming or LACP) if all of the teamed NICs are connected to the same Ethernet switch on your backbone. Let's consider this next.

Static Teaming (also called Generic Teaming or IEEE 802.3ad teaming) requires configuring both the server and Ethernet switch to get the team to work. Generally, only enterprise-class Ethernet switches support this kind of functionality, and since you need to manually configure it on the Ethernet switch, it requires additional work to get it working. Plus, manually configuring something always increases the odds of configuration errors happening if you make some kind of mistake during the setting up process. If at all possible, try to stay away from following this approach to NIC teaming on Windows Server.

LACP (also called IEEE 802.1ax teaming or dynamic teaming, which should not be confused with the new Dynamic load-balancing mode available for NIC teaming in Windows Server 2012 R2) uses the LACP to dynamically identify the network links between the server and the Ethernet switch. This makes LACP superior to Static Teaming because it enables the server to communicate with the Ethernet switch during the team creation process, thus enabling automatic configuration of the team on both the server and Ethernet switch. But whereas most enterprise-class Ethernet switches support LACP, you generally need to enable it on selected switch ports before it can be used. So LACP is less work to configure than Static Teaming, but still more work to set up than switch independent teaming which is the default option for Windows NIC Teaming.

The bottom line then is that Switch Independent teaming is generally your best choice to select for the teaming mode when creating a new NIC Team for two reasons. First, you don't need to perform any configuration on the Ethernet switch to get it working. And second, you can gain two kinds of fault tolerance:

- Protection against the failure of a NIC in the team
- Protection against the failure of an Ethernet switch connected to a teamed NIC (when you are connecting different teamed NICs to different Ethernet switches)

However, there are a couple of scenarios described later where Switch Dependent teaming might be the best choice if your Ethernet switches support such functionality and you're up to configuring it.

Choosing the right load-balancing mode

Let's say you've chosen Switch Independent teaming as the teaming mode for a new NIC team you're creating. Your next decision is which load-balancing mode you're going to use. As described in the previous section, NIC Teaming in Windows Server 2012 supports two different load-balancing modes: Address Hash or Hyper-V Port. Windows Server 2012 R2 adds a third option for load-balancing mode called Dynamic.

First, when should you use Address Hash load-balancing mode?

The main limitation of the Address Hash load-balancing approach is that inbound traffic can only be received by a single member of the team. The reason for this has to do with the underlying operation of how address hashing uses IP addresses and TCP ports to seed the hash function. So a scenario where this could be the best choice would be if your server was running the kind of workload where inbound traffic is light while outbound traffic is heavy.

Sound familiar? That's exactly what a web server like IIS experiences in terms of network traffic. Incoming HTTP/HTTPS requests are generally short streams of TCP traffic. What gets pumped out in response to such requests, however, can include text, images, and video.

So when should you use Hyper-V Port load-balancing mode?

This load balancing approach affinitizes each Hyper-V port (such as each virtual machine) on a Hyper-V host to a single NIC in the team at any given time. Basically what you get here is no load balancing from the virtual machine's perspective. Each virtual machine can only utilize one teamed NIC at a time, so maximum inbound and outbound throughput for the virtual machine is limited to what's provided by a single physical NIC on the host.

When might you use this form of load balancing? A typical scenario might be if the number of virtual machines running on the host is much greater than the number of physical NICs in the team on the host. Just be sure that the physical NICs can provide sufficient bandwidth to the workloads running in the virtual machines.

This discussion only scratches the surface, however, because there are other scenarios you might encounter when considering NIC teaming as a possible solution. For example, if you implement Windows NIC Teaming on a Hyper-V host and your virtual machines need to be able to utilize bandwidth from more than one NIC in the team, then an option for you (if your Ethernet switch supports it) is to configure LACP or Static Teaming as your teaming mode and Address Hash as your load-balancing mode. This is possible because it's how you configure the Ethernet switch that determines how traffic will be distributed across the team members. This scenario is kind of unusual, however, because typically if you have a virtualized workload that requires high bandwidth for both inbound and outbound traffic (such as a huge SQL Server database workload) then you're probably only going to have one or two virtual machines running on the Hyper-V host.

Finally, when should you use the new dynamic load-balancing mode?

Unfortunately, we can't provide guidance concerning this at the time of writing because the documentation on Windows NIC Teaming hasn't yet been updated. So your best bet for more detailed guidance on implementing NIC teaming in different configurations is to keep a watch on the link to this topic in the "Learn more" section at the end of this chapter.

Improved network diagnostics

Networking problems can bring down your private cloud solution and result in losses for your business. Being able to correctly diagnose networking problems makes it easier to quickly resolve them so you can get your business up and running again.

Windows Server 2012 R2 includes new features in Windows PowerShell that can help you troubleshoot network connection problems when they occur. But before we examine some of these improvements, let's start by briefly reviewing some of the network diagnostic capabilities of Windows PowerShell in the previous version Windows Server 2012.

Network diagnostic cmdlets in Windows Server 2012

If you're experiencing what might be a networking issue with one of your servers, the first thing you probably want to check is the configuration of the network adapters. The Get-NetAdapter cmdlet was first introduced in Windows Server 2012 as a way of retrieving the configuration of all physical network adapters in the server.

For example, let's see what happens when we run this command on a Hyper-V host named HOST30.contosol.com that is running Windows Server 2012 R2:

```
PS C:\> Get-NetAdapter

Name                      InterfaceDescription                    ifIndex Statu
                                                                          s
----                      --------------------                    ------- -----
vEthernet (Broadcom Ne... Hyper-V Virtual Ethernet Adapter #2          18 Up
Ethernet                  Broadcom NetXtreme Gigabit Ethernet          12 Di...
Ethernet 2                Broadcom NetXtreme Gigabit Ethernet #2       13 Up
```

Because this is a Hyper-V host, there are probably some virtual machines running on it. On Hyper-V hosts running Windows Server 2012 and later, you can use the Get-VMNetwork-Adapter cmdlet to collect configuration information for the network adapters for these virtual machines. For example, the following command will retrieve information about all virtual machine network adapters on the host:

```
PS C:\> Get-VMNetworkAdapter *

Name                  IsManagementOs VMName       SwitchName
----                  -------------- ------       ----------
Network Adapter False                SRV-STANDARD Broadcom NetXtreme Gigabit Ether...
Network Adapter False                SRV2012R2    Broadcom NetXtreme Gigabit Ether...
Network Adapter False                SRV2012R2
Network Adapter False                SRV2012      Broadcom NetXtreme Gigabit Ether...
Network Adapter False                SRV2012      Broadcom NetXtreme Gigabit Ether...
Network Adapter False                Gen2Test     Broadcom NetXtreme Gigabit Ether...
```

You can also use Get-VMNetworkAdapter with the -VMName option to display network adapters for a specific virtual machine on the host.

Another useful network troubleshooting cmdlet introduced previously in Windows Server 2012 is Get-NetIPAddress, which retrieves the IP addresses configured on the system's network adapters. You can use the Get-NetIPAddress cmdlet both on physical servers and within virtual machines. For example, let's run this command on HOST30 described above:

```
PS C:\> Get-NetIPAddress


IPAddress          : fe80::8843:1e98:a8a6:6fab%12
InterfaceIndex     : 12
InterfaceAlias     : Ethernet
AddressFamily      : IPv6
Type               : Unicast
PrefixLength       : 64
PrefixOrigin       : WellKnown
SuffixOrigin       : Link
AddressState       : Deprecated
ValidLifetime      : Infinite ([TimeSpan]::MaxValue)
PreferredLifetime  : Infinite ([TimeSpan]::MaxValue)
SkipAsSource       : False
PolicyStore        : ActiveStore

IPAddress          : fe80::1905:8ae1:5bfd:7b8e%18
InterfaceIndex     : 18
InterfaceAlias     : vEthernet (Broadcom NetXtreme Gigabit Ethernet #2 -
                     Virtual Switch)
AddressFamily      : IPv6
Type               : Unicast
PrefixLength       : 64
PrefixOrigin       : WellKnown
SuffixOrigin       : Link
AddressState       : Preferred
ValidLifetime      : Infinite ([TimeSpan]::MaxValue)
PreferredLifetime  : Infinite ([TimeSpan]::MaxValue)
SkipAsSource       : False
PolicyStore        : ActiveStore

IPAddress          : fe80::5efe:172.16.11.30%14
InterfaceIndex     : 14
InterfaceAlias     : isatap.{3D53D3DC-9209-4C7F-8AAE-AD8ADCBD93FC}
AddressFamily      : IPv6
Type               : Unicast
PrefixLength       : 128
PrefixOrigin       : WellKnown
SuffixOrigin       : Link
AddressState       : Deprecated
ValidLifetime      : Infinite ([TimeSpan]::MaxValue)
```

```
PreferredLifetime : Infinite ([TimeSpan]::MaxValue)
SkipAsSource      : False
PolicyStore       : ActiveStore

IPAddress         : ::1
InterfaceIndex    : 1
InterfaceAlias    : Loopback Pseudo-Interface 1
AddressFamily     : IPv6
Type              : Unicast
PrefixLength      : 128
PrefixOrigin      : WellKnown
SuffixOrigin      : WellKnown
AddressState      : Preferred
ValidLifetime     : Infinite ([TimeSpan]::MaxValue)
PreferredLifetime : Infinite ([TimeSpan]::MaxValue)
SkipAsSource      : False
PolicyStore       : ActiveStore

IPAddress         : 169.254.111.171
InterfaceIndex    : 12
InterfaceAlias    : Ethernet
AddressFamily     : IPv4
Type              : Unicast
PrefixLength      : 16
PrefixOrigin      : WellKnown
SuffixOrigin      : Link
AddressState      : Tentative
ValidLifetime     : Infinite ([TimeSpan]::MaxValue)
PreferredLifetime : Infinite ([TimeSpan]::MaxValue)
SkipAsSource      : False
PolicyStore       : ActiveStore

IPAddress         : 172.16.11.30
InterfaceIndex    : 18
InterfaceAlias    : vEthernet (Broadcom NetXtreme Gigabit Ethernet #2 -
                    Virtual Switch)
AddressFamily     : IPv4
Type              : Unicast
PrefixLength      : 24
PrefixOrigin      : Manual
SuffixOrigin      : Manual
AddressState      : Preferred
ValidLifetime     : Infinite ([TimeSpan]::MaxValue)
PreferredLifetime : Infinite ([TimeSpan]::MaxValue)
SkipAsSource      : False
PolicyStore       : ActiveStore
```

```
IPAddress          : 127.0.0.1
InterfaceIndex     : 1
InterfaceAlias     : Loopback Pseudo-Interface 1
AddressFamily      : IPv4
Type               : Unicast
PrefixLength       : 8
PrefixOrigin       : WellKnown
SuffixOrigin       : WellKnown
AddressState       : Preferred
ValidLifetime      : Infinite ([TimeSpan]::MaxValue)
PreferredLifetime : Infinite ([TimeSpan]::MaxValue)
SkipAsSource       : False
PolicyStore        : ActiveStore
```

You can see that Get-NetIPAddress returns a lot of useful info you can parse or pipe into other commands for further processing.

Another useful network troubleshooting cmdlet is Get-NetIPConfiguration which can be used to retrieve usable network interfaces, IP addresses, and DNS servers configured on a system. The key value of Get-NetIPConfiguration is that it gives you the "big picture" of the system's network configuration in a concise way. For example, let's see what happens when we run this command on HOST30 without any further options being specified:

```
PS C:\> Get-NetIPConfiguration


InterfaceAlias       : vEthernet (Broadcom NetXtreme Gigabit Ethernet #2 -
                       Virtual Switch)
InterfaceIndex       : 18
InterfaceDescription : Hyper-V Virtual Ethernet Adapter #2
NetProfile.Name      : contoso.com
IPv4Address          : 172.16.11.30
IPv6DefaultGateway   :
IPv4DefaultGateway   : 172.16.11.1
DNSServer            : 172.16.11.50

InterfaceAlias       : Ethernet
InterfaceIndex       : 12
InterfaceDescription : Broadcom NetXtreme Gigabit Ethernet
NetAdapter.Status    : Disconnected
```

To make things even easier, the alias GIP can be used instead of having to type Get-NetIPConfiguration at the command line. For example, let's say we want to retrieve only the DNS Server configuration of the network adapter whose alias begins with "vEthernet" as shown above. Here's how we can do this:

```
PS C:\> $a = GIP 'v*'
PS C:\> $a.DNSServer
```

```
InterfaceAlias           Interface Address ServerAddresses  PSComputerName
                         Index     Family
--------------           --------- ------- ---------------  --------------
vEthernet (Broadcom NetXt...    18 IPv6    {}
vEthernet (Broadcom NetXt...    18 IPv4    {172.16.11.50}
```

Get-NetIPConfiguration can also provide verbose output by specifying the -Detailed option as shown here:

```
PS C:\> GIP -Detailed
```

```
ComputerName                  : HOST30
InterfaceAlias                : vEthernet (Broadcom NetXtreme Gigabit Ethernet
                                #2 - Virtual Switch)
InterfaceIndex                : 18
InterfaceDescription          : Hyper-V Virtual Ethernet Adapter #2
NetAdapter.LinkLayerAddress   : 00-24-E8-50-17-F3
NetAdapter.Status             : Up
NetProfile.Name               : contoso.com
NetProfile.NetworkCategory    : DomainAuthenticated
NetProfile.IPv6Connectivity   : LocalNetwork
NetProfile.IPv4Connectivity   : Internet
IPv6LinkLocalAddress          : fe80::1905:8ae1:5bfd:7b8e%18
IPv4Address                   : 172.16.11.30
IPv6DefaultGateway            :
IPv4DefaultGateway            : 172.16.11.1
NetIPv6Interface.N1MTU        : 1500
NetIPv4Interface.N1MTU        : 1500
NetIPv6Interface.DHCP         : Enabled
NetIPv4Interface.DHCP         : Disabled
DNSServer                     : 172.16.11.50

ComputerName                  : HOST30
InterfaceAlias                : Ethernet
InterfaceIndex                : 12
InterfaceDescription          : Broadcom NetXtreme Gigabit Ethernet
NetAdapter.LinkLayerAddress   : 00-24-E8-50-17-F4
NetAdapter.Status             : Disconnected
```

Network diagnostic cmdlets in Windows Server 2012 R2

Although the above cdmlets can help you troubleshoot a lot of networking issues, they're sometimes hard to apply in certain situations. So let's now examine some of the network troubleshooting improvements introduced in Windows PowerShell in Windows Server 2012 R2.

For many network admins, the first and most useful improvement is the addition of a new cmdlet named Test-NetConnection that can be used to perform ICMP and TCP connectivity tests. Let's now see this in action. We'll perform all our tests from a Windows PowerShell prompt on server HOST30.contoso.com as before.

First, let's test network connectivity between HOST30 and another server named HOST50 on our network:

```
PS C:\> Test-NetConnection HOST50.contoso.com


ComputerName           : HOST50.contoso.com
RemoteAddress          : 172.16.11.50
InterfaceAlias         : vEthernet (Broadcom NetXtreme Gigabit Ethernet #2 -
                         Virtual Switch)
SourceAddress          : 172.16.11.30
PingSucceeded          : True
PingReplyDetails (RTT) : 0 ms
```

The Test-NetConnection cmdlet can also be used to test network connectivity with hosts on remote networks and over the Internet. For example, let's see if HOST30 can establish network connectivity with the Microsoft Xbox website:

```
PS C:\> Test-NetConnection www.xbox.com


ComputerName           : www.xbox.com
RemoteAddress          : 184.29.219.150
InterfaceAlias         : vEthernet (Broadcom NetXtreme Gigabit Ethernet #2 -
                         Virtual Switch)
SourceAddress          : 172.16.11.30
PingSucceeded          : True
PingReplyDetails (RTT) : 26 ms
```

The -TraceRoute option can also be used to trace the exact network route used to establish connectivity with the remote site:

```
PS C:\> Test-NetConnection www.xbox.com -TraceRoute


ComputerName           : www.xbox.com
RemoteAddress          : 184.29.219.150
```

```
InterfaceAlias            : vEthernet (Broadcom NetXtreme Gigabit Ethernet #2 -
                            Virtual Switch)
SourceAddress             : 172.16.11.30
PingSucceeded             : True
PingReplyDetails (RTT)    : 29 ms
TraceRoute                : 172.16.11.1
                            142.161.5.200
                            142.161.5.65
                            4.28.68.21
                            4.69.158.146
                            4.69.138.166
                            4.68.111.70
                            184.29.219.150
```

You can also use Test-NetConnection to test connectivity on a specific TCP port by including the -Port option in your command. For example, let's verify that the Xbox website can be accessed on the standard HTTP port which is TCP port 80:

```
PS C:\> Test-NetConnection www.xbox.com -Port 80


ComputerName              : www.xbox.com
RemoteAddress             : 184.29.219.150
RemotePort                : 80
InterfaceAlias            : vEthernet (Broadcom NetXtreme Gigabit Ethernet #2 -
                            Virtual Switch)
SourceAddress             : 172.16.11.30
PingSucceeded             : True
PingReplyDetails (RTT)    : 28 ms
TcpTestSucceeded          : True
```

You can also use an alias like RDP to verify TCP connectivity with the well-known port for the Remote Desktop Protocol, which is TCP port 3389. For example, let's see if HOST30 can establish connectivity to TCP port 3389 on HOST50:

```
PS C:\> Test-NetConnection HOST50 RDP


ComputerName              : HOST50
RemoteAddress             : 172.16.11.50
RemotePort                : 3389
InterfaceAlias            : vEthernet (Broadcom NetXtreme Gigabit Ethernet #2 -
                            Virtual Switch)
SourceAddress             : 172.16.11.30
PingSucceeded             : True
PingReplyDetails (RTT)    : 0 ms
TcpTestSucceeded          : True
```

The success of the above test indicates that Remote Desktop is enabled on the server HOST50.

Test-NetConnection also lets you use other aliases besides RDP for testing connectivity with well-known TCP ports. For example, you can also use:

- SMB
- HTTP
- PING

Now let's see what happens when we try the RDP test against the server HOST40 on our network:

```
PS C:\> Test-NetConnection HOST40 RDP
WARNING: Ping to HOST40 failed -- Status: TimedOut


ComputerName              : HOST40
RemoteAddress             : 172.16.11.61
RemotePort                : 3389
InterfaceAlias            : vEthernet (Broadcom NetXtreme Gigabit Ethernet #2 -
                            Virtual Switch)
SourceAddress             : 172.16.11.30
PingSucceeded             : False
PingReplyDetails (RTT)    : 0 ms
TcpTestSucceeded          : True
```

Note that RDP connectivity succeeded, but pinging the server failed. This indicates that the server's firewall is active and blocking the inbound ICMP messages that are being sent by HOST30.

The Test-NetConnection cmdlet also supports an -InformationLevel option that allows you to gather more detailed information concerning the connectivity test being performed:

```
PS C:\> Test-NetConnection HOST50 RDP -InformationLevel Detailed


ComputerName              : HOST50
RemoteAddress             : 172.16.11.50
RemotePort                : 3389
AllNameResolutionResults  : 172.16.11.50
                            fe80::396f:7162:ab64:fa82
MatchingIPsecRules        :
NetworkIsolationContext   : Private Network
InterfaceAlias            : vEthernet (Broadcom NetXtreme Gigabit Ethernet #2 -
                            Virtual Switch)
SourceAddress             : 172.16.11.30
NetRoute (NextHop)        : 0.0.0.0
PingSucceeded             : True
```

```
PingReplyDetails (RTT)    : 0 ms
TcpTestSucceeded          : True
```

Or you can use -InformationLevel to suppress all output except whether the desired test was successful or not:

```
PS C:\> Test-NetConnection HOST40 RDP -InformationLevel Quiet
WARNING: Ping to HOST40 failed -- Status: TimedOut
True
PS C:\>
```

One final note about Test-NetConnection is that you can also run it with no parameters like this:

```
PS C:\> Test-NetConnection
```

```
ComputerName              : internetbeacon.msedge.net
RemoteAddress             : 131.253.3.197
InterfaceAlias            : vEthernet (Broadcom NetXtreme Gigabit Ethernet #2 -
                            Virtual Switch)
SourceAddress             : 172.16.11.30
PingSucceeded             : True
PingReplyDetails (RTT)    : 49 ms
```

Doing this simply tests whether your server has a network connection with the Internet by testing connectivity with a remote server belonging to the DNS domain msedge.net, which is registered by Microsoft.

Another new network diagnostic cmdlet introduced in Windows Server 2012 R2 is Test-VMNetworkAdapter, which lets you diagnose network connectivity issues in the tenant network of a Hyper-V Virtual Network environment. At the time of writing, the documentation for this cmdlet had not been published, so we'll refer you to the link on this topic in the "Learn more" section of this chapter for more information when it becomes available.

IPAM enhancements

Enterprise networks today tend to be a lot more complex than they were 20 or even 10 years ago. With the advent of virtualization technologies like Hyper-V, network administrators have to deal with both physical networks and virtual networks. Nodes on both kinds of networks need IP addresses in order to be reachable, and these IP addresses can be assigned statically (manually), dynamically using DHCP, dynamically using Automatic Private IP Addressing (APIPA), or more typically, using some combination of these three methods. DNS is also needed in order to provide name resolution services so servers can have easy-to-remember friendly names like SRV-A instead of hard-to-memorize IP addresses like 169.254.115.33.

DHCP simplifies the task of allocating IP addresses to clients on a network (and to servers by using DHCP reservations), but large organizations can have multiple DHCP servers with each server having dozens or more scopes and each scope having its own special set of options. Similarly, DNS simplifies management of fully-qualified domain names (FQDNs) for both servers and clients, but large organizations can have multiple DNS servers with each one authoritative over dozens of zones and each zone containing thousands of resource records.

How does one manage all this? On the Windows Server platform, you can use the DHCP Server snap-in to manage all the DHCP servers in your organization, but the snap-in really isn't efficient when it comes to managing large numbers of DHCP servers. Similarly, you can use the DNS Server snap-in to manage all your DNS servers, but again this snap-in isn't efficient for managing large numbers of DNS servers.

For example, on large networks neither the DHCP snap-in nor DNS snap-in are very useful for helping you get quick answers to any of the following questions:

- Which DHCP servers in my organization manage which blocks of the IP address space?
- Which IP addresses are actually being used at each site where my company has a physical presence?
- Which IP addresses have been assigned to virtual network adapters of virtual machines running on Hyper-V hosts?
- How can I modify a particular scope option for a certain number of scopes residing on several different DHCP servers?
- How can I determine which subnets of an IP address range being managed by a certain DHCP server are not being used?
- How can I determine how many free IP addresses are available for leasing for certain scopes on certain DHCP servers?
- How can I find all scopes that have 95 percent or more of their address pool leased out to clients?
- How can I track all the IP addresses that have been assigned over the last 12 months to a certain server on my network?
- How can I find DNS servers that don't have a certain server option configured?

Administrators of large enterprises often want answers like these—and want them quickly. However, it can be difficult for them to keep track of their IP addressing schemes, DHCP server configurations, and DNS server configurations. Cloud hosting providers can have even greater difficulties keeping track of such information because their environments include both physical and virtual networks, and because of the address space reuse that often happens in multitenant cloud environments.

In the past, most large enterprises and hosters have relied on either spreadsheets, custom software developed in-house, or third-party commercial programs for keeping track of IP addressing schemes, DHCP server configurations, and DNS server configurations. Beginning with Windows Server 2012, however, Microsoft introduced an in-box solution for performing these kinds of tasks. That in-box solution is IPAM.

IPAM in Windows Server 2012

IPAM is an integrated set of tools that helps you plan, deploy, manage, and monitor your IP address infrastructure. IPAM includes functionality for performing address space management in multiserver environments and includes monitoring and network auditing capabilities. IPAM can automatically discover the IP address infrastructure of servers on your network and allows you to manage them from a central interface that is integrated into Server Manager. IPAM is an agentless technology that works together with the Active Directory Domain Services (AD DS), DHCP Server, DNS Server, and Network Policy Server (NPS) roles of the Windows Server platform.

Some of the capabilities of IPAM in Windows Server 2012 include:

- Integrates management of IP addresses, domain names, and device identities
- Organizes, assigns, monitors, and manages static and dynamic IPv4 and IPv6 addresses
- Automatic discovery of domain controllers, DHCP and DNS servers, and dynamic IP addresses in use
- Provides custom IP address space display, reporting, and management
- Tightly integrates with Microsoft DNS and DHCP servers
- Centralizes configuration and update of Microsoft DHCP and DNS servers
- Monitors and manages specific scenario-based DHCP and DNS services
- Tracks and audits changes and provides real-time view of status
- Audits server configuration changes and tracks IP address use

Although IPAM in Windows Server 2012 provided enough functionality for some organizations, other organizations (especially hosters) wanted something more. That something more has now arrived with the enhanced IPAM included in Windows Server 2012 R2.

IPAM in Windows Server 2012 R2

IPAM in Windows Server 2012 R2 represents a significant step forward in simplifying the management of addressing and DNS/DHCP server management both for large enterprises and especially for cloud hosting providers. Let's examine some of these improvements now.

First and perhaps most importantly, IPAM in Windows Server 2012 R2 now allows you to manage your virtual address space in addition to its physical address space. This means that enterprises that have a mixture of physical and virtual environments now have an in-box unified IP address management solution. Figure 5-5 shows the new Virtualized IP Address Space option in the IPAM page of Server Manager and some of the available configuration options.

This enhancement should be especially useful to very large enterprises and to hosters whose networks often consist of multiple data centers in different geographical locations. Such networks typically consist of an underlying fabric layer of infrastructure resources with a multitenant virtual network layered on top.

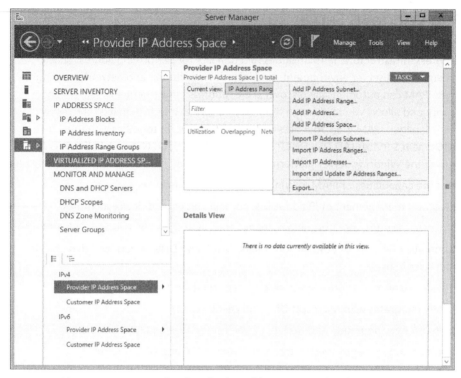

FIGURE 5-5 You can now manage the Virtualized IP Address Space option for IPAM using Server Manager.

For hosters that have built their cloud using the Windows Server platform, IPAM in Windows Server 2012 R2 offers the additional advantage of tight integration between IPAM and System Center Virtual Machine Manager (VMM) 2012 R2. Because IPAM basically knows everything about your physical network, such as its subnets, virtual LANs (VLANs), and pools, IPAM can make all this information available to VMM for the rapid provisioning of new virtual networks.

Another very important enhancement to IPAM in Windows Server 2012 R2 is the introduction of role-based access control. Role-based access control provides the organization with a mechanism for specifying access to objects and capabilities in terms of the organizational structure. Instead of assigning certain rights and permissions to a user or group of users, role-based access control allows you to assign a certain role instead. The role aligns with the kinds of tasks a certain type of user needs to be able to perform, and assigning the role to a user automatically grants that user all the necessary rights and permissions he or she needs to do the job.

For example, let's say your organization is very large and you have a fairly large IT staff to manage your network. You want to assign the job of being able to manage the IP address space for your network to three individuals, and you want to give the job of managing network infrastructure servers (DHCP and DNS) to two other people. Role-based access control in IPAM now makes doing these things simple.

Role-based access control in IPAM is also highly granular. For example, let's say that you want to allow a junior administrator to be able to manage only a certain DHCP scope on a certain DHCP server. Role-based access control in IPAM allows you to grant such access to the user while preventing her from having any other IP address management capabilities in your organization.

Role-based access control also includes the ability to delegate administrative privileges. This means that a senior administrator can delegate to junior administrators the ability to perform certain kinds of address management tasks in your organization.

To understand how role-based access control is integrated into the capabilities of IPAM, Figure 5-6 shows the basic architecture for how IPAM works. At the top is an administrator whose computer is running Windows 8.1 and has the Remote Server Administration Tools (RSAT) for Windows 8.1 installed. The administrator opens Server Manager on his computer and selects the IPAM page of Server Manager, as shown previously in Figure 5-5. The tasks available for the administrator to perform will depend on the specific role assigned to the administrator—for example, whether he is a network administrator, fabric administrator, system administrator, forensics investigator, and so on.

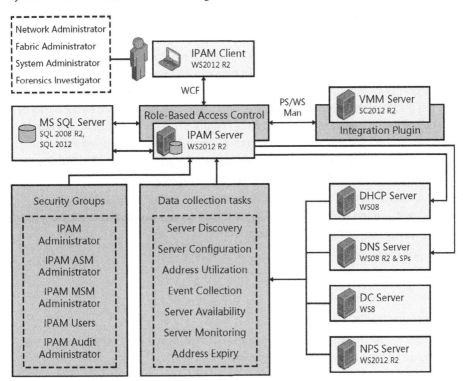

FIGURE 5-6 An example of how role-based access control is integrated into the capabilities of IPAM in Windows Server 2012 R2.

The IPAM client (in Server Manager) communicates with the IPAM server using Windows Communication Foundation (WCF)—a framework for building service-oriented applications. All communications between the IPAM client and IPAM server must go through the role-based access control component, which controls what tasks the administrator is able to perform.

The IPAM server performs various data-collection tasks including performing server discovery and monitoring, determining the configuration and availability of servers, performing event collection, determining address utilization, checking for expired addresses, and so on. To perform these different tasks, IPAM communicates with the DHCP servers, DNS servers, NPS servers, and domain controllers on your network.

As described earlier, the IPAM server can also communicate with one or more VMM servers. Such communications are made possible by using an IPAM integration plug-in included in VMM 2012 R2.

Although role-based access control should be the way to use IPAM going forward, IPAM in Windows Server 2012 R2 still includes the various IPAM security groups that were used in the previous version of IPAM for granting administrative privileges to users and groups.

The IPAM server stores the information it collects about your organization's network in a database. In the previous version of IPAM in Windows Server 2012, addressing information that was collected could only be stored in the Windows Internal Database (WID). IPAM in Windows Server 2012 R2, however, can now store data in a Microsoft SQL Server database running either on the local IPAM server or on an external server. This means that you can now ensure that the IPAM database is highly available, back the database up more easily, perform custom queries against it using T-SQL, and so on. As Figure 5-7 shows, when you provision a Windows Server 2012 R2 system as an IPAM server, you have the option of using either the WID or a SQL server for storing the data that IPAM collects for your network. The SQL Server database for IPAM must be on SQL Server 2008 R2 or SQL Server 2012.

IPAM in Windows Server 2012 R2 also includes extensive capabilities for allowing you to monitor and manage the activity of the DHCP and DNS servers on your network. For example, IPAM allows you to monitor such things as:

- Server availability
- DHCP Scope utilization
- DNS Zone replication health
- DHCP Failover health

IPAM also enables you to enable/disable features, activate/deactivate entities, allow/deny actions, and so on relating to DNS and DHCP servers.

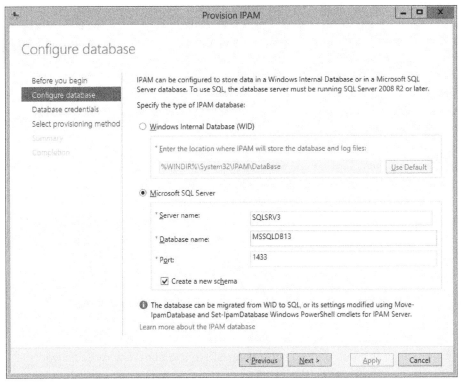

FIGURE 5-7 IPAM in Windows Server 2012 R2 can now store data in a Microsoft SQL Server database.

In terms of management capability, IPAM in Windows Server 2012 R2 makes it easy for administrators to manage from a central user interface and for a whole organization such things as:

- DHCP servers
- DHCP scopes
- DHCP properties
- DHCP options
- DHCP filters
- DHCP failover relationships
- DHCP policies
- DHCP classes
- DHCP reservations
- DNS resource records

Just imagine how much easier this is compared to using the DHCP or DNS snap-ins for performing such tasks!

IPAM in Windows Server 2012 R2 is also fully integrated with Windows PowerShell. In fact, there is 100 percent parity between what you can do using the IPAM page in Server Manager and the IPAM cmdlets in Windows PowerShell. The IPAM Windows PowerShell provider also facilitates integration with other platforms such as System Center Configuration Manager and the Microsoft Assessment and Planning (MAP) Toolkit. Such integration can simplify and speed the network discovery of the IP address inventory of your network. And you can also leverage an Internet Control Message Protocol (ICMP)–based discovery module for performing network discovery as well.

IPAM in Windows Server 2012 R2 also integrates with Active Directory Domain Services (AD DS). Specifically, IPAM enables synchronization of Active Directory Sites and Subnets information from Active Directory to IPAM. This too makes it quick and easy for IPAM to determine the subnet structure of your organization's network.

IPAM in Windows Server 2012 R2 is clearly a cost-effective, scalable, and customizable solution for unified management of physical and virtual network IP address spaces, and DHCP and DNS services in both enterprise and hoster environments.

Hyper-V Network Virtualization enhancements

Hyper-V Network Virtualization was introduced in Windows Server 2012 as a key part of Microsoft's vision for software-defined networking (SDN). Traditional enterprise networks typically had many different physical networking devices such as Ethernet switches, routers, virtual private networking (VPN) gateways, hardware firewalls, and other kinds of network appliances. And of course they needed lots of wires to connect all the network hosts (servers and appliances) together.

The modern data center network is no longer like that. Instead of dozens of network devices and hundreds or thousands of servers, the modern data center might consist of only a dozen or so very powerful virtualization host systems, a handful of 10 GbE switches, and a couple of perimeter firewalls. Instead of thousands of individual physical servers, you now have thousands of virtual machines running on relatively few Hyper-V hosts. One reason this change is possible is because of server virtualization and consolidation, which enables organizations to virtualize workloads that previously needed to run on physical server systems. Another reason it's possible, however, is because of SDN technologies like network virtualization that allow you to consolidate multiple physical network devices onto a single physical networking device in a similar fashion to how server virtualization lets you consolidate multiple physical servers onto a single physical virtualization host. The basic idea of network virtualization is nothing new, and Hyper-V Network Virtualization is simply Microsoft's implementation of the concept of network virtualization.

How Hyper-V Network Virtualization works

The basic idea behind network virtualization is that it allows multiple virtual machine networks to overlay a cloud hosting provider's underlying physical network (see Figure 5-8). Each virtual machine network, which can be composed of one or more virtual subnets, is independent of all other virtual machine networks and also of the hoster's underlying physical network. In other words, the exact physical location of an IP subnet on the hoster's physical network is decoupled from the virtual network topology of each customer's network.

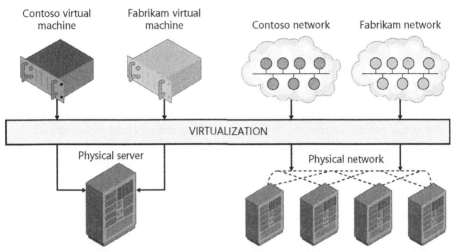

FIGURE 5-8 Hyper-V Network Virtualization allows multiple virtual machine networks to overlay a cloud hosting provider's underlying physical network.

The benefit of this decoupling is that customers can easily move physical server workloads to a hoster's cloud while preserving the IP addresses and network topology of their workloads. For example, let's say that your organization has three physical servers residing on-premises and having private IP addresses of 192.168.33.45, 192.168.33.46, and 192.168.33.47. You want to virtualize these servers by converting them into virtual machines, which you will move to the hoster's cloud. Your physical servers are currently using 192.168.0.0/16 as their address space, while the hoster uses 10.0.0.0/24 for its physical network.

If the hoster is using Hyper-V hosts running Windows Server 2012, your servers can keep their existing IP addresses in the 192.168.0.0/16 address space when their workloads are moved into the hoster's cloud. This means that your existing clients, which are used to accessing physical servers located on the 192.168.0.0/16 subnet, will still be able to do so with no modifications needed to your routing infrastructure, management platform, or network security policies. All that is required is a gateway be used to connect the physical networks where your clients and the resources they need reside with the virtual network on which your virtualized workloads are running on the hoster's physical network.

The ability of Hyper-V Network Virtualization to preserve your network infrastructure (addressing and subnet scheme) allows existing services to continue to work while being unaware of the physical location of the subnets. The way this works is that network virtualization enables you to assign two different IP addresses to each virtual machine running on a Windows Server 2012 Hyper-V host. These two addresses are:

- **Customer Address (CA)** This is the IP address that the server had when it resided on the customer's premises before it was migrated into the cloud. In the above example, this might be the 192.168.33.45 address for a particular server that the customer wants to move to the cloud.

- **Provider Address (PA)** This is the IP address assigned by the cloud provider to the server once the server has been migrated to the provider's data center. In the above example, this might be 10.44.2.133, or some other address in the 10.0.0.0/24 address space.

The CA for each virtual machine is mapped to the PA for the underlying physical host on which the virtual machine is running. Virtual machines communicate over the network by sending and receiving packets in the CA space. The virtual machine's packets are then encapsulated into new packets that have a PA as source and destination address so they can be routed over the hoster's physical network. The standards-based Network Virtualization Generic Routing Encapsulation (NVGRE) protocol is used by Hyper-V Network Virtualization, in Windows Server 2012, to encapsulate the virtual machine's packet inside a new packet. The header of this new packet has the appropriate source and destination PA, in addition to the virtual subnet ID, which is stored in the Key field of the GRE header. The virtual subnet ID in the GRE header allows hosts to identify the customer virtual machine for any given packet even though the PAs and the CAs on the packets may overlap. In other words, Hyper-V Network Virtualization keeps track of CA-to-PA mappings to enable hosts to differentiate packets for virtual machines of different customers. All virtual machines on the same host can therefore share a single PA, which helps increase network scalability because you only need as few as a single IP address per host, which lowers the burden on switches in the hoster's network.

The result is that Hyper-V Network Virtualization allows the hoster to run multiple customer virtual networks on top of a single underlying physical network in much the same way as server virtualization lets you run multiple virtual servers on a single physical server. Network virtualization isolates each virtual network from every other virtual network so that each virtual network has the illusion that it is a completely separate network. Multiple customers can even use the exact same addressing scheme for their virtual networks; customer networks will be fully isolated from one another and will function as if each network is the only one present with that particular addressing scheme.

Hyper-V Network Virtualization also makes it easier for large enterprise to move server workloads between multiple data centers where overlapping addressing schemes exist between these data centers. Hyper-V Network Virtualization thus provides increased virtual machine mobility across data centers, hosting provider clouds, and Windows Azure.

Hyper-V Network Virtualization enhancements in Windows Server 2012 R2

Although Windows Server 2012 provided the base functionality for implementing network virtualization, Windows Server 2012 R2 includes some new features and enhancements that not only make network virtualization easier to implement and manage but also provide customers with a more comprehensive and integrated SDN solution.

One key enhancement with Hyper-V Network Virtualization in Windows Server 2012 R2 is that it can now dynamically learn the IP addresses on the virtual machine networks. This improvement provides several new benefits such as increasing the high availability options available when deploying a network virtualization solution. For example, with Hyper-V Network Virtualization in Windows Server 2012 R2, you can now use guest clustering inside a virtual network, something you couldn't do before using Hyper-V Network Virtualization in Windows Server 2012. Another benefit is that you can now deploy domain controllers, DNS servers, and DHCP servers as virtual machines on your virtual network running on top of your cloud hoster's physical network infrastructure.

Hyper-V Network Virtualization in Windows Server 2012 R2 also includes several performance enhancements over how this technology worked in Windows Server 2012. For example, you now have the option to be able to load balance NVGRE traffic across multiple NICs. This means that customers who move their workloads into a hoster's cloud now have new options for load-balancing network traffic and providing failover capability to ensure the availability of the virtual network at all times.

Another performance improvement with Hyper-V Network Virtualization in Windows Server 2012 R2 involves work Microsoft is doing with network hardware vendor partners to help bring new network adapter hardware to market that has the capability of offloading NVGRE processing from the host system's processor to the network adapter. These NVGRE Task Offload Enabled NICs will soon be available and should provide significantly better performance for Hyper-V Network Virtualization solutions over current network adapters that don't let you offload NVGRE processing from the host system's processors to the adapter. Emulex is one such network adapter hardware vendor, and you can read its analysis of the performance gains that can be achieved using NVGRE Task Offload Enabled NICs on its blog at *http://o-www.emulex.com/blogs/labs/2013/06/03/benefits-network-virtualization-offload-technologies-optimize-performance-nvgre/*.

The architecture of the Hyper-V Extensible Switch has also been modified in Windows Server 2012 R2 to provide new functionality for customers that implement Hyper-V Network Virtualization solutions. Microsoft introduced the Hyper-V Extensible Switch in Windows Server 2012 to provide new capabilities for tenant isolation, traffic shaping, protection against malicious virtual machines, and hassle-free troubleshooting. The Hyper-V Extensible Switch was also designed to allow third parties to develop plug-in extensions to emulate the full capabilities of hardware-based switches and support more complex virtual environments and solutions. It does this by allowing custom Network Driver Interface Specification (NDIS) filter drivers (called *extensions*) to be added to the driver stack of the virtual switch. This means that networking independent software vendors (ISVs) can create extensions that can be installed in the virtual switch to perform different actions on network packets being processed by the switch.

The Hyper-V Extensible Switch supports three kinds of extensions:

- **Capturing extensions**   These can capture packets to monitor network traffic but cannot modify or drop packets.
- **Filtering extensions**   These are like capturing extensions but also can inspect and drop packets.
- **Forwarding extensions**   These allow you to modify packet routing and enable integration with your physical network infrastructure.

The Hyper-V Extensible Switch also lets you use the built-in Wfplwfs.sys filtering extension of the Windows Filtering Platform (WFP) to intercept packets as they travel along the data path. Networking ISVs can use this functionality to develop applications that can perform packet inspection on a virtual network.

In Windows Server 2012, however, the Hyper-V Extensible Switch was layered above Hyper-V Network Virtualization functionality as shown on the left in Figure 5-9. This meant that capturing, filtering, or forwarding extensions installed in the switch could only see the CA packets, that is, the packets that the virtual machine sees on its virtual network. The extensions could not see or manipulate the PA packets, that is, the packets that the Hyper-V host sees on the hosting provider's underlying physical network.

However, in Windows Server 2012 R2 network virtualization, functionality now resides in the Hyper-V Extensible Switch, as shown on the right in Figure 5-8. This means that third-party extensions can now process network packets using either CA or PA addresses as desired. This enables new types of scenarios, such as hybrid forwarding, whereby Hyper-V Network Virtualization forwards the network virtualization traffic while a third-party extension forwards non-network virtualization traffic. Another possibility might be a networking ISV developing a firewall application that drops certain kinds of packets on the customer's network and other types of packets on the provider's network. It also allows third-party ISVs to use the Hyper-V Extensible Switch to implement their own network virtualization solutions using Hyper-V instead of needing to use the in-box Hyper-V Network Virtualization approach from Microsoft.

Finally, if you wanted to implement a network virtualization solution using Hyper-V in Windows Server 2012, you needed to use third-party gateway products to do this. That's because Windows Server 2012 doesn't include an in-box gateway, and a gateway is needed to provide connectivity between virtual machines running on the virtual network and resources on physical networks at local or remote sites. The result is that Hyper-V Network Virtualization by itself in Windows Server 2012 creates virtual subnets that are separated from the rest of the network the way islands are separated from the mainland.

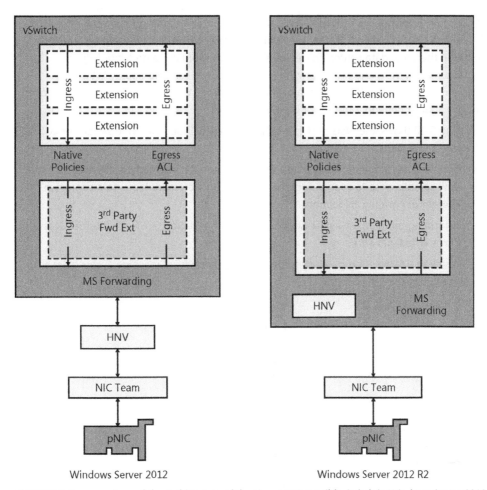

FIGURE 5-9 A comparison of the architecture of the Hyper-V Extensible Switch in Windows Server 2012 and Windows Server 2012 R2.

Beginning with Windows Server 2012 R2, however, Hyper-V Network Virtualization now includes an in-box component called Windows Server Gateway (WSG), a virtual machine-based software router that allows cloud hosters to route data center and cloud network traffic between virtual and physical networks including the Internet. WSG can be used to route network traffic between physical and virtual networks at the same physical location or at multiple different physical locations. This allows organizations to implement new kinds of scenarios. For example, if your organization has both a physical network and a virtual network at the same location, you can now deploy a Hyper-V host configured with a WSG virtual machine and use it to route traffic between your virtual and physical networks. As a second example, if your virtual networks reside in a hoster's cloud built using Hyper-V in Windows Server 2012 R2, the hoster can now deploy a WSG that allows you to create a VPN connection between your VPN server and the hoster's WSG to allow your users to connect to your organization's virtual resources in the cloud using the VPN connection.

WSG is fully integrated with Hyper-V Network Virtualization in Windows Server 2012 R2 and allows routing of network traffic, even when multiple customers are running tenant networks in the same data center. To deploy WSG, you should use a dedicated Hyper-V host that runs only WSG and no other virtual machines. You can also deploy WSG on a failover cluster of Hyper-V hosts to create a highly available WSG solution to provide failover protection against network outages or hardware failure.

As Figure 5-10 shows, the WSG of Hyper-V Network Virtualization in Windows Server 2012 R2 can be used to implement three types of gateway solutions:

- Implementing a multitenant-aware VPN for site-to-site connectivity, for example, to allow an enterprise to span a single virtual network across multiple data centers in different geographical locations.

- Performing multitenant-aware network address translation (NAT) for Internet access from a virtual network.

- Providing a forwarding gateway for in-data center physical machine access from a virtual network.

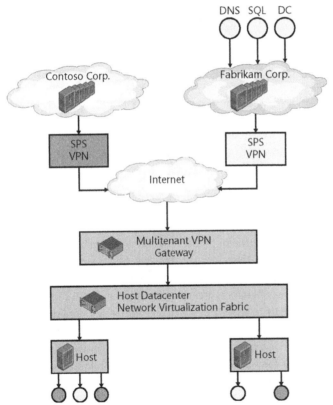

FIGURE 5-10 Windows Server Gateway implements three types of solutions.

Hyper-V Virtual Switch enhancements

The Hyper-V Virtual Switch is the software-based layer-2 network switch on Hyper-V hosts. Windows Server 2012 previously added many new capabilities to the Hyper-V Virtual Switch, perhaps most importantly by making the switch extensible, but also other improvements for tenant isolation, traffic shaping, protection against malicious virtual machines, and hassle-free troubleshooting. Let's review these earlier improvements before describing the new ones introduced in Windows Server 2012 R2.

Hyper-V Virtual Switch in Windows Server 2012

Versions of Hyper-V earlier than Windows Server 2012 allowed you to implement complex virtual network environments by creating virtual network switches that worked like physical layer-2 Ethernet switches. You could create external virtual networks to provide VMs with connectivity with externally located servers and clients, internal networks to allow VMs on the same host to communicate with each other as well as the host, or private virtual networks (PVLANs) that you could use to completely isolate all VMs on the same host from each other and allow them to communicate only via external networks.

The Hyper-V Virtual Switch introduced in Windows Server 2012 facilitated the creation of virtual networks that could be implemented in even more ways to provide greater flexibility in how you could design your virtualized infrastructure. For example, you could configure a guest operating system within a virtual machine to have a single virtual network adapter associated with a specific switch or multiple virtual network adapters (each associated with a different switch), but you couldn't connect the same switch to multiple network adapters.

Extensibility was added to the Hyper-V Virtual Switch in Windows Server 2012 in several ways. First, you could install custom Network Driver Interface Specification (NDIS) filter drivers (called extensions) into the driver stack of the virtual switch. For example, you could create an extension that captures, filters, or forwards packets to extensible switch ports. Specifically, the extensible switch allows for using the following kinds of extensions:

- **Capturing extensions** These can capture packets to monitor network traffic but cannot modify or drop packets
- **Filtering extensions** These are like capturing extensions but also can inspect and drop packets
- **Forwarding extensions** These allow you to modify packet routing and enable integration with your physical network infrastructure

Second, you can use the capabilities of the Windows Filtering Platform (WFP) by using the built-in Wfplwfs.sys filtering extension to intercept packets as they travel along the data path of the extensible switch. You might use this approach, for example, to perform packet inspection within your virtualized environment.

These different extensibility capabilities of the Hyper-V Virtual Switch were intended primarily for Microsoft partners and independent software vendors (ISVs) so they could update their existing network monitoring, management, and security software products so they could work not just with physical hosts, but also with VMs deployed within any kind of virtual networking environment that you might possibly create using Hyper-V in Windows Server 2012.

In addition, being able to extend the functionality of the Hyper-V networking by adding extensions made it easier to add new networking functionality to Hyper-V without needing to replace or upgrade the switch. You'd also be able to use the same tools for managing these extensions that you use for managing other aspects of Hyper-V networking, namely the Hyper-V Manager console, Windows PowerShell, and Windows Management Instrumentation (WMI). And because these extensions integrate into the existing framework of Hyper-V networking, they automatically work with other capabilities, like Live Migration.

A number of other advanced capabilities were also integrated by Microsoft into the Hyper-V Virtual Switch in Windows Server 2012 to help enhance security, monitoring, and troubleshooting functionality. These additional capabilities included the following:

- **DHCP guard** Helps safeguard against Dynamic Host Configuration Protocol (DHCP) man-in-the-middle attacks by dropping DHCP server messages from unauthorized VMs pretending to be DHCP servers

- **MAC address spoofing** Helps safeguard against attempts to use ARP spoofing to steal IP addresses from VMs by allowing VMs to change the source media access control (MAC) address in outgoing packets to an address that is not assigned to them

- **Router guard** Helps safeguard against unauthorized routers by dropping router advertisement and redirection messages from unauthorized VMs pretending to be routers

- **Port mirroring** Enables monitoring of a VM's network traffic by forwarding copies of destination or source packets to another VM being used for monitoring purposes

- **Port ACLs** Helps enforce virtual network isolation by allowing traffic filtering based on MAC or IP address ranges

- **Isolated VLANs** Allows segregation of traffic on multiple VLANs to facilitate isolation of tenant networks through the creation of PVLANs

- **Trunk mode** Allows directing traffic from a group of VLANs to a specific VM

- **Bandwidth management** Allows guaranteeing a minimum amount of bandwidth and/or enforcing a maximum amount of bandwidth for each VM

- **Enhanced diagnostics** Allows packet monitoring and event tracing through the extensible switch using ETL and Unified Tracing

Hyper-V Virtual Switch in Windows Server 2012 R2

Besides adding the vRSS capability described earlier in this chapter, Windows Server 2012 R2 builds on the many improvements added to the Hyper-V Virtual Switch in the previous Windows Server version by adding other new capabilities:

- **Enhanced extended port ACLs**   Hyper-V Virtual Switch Extended Port ACLs now allow you to specify the socket port number when you create new port ACL rules. You can also configure unidirectional port rules and include a timeout parameter. These improvements make port ACLs more useful for safeguarding data center resources in multitenant cloud environments and for enforcing security policies for tenants.

- **Dynamic load balancing of network traffic**   The Hyper-V Virtual Switch now automatically performs dynamic load balancing in order to move traffic streams between different NICs within a NIC team in order to share the network traffic load as equitably as possible. Previously in Windows Server 2012, the Hyper-V Virtual Switch provided simultaneous failover and load distribution capabilities, but it didn't ensure load distribution for teamed NICs in a balanced manner.

- **Coexistence with third-party forwarding extensions**   To better support Hyper-V Network Virtualization scenarios in multitenant environments, the Hyper-V Virtual Switch now allows third-party forwarding extensions installed on the switch to forward packets for either the customer address space or the physical address space using hybrid forwarding. Third-party forwarding extensions can also apply other policies, such as ACLs and QoS, to both the NVGRE and the non NVGRE-encapsulated traffic.

- **Improved network tracing**   To better enable troubleshooting problems that might arise, network traces now contain switch and port configuration information.

Learn more

You can learn more about the new Failover Clustering features and enhancements in Windows Server 2012 R2 by checking out the following topics on Microsoft TechNet:

- "What's New in Networking in Windows Server 2012 R2" at *http://technet.microsoft .com/en-us/library/dn313100.aspx*.

- "What's New in Hyper-V Network Virtualization in Windows Server 2012 R2" at *http://technet.microsoft.com/en-us/library/dn383586.aspx*.

- "What's New in Hyper-V Virtual Switch in Windows Server 2012 R2" at *http://technet.microsoft.com/en-us/library/dn343757.aspx*.

- "Windows Server Gateway" at *http://technet.microsoft.com/en-us/library/dn313101 .aspx*.

The following Microsoft TechNet and MSDN blog posts also have lots of information about the new Failover Clustering features and enhancements in Windows Server 2012 R2:

- "What's New in Hyper-V Network Virtualization in R2" at *http://blogs.technet.com/b/networking/archive/2013/07/31/what-s-new-in-hyper-v-network-virtualization-in-r2.aspx.*

- "New Networking Diagnostics with PowerShell in Windows Server R2" at *http://blogs.technet.com/b/networking/archive/2013/07/31/new-networking-diagnostics-with-powershell-in-windows-server-r2.aspx.*

- "Drive Up Networking Performance for Your Most Demanding Workloads with Virtual RSS" at *http://blogs.technet.com/b/networking/archive/2013/07/31/drive-up-networking-performance-for-your-most-demanding-workloads-with-virtual-rss.aspx.*

- "Hyper-V Extensible Switch Enhancements in Windows Server 2012 R2" at *http://blogs.technet.com/b/networking/archive/2013/07/31/hyper-v-extensible-switch-enhancements-in-windows-server-2012-r2.aspx.*

- "Transforming Your Datacenter—Networking in the R2 Release" at *http://blogs.technet.com/b/networking/archive/2013/07/31/transforming-your-datacenter-networking.aspx.*

- "Cloud Scale Multitenant Networking Stack" at *http://blogs.technet.com/b/networking/archive/2013/08/03/cloud-scale-multitenant-networking-stack-and-service.aspx.*

- "Enable the Forwarding Function on Windows Server Gateway: A Use Case Study" at *http://blogs.technet.com/b/networking/archive/2013/09/06/enable-forwarding-function-on-windows-server-gateway-a-use-case-study.aspx.*

Be sure also to check out the following videos from TechEd 2013 on Channel 9:

- "What's New in Windows Server 2012 R2 Networking" at *http://channel9.msdn.com/Events/TechEd/NorthAmerica/2013/MDC-B216.*

- "Networking for Cloud Services in Windows Server 2012 R2" at *http://channel9.msdn.com/Events/TechEd/NorthAmerica/2013/MDC-B376.*

CHAPTER 6

Active Directory

Active Directory is the core identity and access control technology used for the IT infrastructure of most businesses today. Active Directory on the Windows Server platform collectively consists of the following server roles:

- **Active Directory Domain Services (AD DS)** Provides organizations with a scalable, secure, and manageable infrastructure for user and resource management and support for directory-enabled applications like Microsoft Exchange Server.

- **Active Directory Federation Services (AD FS)** Provides organizations with simple and secure identity federation and web single sign-on (SSO) capabilities.

- **Active Directory Lightweight Directory Services (AD LDS)** Provides an implementation of the Lightweight Directory Access Protocol (LDAP) so organizations can deploy a directory service that doesn't include the dependencies and domain-related restrictions of AD DS.

- **Active Directory Rights Management Services (AD RMS)** Provides organizations with tools for implementing and managing encryption, certificates, and authentication so they can implement reliable information protection solutions.

- **Active Directory Certificate Services (AD CS)** Enables organizations to implement a public key infrastructure (PKI) so they can deploy and manage public key cryptography, digital certificates, and digital signature capabilities for users and devices.

Microsoft has steadily enhanced the identity and access capabilities of the Windows Server platform over the years, and Windows Server 2012 R2 adds some exciting new capabilities we'll examine in a moment. But first let's briefly review how Active Directory was enhanced in the previous platform of Windows Server 2012.

Previous enhancements to Active Directory

Microsoft added a number of new features and enhancements to Active Directory in Windows Server 2012 that helped simplify the task of deploying, managing, and maintaining an Active Directory environment. Some of the key enhancements to AD DS included:

- Virtualizing domain controllers in previous versions of Windows Server sometimes resulted in problems with the logical clocks used by domain controllers to determine relative levels of convergence. Beginning with Windows Server 2012, however, virtual domain controllers employed a unique identifier called the virtual machine GenerationID. This unique identifier is exposed by the hypervisor to the virtual machine's address space within its BIOS so it can be made available to the guest operating system. When the guest operating system of a virtual domain controller boots, the current value of this identifier is compared with the value stored in AD DS. If a mismatch is detected, a rollback takes place to ensure that the virtual domain controller will properly converge with other domain controllers in the forest. The result of this improvement is to make virtualizing domain controllers safe for enterprises who want to implement this kind of scenario.

- Beginning with Windows Server 2012, organizations were able to deploy replica virtual domain controllers by cloning existing virtual domain controllers. The cloning process involved creating a copy of the existing source virtual domain controller, authorizing the source domain controller in AD DS, and using Windows PowerShell to create a configuration file for performing the domain controller promotion operation.

- The process for deploying domain controllers was also made faster and more flexible in Windows Server 2012. The Dcpromo.exe wizard of previous versions of Windows Server was replaced with a new Active Directory Domain Services Configuration Wizard built entirely upon Windows PowerShell. This redesign provides a number of benefits. For example, you can now install the AD DS server role binaries remotely using Server Manager or with the new AD DS PowerShell cmdlets. You can also install the binaries on multiple servers at the same time. Adprep.exe is also integrated into the Active Directory installation process to make it easier to prepare your existing Active Directory environment for upgrading to Windows Server 2012. And the Active Directory Domain Services Configuration Wizard performs validation to ensure that the necessary prerequisites have been met before promoting a server to a domain controller.

- The Active Directory Administrative Center (ADAC) that was first introduced in Windows Server 2008 R2 as a central management console for Active Directory administrators was also enhanced in Windows Server 2012 with new GUI elements for managing the Active Directory Recycle Bin and fine-grained password policies. In addition, a feature called Windows PowerShell History Viewer was added to help you quickly create Windows PowerShell scripts to automate Active Directory administration tasks by viewing and utilizing the Windows PowerShell commands underlying any actions performed using the user interface of ADAC.

Let's now look at some of the new capabilities in Active Directory in Windows Server 2012 R2.

Workplace Join

One of the key Active Directory enhancements in Windows Server 2012 R2 is called Workplace Join. Basically, what this means is that companies can now provide an SSO experience for all workplace-joined devices, which at present includes Windows and iOS devices.

The way it works is that users join their personal devices to their workplace by making their devices known to the company's Active Directory. The goal of doing this is to allow users to be able to easily and securely access resources and services on the company network so they can perform their job better.

Workplace Join associates the device with the user and enables a better user experience by providing a seamless second factor authentication. Users sign in once from any application running on their workplace-joined devices. They are not prompted for credentials by every company application when they are using their workplace-joined devices. This provides both the user and the company with some major benefits in the areas of usability and security, namely:

- Usability is enhanced because the user no longer has to repeatedly enter his or her credentials into the device to access resources on the company network.

- Security is enhanced because the risks involved in saving passwords with each application on the user's device are avoided.

When a user's device is workplace-joined, the attributes of the device are stored in Active Directory and can be retrieved to issue security tokens for the applications running on the user's device. This enables the company to grant the appropriate rights and permissions for the user's application to securely access company resources and services.

Workplace Join enables new scenarios for organizations that want to take advantage of bring-your-own-device (BYOD) to enhance user productivity. As Figure 6-1 shows, Workplace Join represents a middle-of-the-road approach to device manageability and security for enterprises.

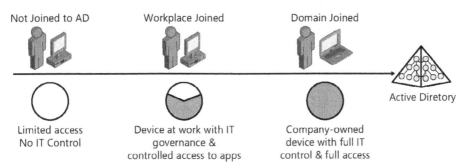

FIGURE 6-1 Workplace Join represents a middle-of-the-road approach to device manageability and security for enterprises.

Implementing Workplace Join

Workplace Join uses the new capabilities of the AD FS role in Windows Server 2012 R2. Specifically, AD FS now includes a new service called the Device Registration Service that creates a device object in Active Directory when the user registers the device at a special website on the corporate network. The attributes of the device object are then used to provide conditional access to resources the user tries to access and to applications the user tries to run.

The steps for implementing Workplace Join are fairly straightforward but you'll need three servers to set things up. Here's a quick summary:

1. You need a domain controller running Windows Server 2012 R2.

2. You need to create a Group Managed Service Account (GMSA) account, which is basically a service account that can be used across a domain environment.

3. You need to obtain a server SSL certificate from a certificate authority (CA) and install it on a second server running Windows Server 2012 R2.

4. You need to install and configure the AD FS role on the second server.

5. You need to enable and configure the Device Registration Service on the second server.

6. You need to perform some additional tasks on your DNS server.

7. You need to install the IIS (Web Server) role and the Windows Identity Foundation feature on a third server running Windows Server 2012 R2.

8. You need to install the Windows Identity Foundation SDK on the third server.

9. You need to perform some additional steps involving IIS configuration and using the AD FS Management console.

Now you're all ready to go. Let's say a user wants to join his iPhone to your corporate network. Here's all the user needs to do:

1. Install an SSL certificate on his phone by browsing to a website specified by your administrator.

2. Open Safari on his phone and navigate to a web page by opening a special URL on your corporate network.

3. Log on to the web page using his domain credentials.

4. Accept the prompt to install a profile on his phone.

5. Re-enter his PIN to unlock his phone.

That's basically it and you can find more detail concerning the above steps in the Microsoft TechNet articles listed in the "Learn more" section at the end of this chapter.

Multi-factor access control

The AD FS server role has been enhanced in Windows Server 2012 R2 to support multi-factor access control that includes user, device, location, and authentication data. The result is that organizations that use AD FS can now control access to network resources based on such things as:

- User identity
- Group membership
- Network location
- Whether the device is workplace-joined
- Whether multi-factor authentication (MFA) has been performed

Access can be permitted or denied based on any of the above.

Multi-factor access control provides organizations with greater flexibility in how they craft their authorization policies. A rich claims language is provided, and Windows PowerShell can be used for more advanced claims scenarios.

Other enhancements include:

- A global authentication policy that can be applied to all applications and services that are secured by AD FS. The global policy can also be used to enable device authentication for seamless second-factor authentication.
- A simple and intuitive GUI-based AD FS MMC snap-in that is easy to use.
- Windows PowerShell support for automating mundane tasks.
- Support for custom MFA providers for organizations that leverage third-party MFA methods.

Web Application Proxy

Web Application Proxy is a new role service of the Remote Access server role in Windows Server 2012 R2 (see Figure 6-2). With a Web Application Proxy your organization can publish applications for external access, for example, in order to make your on-premises web resources available over the Internet so users outside your organization can access applications and services running on servers inside your corporate network.

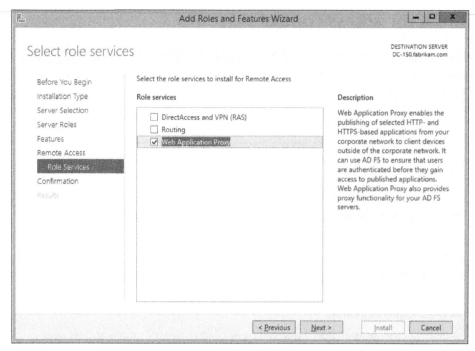

FIGURE 6-2 Installing the Web Application Proxy role service of the Remote Access server role.

Web Application Proxy works by acting as both a reverse proxy and an AD FS proxy. In the previous version of Windows Server 2012, a role service called Federation Proxy Service was available for installation when you installed the AD FS server role. In Windows Server 2012 R2, this role service has been removed from the AD FS role and moved to the Remote Access role, and additional reverse proxy functionality has been added. Because you cannot install both Web Application Proxy and AD FS on the same server, remote access solutions based on Windows Server 2012 R2 are now made more secure by controlling authentication and authorization policies separately in AD FS.

Web Application Proxy works with any kind of user device. This means for example that Web Application Proxy can be used to enable your users to work from home or on the road using their personal computer, tablet, or smartphone. And because Web Application Proxy also provides reverse proxy functionality, the experience from the user's point of view is the same as if her device was connecting directly to the server running the application.

Implementing Web Application Proxy

Web Application Proxy is typically deployed on a server in the perimeter network of your organization (see Figure 6-3). Placing the Web Application Proxy on your perimeter network affords greater security because of the double nature of the firewall protection being provided.

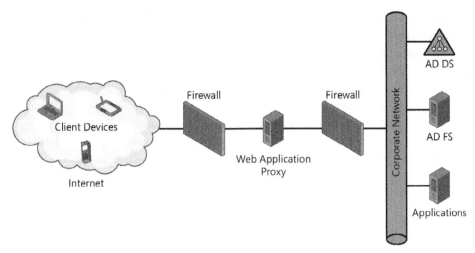

FIGURE 6-3 Deploying a Web Application Proxy on your perimeter network.

Once you've deployed and configure AD FS in your environment and have installed Web Application Proxy on the perimeter network server, your next step is to configure the Web Application Proxy. The Web Application Proxy Configuration Wizard shown in Figure 6-4 can be used for this purpose. Configuring the Web Application Proxy involves providing information that can be used to connect Web Application Proxy with your AD FS server.

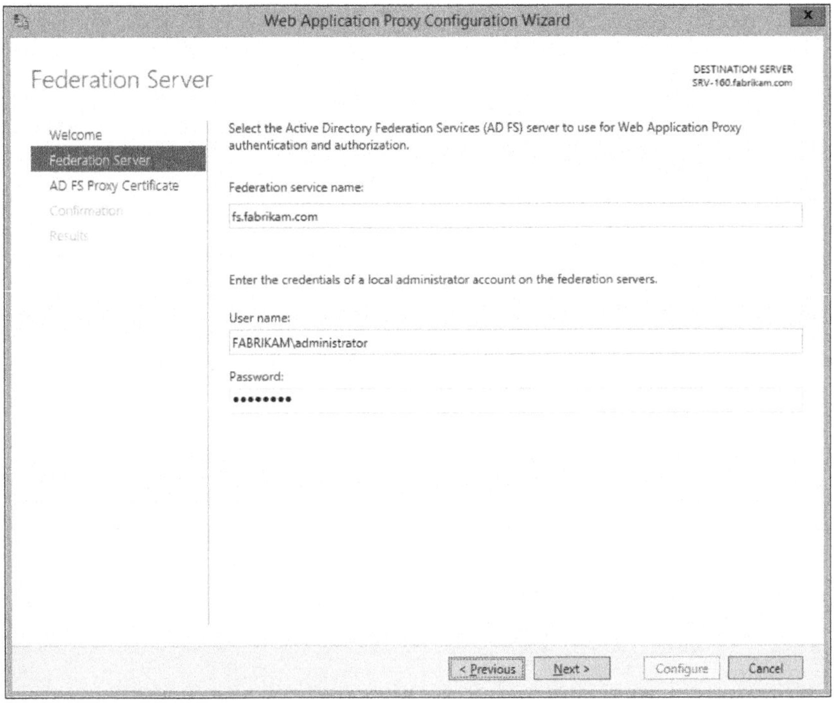

FIGURE 6-4 Configuring the Web Application Proxy.

Once Web Application Proxy has been configured, you can use the Remote Access Management console to publish your internal applications so external users can access them via Web Application Proxy. Applications are published by using the Publish New Application Wizard. On the Preauthentication page, as shown in Figure 6-5, you choose which method Web Application Proxy should use for preauthentication. The options here are either Pass-through, which simply forwards all requests to the backend application server without performing any preauthentication, or AD FS, which redirects all requests to your federation server. If you choose AD FS, requests that have been successfully preauthenticated are then forwarded to the backend server.

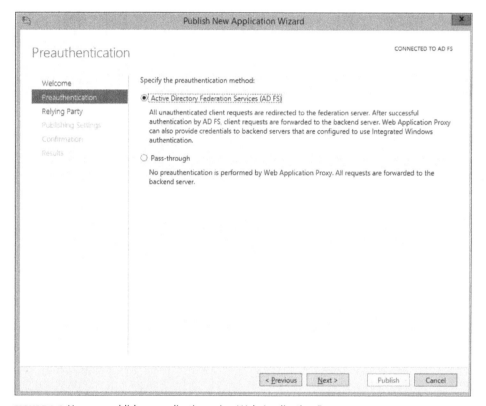

FIGURE 6-5 You can publish an application using Web Application Proxy.

After choosing the preauthentication method you wish to use for publishing applications, you then specify the relying party. Since we selected AD FS as the preauthentication method, the relying party is the Device Registration Service (see Figure 6-6).

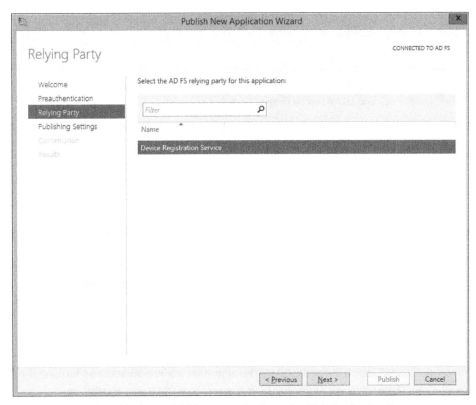

FIGURE 6-6 A continued look at publishing an application using Web Application Proxy.

The Publishing Settings page allows you to specify a name, external URL, external certificate, and backend server URL for the application you are publishing. Once you've completed the wizard, the internal application will be accessible for external users to access provided they have been properly authorized to do so.

Improved LDAP search performance

Lightweight Directory Access Protocol (LDAP) is the industry-standard protocol used by Active Directory clients when performing searches against the directory. To query AD DS, the client composes a search query using the LDAP syntax and then submits it to the directory for processing. One of the many under-the-hood improvements introduced in Windows Server 2012 R2 is some changes to the LDAP query optimizer algorithm. As the following sidebar contributed by one of our Microsoft insiders shows, these changes can result in better performance for even complex queries against AD DS.

LDAP query optimizer changes

The LDAP query optimizer algorithm was reevaluated and further optimized in Windows Server 2012 R2. The result is a performance improvement in LDAP search efficiency and LDAP search time of complex queries.

These improvements in the performance of searches are a result of improvements in the mapping from LDAP query to ESE query. LDAP filters beyond a certain level of complexity prevent optimized index selection, resulting in drastically decreased performance (1000x or more). This change alters the way in which we select indices for LDAP queries to avoid this problem.

Background

The ability to search Active Directory is one of the core services provided by domain controllers. Many services and line-of-business applications rely on this service. Business operations can cease to a halt if this feature is not available. As a core and heavily used service, it is imperative that domain controllers handle LDAP search traffic efficiently.

The LDAP query optimizer algorithm attempts to make LDAP searches efficient as possible by mapping LDAP search filters to a result set that can be satisfied via records already indexed in the database. This algorithm was reevaluated and further optimized. The result is the performance improvement in LDAP search efficiency and LDAP search time of complex queries.

Details of change

An LDAP search contains a location (NC head, OU, Object) within the hierarchy to begin the search, a search filter, and a list of attributes to return. The search process can be summarized as follows:

1. Simplify the search filter, if possible.
2. Select a set of index keys that will return the smallest covered set.
3. Perform one or more intersections of index keys to reduce the covered set.
4. For each record in the covered set, evaluate the filter expression as well as the security. If the filter evaluates to TRUE and access is granted, then return this record to the client.

The LDAP query optimization work modifies steps 2 and 3 so as to reduce the size of the covered set. More specifically, the current implementation selects duplicate index keys and performs redundant intersections.

- Select a set of index keys that will return the smallest covered set.
- Perform one or more intersections of index keys to reduce the covered set.

Sample results using the old algorithm

The target of the inefficient LDAP search in the following example is a Windows Server 2012 domain controller. The search completes in approximately 44 seconds as a result of failing to find a more efficient index.

```
adfind -b dc=blue,dc=contoso,dc=com -f "(| (& (|(cn=justintu)
(postalcode=80304) (userprincipalname=justintu@blue.contoso.com))
(|(objectclass=person) (cn=justintu)) )
(&(cn=justintu)(objectclass=person)))" -stats >>adfind.txt


Using server: WINSRV-DC1.blue.contoso.com:389


...<removed search results>


Statistics
==================================
Elapsed Time: 44640 (ms)
Returned 324 entries of 553896 visited - (0.06%)


Used Filter:
 ( | ( & ( | (cn=justintu) (postalCode=80304)
(userPrincipalName=justintu@blue.contoso.com) ) ( |
(objectClass=person) (cn=justintu) ) ) ( & (cn=justintu)
(objectClass=person) ) )


Used Indices:
 DNT_index:516615:N


Pages Referenced          : 4619650
Pages Read From Disk       : 973
Pages Pre-read From Disk   : 180898
Pages Dirtied              : 0
Pages Re-Dirtied           : 0
Log Records Generated      : 0
Log Record Bytes Generated: 0
```

Sample results using the new algorithm

Here we repeat the exact same search as above but target a Windows Server 2012 R2 domain controller. The same search completes in less than a second due to the improvements in the LDAP query optimizer algorithm.

```
adfind -b dc=blue,dc=contoso,dc=com -f "(| (& (|(cn=justintu)
(postalcode=80304) (userprincipalname=dhunt@blue.contoso.com))
(|(objectclass=person) (cn=justintu)) )
(&(cn=justintu)(objectclass=person)))" -stats >>adfindBLUE.txt
```

```
Using server: winblueDC1.blue.contoso.com:389

....<removed search results>

Statistics
==================================
Elapsed Time: 672 (ms)
Returned 324 entries of 648 visited - (50.00%)

Used Filter:
 ( |  ( &  ( |  (cn=justintu)  (postalCode=80304)
(userPrincipalName=justintu@blue.contoso.com) )  ( |
(objectClass=person)  (cn=justintu) ) )  ( &  (cn=justintu)
(objectClass=person) ) )

Used Indices:
 idx_userPrincipalName:648:N
 idx_postalCode:323:N
 idx_cn:1:N


Pages Referenced           : 15350
Pages Read From Disk        : 176
Pages Pre-read From Disk    : 2
Pages Dirtied              : 0
Pages Re-Dirtied           : 0
Log Records Generated      : 0
Log Record Bytes Generated: 0
```

Optimization of paged queries

The handling of paged queries was changed completely.

From a sample paged query that gets 112 out of 10,000+ groups based on a CN filter and a page size of 6:

```
Statistics
==================================
Elapsed Time: 0 (ms)
Returned 112 entries of 113 visited - (99.12%)

Used Filter:
( |  ( &  ( |  (cn=SFU-GRP-Test73*)  (userPrincipalName=add-t*) )  ( |
(objectClass=person)  (objectClass=group) (cn=add-t*) ) )
( &  (cn=add-t*)  (objectClass=person) ) )

Used Indices:
idx_cn:113:N
```

```
idx_cn:1:N
idx_userPrincipalName:1:N

Pages Referenced          : 3223
Pages Read From Disk      : 0
Pages Pre-read From Disk  : 0
Pages Dirtied             : 0
Pages Re-Dirtied          : 0
Log Records Generated     : 0
Log Record Bytes Generated: 0
...
Filter Breakdown:

(
(|
  (&
   (|
     (cn=SFU-GRP-Test73*)
     (userPrincipalName=add-t*)
   )
   (|
     (objectClass=person)
     (objectClass=group)
     (cn=add-t*)
   )
  )
  (&
   (cn=add-t*)
   (objectClass=person)
  )
)
)
```

In the network frames, the cookie is just 6 bytes now in contrast to several hundred bytes before controls:

```
ControlType: 1.2.840.113556.1.4.319 (LDAP_PAGED_RESULT_OID_STRING)
```

```
31 2E 32 2E 38 34 30 2E 31 31 33 35 35 36 2E 31 2E 34 2E 33 31 39 01 01
FF 04 0F 30 84 00 00 00 09 02 01 06 04 04 33 0B 00 00 01
1.2.840.113556.1.4.319..ÿ..0,.........3....
```

This means we can now optimize paged queries just like non-paged queries.

Justin Turner
Support Topic Lead for Active Directory, Windows DSYS TX

Learn more

You can learn more about the new Active Directory features and enhancements in Windows Server 2012 R2 by checking out the following topics on Microsoft TechNet:

- "What's New in Active Directory in Windows Server 2012 R2" at *http://technet .microsoft.com/en-us/library/dn268294.aspx*.

Be sure also to check out the following videos from TechEd 2013 on Channel 9:

- "Understanding Access and Information Protection" at *http://channel9.msdn.com/ Events/TechEd/NorthAmerica/2013/WCA-B207*.

- "Identity Infrastructure Fundamentals and Essential Capabilities" at *http://channel9 .msdn.com/Events/TechEd/NorthAmerica/2013/ATC-B209*.

- "Enable Work from Anywhere without Losing Sleep: Remote Access with the Web Application Proxy and VPN Solutions" at *http://channel9.msdn.com/Events/TechEd/ NorthAmerica/2013/WCA-B333*.

- "Active Directory Enables User Productivity and IT Risk Management Strategies Across a Variety of Devices" at *http://channel9.msdn.com/Events/TechEd/NorthAmerica/2013/ WCA-B204*.

CHAPTER 7

Group Policy

For many organizations, Group Policy is the key technology they utilize to lock down their environments. Composed of thousands of different policy settings and dozens of categories of preference items, a thorough knowledge of what Group Policy can do and how to configure, optimize and maintain its operations is an essential part of the administrator's job.

Previous enhancements to Group Policy

Group Policy received a lot of new functionalities in Windows Server 2012 and Windows 8. Some of the more important enhancements included:

- **Remote Group Policy update**   Windows Server 2012 enabled the use of the Group Policy Management Console (GPMC) to refresh the computer and user Group Policy settings (including security settings) on all remote computers in an organizational unit (OU). It did this by scheduling a task that ran an update.exe on the remote computers. You could also use the Invoke-GPUpdate Windows PowerShell cmdlet to automate the remote Group Policy update. These functionalities helped when you needed to push out a new Group Policy setting immediately to users or computers in your environment.

- **Group Policy infrastructure status**   You could use the GPMC to view the status of Active Directory and SYSVOL replication for all Group Policy Objects (GPOs) or for a selected GPO. This included viewing the security descriptors, GPO version details, and number of GPOs listed in Active Directory and SYSVOL for each domain controller. This functionality was helpful for monitoring and diagnosing replication issues related to Group Policy at the domain level.

- **Fast Startup**   Computers running Windows 8 and later are configured by default to use Fast Startup, a new boot mode that is a hybrid of traditional cold boot and resuming from hibernate. Fast Startup closes all user sessions on shutdown, but hibernates the kernel session instead of closing it. This enabled Windows 8 computers to shut down and start up more quickly than in previous versions of Windows. Although Fast Startup can help speed up Group Policy processing, some policy settings or scripts processed during startup or shutdown might not be applied when Fast Startup is enabled.

- **New Group Policy starter GPOs** Windows Server 2012 included two new starter GPOs that can make configuring Group Policy firewall port requirements a lot easier. These starter GPOs are named Group Policy Reporting Firewall Ports and Group Policy Remote Update Firewall Ports. You could import these starter GPOs when you created a new GPO for this purpose.
- **Local Group Policy support for Windows RT** Group Policy can be used to manage devices that run Windows RT. By default, the Group Policy Client service was disabled on Windows RT devices and must be enabled and configured to start automatically using the Services snap-in.

Additionally, there were lots of new policy settings and preferences added to Group Policy in Windows Server 2012, including settings and preferences for Internet Explorer 10 and many other Windows components and capabilities.

As far as enhancements in Windows Server 2012 R2 go, this time around it's more of a fine-tuning of Group Policy capabilities rather than a lot of new functionality. Let's examine some of the changes now.

Group Policy caching

One of the key enhancements in Windows Server 2012 R2 is policy caching, which can significantly reduce the amount of time it takes to process Group Policy on a client. Policy caching works by having the client download the policy from a domain controller and save a copy of the policy to a local store on the client. Then, when the next Group Policy processing occurs, the client can apply the policy cached in the local store instead of having to download the policy again from the network.

By speeding up Group Policy processing, policy caching can shorten boot times for clients. This can be especially helpful in scenarios where the network connection experiences latency or is connecting from off-premises over the Internet, for example, in a DirectAccess scenario. Note that policy caching only works when Group Policy is running in synchronous mode.

Policy caching is disabled by default in Windows Server 2012 R2. To enable and configure policy caching, configure the following policy setting named Enable Group Policy Caching For Servers as shown in Figure 7-1. This policy setting can be found under:

Computer Configuration\Policies\Administrative Templates\System\Group Policy

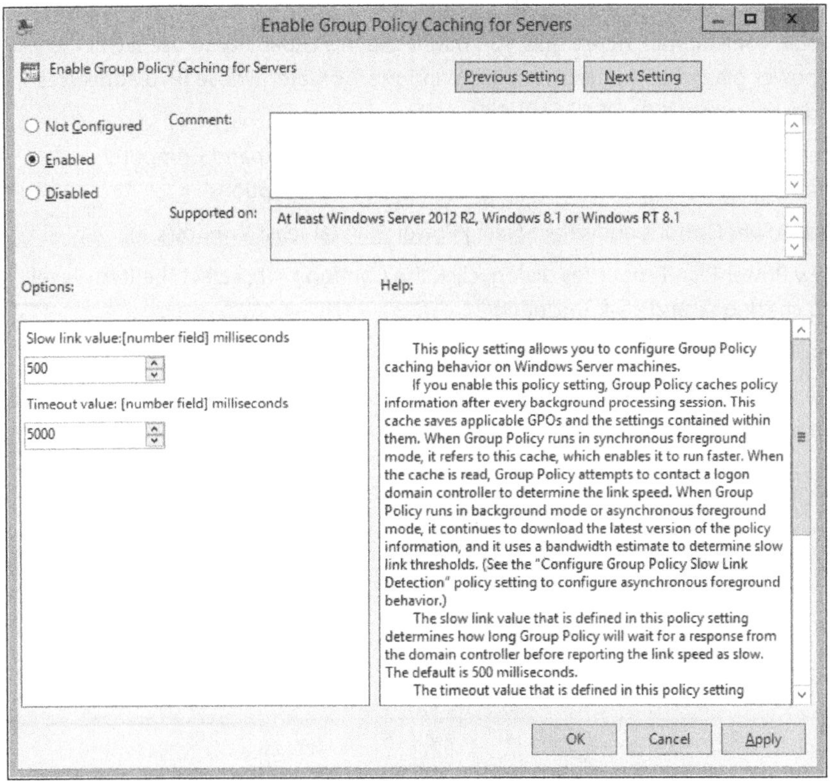

FIGURE 7-1 The new Enable Group Policy Caching For Servers policy setting.

Group Policy Preferences and IPv6

Another important area where Group Policy has been enhanced in Windows Server 2012 R2 is in regards to Internet Protocol version 6 (IPv6) support. An increasingly important part of the job of the Windows Server administrator is to prepare the organization's network for migration to IPv6. The reasons for this include the exponential growth of the Internet, the proliferation of mobile devices that need to be able to connect to the corporate network, and the exhaustion of the IPv4 address space. Windows Server 2012 included a number of new IPv6 capabilities such as built-in support for NAT64/DNS64 when implementing DirectAccess, new Windows PowerShell cmdlets that supersede the Netsh.exe command-line utility of earlier Windows versions, and improved Internet connectivity by marking well-known IPv6 Internet resources Windows can't reach as unreachable so that in the future only IPv4 is used for connecting to them.

With Windows Server 2012 R2, however, IPv6 has now made more inroads into Group Policy functionality on the platform. For example, you can now specify an IPv6 address when using item-level targeting with Group Policy Preferences (GPP). This allows you to configure the scope of individual preference items so they apply only to computers that have a specific IPv6 address range. For example, here's how you might use this capability to use a GPO to apply a certain power plan to computers running Windows 7 or later whose IPv6 addresses fall within the address range 2001:DB8:3FA9:/48:

1. Open the GPO in the Group Policy Management Editor and expand Computer Configuration | Preferences | Control Panel Settings | Power Options.

2. Right-click Power Options and select New | Power Plan (at least Windows 7).

3. In the New Power Plan Properties dialog, click the Common tab, select the Item-level Targeting check box, and click Targeting.

4. In the Targeting Editor, click New Item | IP Address Range.

5. Select the Use IPv6 check box, as shown in Figure 7-2, and specify the IPv6 address and prefix length.

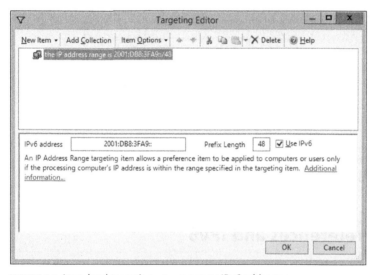

FIGURE 7-2 Item-level targeting now supports IPv6 addresses.

Support for IPv6 has been introduced into other areas of Group Policy as well. For example, when you create a new TCP/IP Printer preference item, you can specify an IPv6 address of the network printer, as shown in Figure 7-3.

FIGURE 7-3 You can now specify an IPv6 address for a network printer.

Another example of IPv6 support in Group Policy can be found when you create a new VPN Connection preference item, as shown in Figure 7-4.

FIGURE 7-4 You can now specify an IPv6 address when creating a new VPN connection.

New policy settings

Finally, as one might expect, there are a number of new policy settings available for Group Policy in Windows Server 2012 R2. Although the sections below don't cover all of these new policy settings, the ones described will definitely be of interest for administrators to learn. Some of these policy settings are specific to Windows 8.1 client computers, whereas others are applicable to both clients and servers. The policy settings have been roughly grouped together according to the areas of functionality to which they apply.

Start screen

There are several new policy settings that can be used for customizing the behavior of the Start screen only on computers running Windows Server 2012 R2, Windows 8.1, or Windows RT 8.1. The ones we'll look at here are:

- Start Screen Layout
- Force a specific Start background
- Force a specific background and accent color
- Show the Apps view automatically when the user goes to Start

Start Screen Layout

This policy setting specifies the Start screen layout for users and is located at:

Computer Configuration\Start Menu and Taskbar

User Configuration\Start Menu and Taskbar

This setting lets you specify the Start screen layout for users and prevents them from changing its configuration. The Start screen layout you specify must be stored in an XML file that was generated by the Export-StartLayout Windows PowerShell cmdlet.

To use this setting, you must first manually configure a device's Start screen layout to the desired look and feel. Once you are done, run the Export-StartLayout Windows PowerShell cmdlet on that same device. The cmdlet will generate an XML file representing the layout you configured.

Once the XML file is generated and moved to the desired file path, type the fully qualified path and name of the XML file. You can type a local path, such as C:\StartLayouts\myLayout.xml or a UNC path, such as \\Server\Share\Layout.xml. If the specified file is not available when the user logs on, the layout won't be changed. Users cannot customize their Start screen while this setting is enabled.

If you disable this setting or do not configure it, the Start screen layout won't be changed and users will be able to customize it.

Force a specific Start background

This policy setting forces the Start screen to use a specific background and is located at:

Computer Configuration\Control Panel\Personalization

Specifically, it forces the Start screen to use one of the available backgrounds, 1 through 20, and prevents the user from changing it.

If this setting is set to zero or not configured, then Start uses the default background and users can change it.

If this setting is set to a nonzero value, then Start uses the specified background and users cannot change it. If the specified background is not supported, the default background is used.

Force a specific background and accent color

This policy setting forces Windows to use the specified colors for the background and accent. It is located at:

Computer Configuration\Control Panel\Personalization

When configuring this policy setting, the color values are specified in hex as #RGB.

By default, users can change the background and accent colors.

If this setting is enabled, the background and accent colors of Windows will be set to the specified colors and users cannot change those colors. This setting will not be applied if the specified colors do not meet a contrast ratio of 2:1 with white text.

Show the Apps view automatically when the user goes to Start

This policy setting allows the Apps view to be opened by default when the user goes to Start. It is located at:

User Configuration\Start Menu and Taskbar

If you enable this policy setting, the Apps view will appear whenever the user goes to Start. Users will still be able to switch between the Apps view and the Start screen.

If you disable or don't configure this policy setting, the Start screen will appear by default whenever the user goes to Start, and the user will be able to switch between the Apps view and the Start screen. Also, the user will be able to configure this setting.

Multi-monitor display

There is an additional policy setting for the Start screen that only applies when the user is using a multimonitor display. This policy setting also applies only to computers running Windows Server 2012 R2, Windows 8.1, or Windows RT 8.1.

Show Start on the display the user is using when they press the Windows logo key

This policy setting allows the Start screen to appear on the display the user is using when they press the Windows logo key. It is located at:

User Configuration\Start Menu and Taskbar

If you enable this policy setting, the Start screen will appear on the display the user is using when they press the Windows logo key.

If you disable or don't configure this policy setting, the Start screen will always appear on the main display when the user presses the Windows logo key. Users will still be able to open Start on other displays by pressing the Start button on that display. Also, the user will be able to configure this setting.

Apps

There are a couple of new policy settings that deal with how apps are displayed and searched for from the Start screen:

- Do not show recent apps when the mouse is pointing to the upper-left corner of the screen
- Search just apps from the Apps view

These new policy settings apply only to computers running Windows Server 2012 R2, Windows 8.1, or Windows RT 8.1.

Do not show recent apps when the mouse is pointing to the upper-left corner of the screen

This policy setting allows you to prevent the last app and the list of recent apps from appearing when the mouse is pointing to the upper-left corner of the screen. It is located at:

User Configuration\Windows Components\Edge UI

If you enable this policy setting, the user will no longer be able to switch to recent apps using the mouse. The user will still be able to switch apps using touch gestures, keyboard shortcuts, and the Start screen.

If you disable or don't configure this policy setting, the recent apps will be available by default and the user can configure this setting.

Search just apps from the Apps view

This policy setting prevents the user from searching apps, files, and settings (and the web if enabled) when the user searches from the Apps view. It is located at:

User Configuration\Start Menu and Taskbar

This policy setting is only applied when the Apps view is set as the default view for Start.

If you enable this policy setting, searching from the Apps view will only search the list of installed apps.

If you disable or don't configure this policy setting, the user can configure this setting.

Sync your settings

There is one new Group Policy setting that can be used to configure the behavior of how Sync Your Settings works for users. This new policy setting applies only to computers running Windows Server 2012 R2, Windows 8.1, or Windows RT 8.1.

Do not sync Start settings

This policy setting can prevent the "Start layout" group from syncing to and from this PC. This turns off and disables the "Start layout" group on the "sync your settings" page in PC settings. It is located at:

Computer Configuration\Windows Components\Sync your settings

If you enable this policy setting, the "Start layout" group will not be synced.

If you do not set or disable this setting, syncing of the "Start layout" group is on by default and configurable by the user.

Use the option "Allow users to turn start syncing on" so that syncing is turned off by default but not disabled.

Work Folders

As described previously in Chapter 3, "Storage," Work Folders is a new storage feature introduced in Windows Server 2012 R2 that can help your organization address bring-your-own device (BYOD) scenarios typical of the modern workplace. There are two new Group Policy settings you can use to configure the behavior of this new feature:

- Force automatic setup for all users
- Specify Work Folders settings

Both of these new policy settings apply only to computers running Windows 8.1 or Windows RT 8.1.

Force automatic setup for all users

This policy setting specifies whether Work Folders should be set up automatically for all users of the affected computer. It is located at:

Computer Configuration\Windows Components\Work Folders

If you enable this policy setting, Work Folders will be set up automatically for all users of the affected computer. This prevents users from choosing not to use Work Folders on the computer; it also prevents them from manually specifying the local folder in which Work Folders store files. Work Folders will use the settings specified in the "Specify Work Folders settings" policy setting in User Configuration\Administrative Templates\Windows Components\WorkFolders. If the "Specify Work Folders settings" policy setting does not apply to a user, Work Folders is not automatically set up.

If you disable or do not configure this policy setting, Work Folders uses the "Force automatic setup" option of the "Specify Work Folders settings" policy setting to determine whether to automatically set up Work Folders for a given user.

Specify Work Folders settings

This policy setting specifies the Work Folders server for affected users, as well as whether or not users are allowed to change settings when setting up Work Folders on a domain-joined computer. It is located at:

User Configuration\Windows Components\Work Folders

If you enable this policy setting, affected users receive Work Folders settings when they sign in to a domain-joined PC.

The "Work Folders URL" (see Figure 7-5) can specify either the URL used by the organization for Work Folders discovery, or the specific URL of the file server that stores the affected users' data.

The "Force automatic setup" option specifies that Work Folders should be set up automatically without prompting users. This prevents users from choosing not to use Work Folders on the computer; it also prevents them from manually specifying the local folder in which Work Folders stores files. By default, Work Folders is stored in the "%USERPROFILE%\ Work Folders" folder. If this option is not specified, users must use the Work Folders Control Panel item on their computers to set up Work Folders.

If this policy setting is disabled or not configured, no Work Folders settings are specified for the affected users, though users can manually set up Work Folders by using the Work Folders Control Panel item.

Kerberos authentication

There are three new policy settings related to how Kerberos authentication can be performed in Active Directory environments:

- Request compound authentication
- Always send compound authentication first
- Restrict delegation of credentials to remote servers

These new policy settings apply only to computers running Windows Server 2012 R2, Windows 8.1, or Windows RT 8.1.

Request compound authentication

This policy setting allows you to configure a domain controller to request compound authentication. It is located at:

Computer Configuration\System\KDC

If you enable this policy setting, domain controllers will request compound authentication. The returned service ticket will contain compound authentication only when the account is explicitly configured. This policy should be applied to all domain controllers to ensure consistent application of this policy in the domain.

If you disable or do not configure this policy setting, domain controllers will return service tickets that contain compound authentication any time the client sends a compound authentication request regardless of the account configuration.

> **NOTE** For a domain controller to request compound authentication, the policy "KDC support for claims, compound authentication, and Kerberos armoring" must be configured and enabled.

Always send compound authentication first

This policy setting controls whether a device always sends a compound authentication request when the resource domain requests compound identity. It is located at:

Computer Configuration\System\Kerberos

If you enable this policy setting and the resource domain requests compound authentication, devices that support compound authentication always send a compound authentication request.

If you disable or do not configure this policy setting and the resource domain requests compound authentication, devices will send a non-compounded authentication request first, and then a compound authentication request when the service requests compound authentication.

> **NOTE** For a domain controller to request compound authentication, the policies "KDC support for claims, compound authentication, and Kerberos armoring" and "Request compound authentication" must be configured and enabled in the resource account domain.

Restrict delegation of credentials to remote servers

This policy setting is used to configure restricted mode. It is located at:

Computer Configuration\System\Credentials Delegation

When running in restricted mode, participating apps do not expose credentials to remote computers (regardless of the delegation method). Restricted mode may limit access to resources located on other servers or networks beyond the target computer because credentials are not delegated. Participating apps include Remote Desktop Client.

If you enable this policy setting, restricted mode is enforced and participating apps will not delegate credentials to remote computers.

If you disable or do not configure this policy setting, restricted mode is not enforced and participating apps can delegate credentials to remote computers.

> **NOTE** To disable most credential delegation, it may be sufficient to deny delegation in Credential Security Support Provider (CredSSP) by modifying Administrative template settings (located at Computer Configuration\Administrative Templates\System\Credentials Delegation).

Logon scripts

There is one new Group Policy setting that can be used to configure the behavior of how logon scripts are processed in your environment. This new policy setting applies only to computers running Windows Server 2012 R2, Windows 8.1, or Windows RT 8.1.

Configure Logon Script Delay

This policy setting allows you to configure how long the Group Policy client waits after logon before running scripts. It is located at:

Computer Configuration\System\Group Policy

By default, the Group Policy client waits five minutes before running logon scripts. This helps create a responsive desktop environment by preventing disk contention.

If you enable this policy setting, Group Policy will wait for the specified amount of time before running logon scripts.

If you disable this policy setting, Group Policy will run scripts immediately after logon.

If you do not configure this policy setting, Group Policy will wait five minutes before running logon scripts.

Enter "0" to disable Logon Script Delay.

Windows Update

There is one new Group Policy setting that can be used to configure the behavior of how Windows Update works in your environment. This new policy setting applies only to computers running Windows Server 2012 R2, Windows 8.1, or Windows RT 8.1.

Do not connect to any Windows Update Internet locations

This policy setting is located at:

Computer Configuration\Windows Components\Windows Update

Enabling this policy will disable that functionality and may cause connection to public services such as the Windows Store to stop working.

Even when Windows Update is configured to receive updates from an intranet update service, it will periodically retrieve information from the public Windows Update service to enable future connections to Windows Update, and other services like Microsoft Update or the Windows Store.

> **NOTE** This policy applies only when this PC is configured to connect to an intranet update service using the "Specify intranet Microsoft update service location" policy.

Windows Runtime apps

There is one new Group Policy setting that can be used to configure the behavior of Windows runtime apps for your environment. This new policy setting applies only to computers running Windows Server 2012 R2, Windows 8.1, or Windows RT 8.1.

Allow Windows Runtime apps to revoke enterprise data

This policy setting is located at:

User Configuration\Windows Components\File Revocation

Windows Runtime applications can protect content which has been associated with an enterprise identifier (EID), but can only revoke access to content it protected. To allow an application to revoke access to all content on the device that is protected by a particular enterprise, add an entry to the list on a new line that contains the enterprise identifier, separated by a comma, and the Package Family Name of the application. The EID must be an internet domain belonging to the enterprise in standard international domain name format. An example value might be:

Contoso.com,ContosoIT.HumanResourcesApp_m5g0r7arhahqy

If you enable this policy setting, the application identified by the Package Family Name will be permitted to revoke access to all content protected using the specified EID on the device.

If you disable or do not configure this policy setting, the only Windows Runtime applications that can revoke access to all enterprise-protected content on the device are Windows Mail and the user-selected mailto protocol handler app. Any other Windows Runtime application will only be able to revoke access to content it protected.

> **NOTE** File revocation applies to all content protected under the same second level domain as the provided enterprise identifier. So, revoking an enterprise ID of mail.contoso.com will revoke the user's access to all content protected under the contoso.com hierarchy.

Microsoft accounts

There is one new Group Policy setting that can be used to configure the behavior of Microsoft accounts for users. This new policy setting applies only to computers running Windows Server 2012 R2, Windows 8.1, or Windows RT 8.1.

Allow Microsoft accounts to be optional

This policy setting lets you control whether Microsoft accounts are optional for Windows Store apps that require an account to sign in. It is located at:

Computer Configuration\Windows Components\App runtime

User Configuration\Windows Components\App runtime

If you enable this policy setting, Windows Store apps that typically require a Microsoft account to sign in will allow users to sign in with an enterprise account instead.

If you disable or do not configure this policy setting, users will need to sign in with a Microsoft account.

> **NOTE** This policy only affects Windows Store apps that support it.

Automatic sign-in

An interesting new Group Policy setting is now available to configure what happens if Windows initiates a restart while the user is logged on to his or her computer. This new policy setting applies only to computers running Windows Server 2012 R2, Windows 8.1, or Windows RT 8.1.

Sign-in last interactive user automatically after a system-initiated restart

This policy setting controls whether a device will automatically sign-in the last interactive user after Windows Update restarts the system. It is located at:

Computer Configuration\Windows Components\Windows Logon Options

If you enable or do not configure this policy setting, the device securely saves the user's credentials (including the user name, domain and encrypted password) to configure automatic sign-in after a Windows Update restart. After the Windows Update restart, the user is automatically signed-in and the session is automatically locked with all the lock screen apps configured for that user.

If you disable this policy setting, the device does not store the user's credentials for automatic sign-in after a Windows Update restart. The users' lock screen apps are not restarted after the system restarts.

Windows SkyDrive

Two new Group Policy settings can be used to configure the behavior of Windows SkyDrive for users:

- Prevent the usage of SkyDrive for file storage
- Save documents and pictures to the local PC by default

These new policy settings apply only to computers running Windows 8.1 or Windows RT 8.1.

Prevent the usage of SkyDrive for file storage

This policy setting lets you prevent apps and features from working with files on SkyDrive. It is located at:

Computer Configuration\Windows Components\SkyDrive

If you enable this policy setting, the following happens:

- Users can't access SkyDrive from the SkyDrive app and file picker.
- Windows Store apps can't access SkyDrive using the WinRT API.
- SkyDrive doesn't appear in the navigation pane in File Explorer.
- SkyDrive files aren't kept in sync with the cloud.
- Users can't automatically upload photos and videos from the camera roll folder.

If you disable or do not configure this policy setting, apps and features can work with SkyDrive file storage.

Save documents and pictures to the local PC by default

This policy setting lets you select the local PC as the default save location. It does not prevent apps and users from saving files on SkyDrive. It is located at:

Computer Configuration\Windows Components\SkyDrive

If you enable this policy setting, files will be saved locally by default. Users will still be able to change the value of this setting to save to SkyDrive by default. They will also be able to open and save files on SkyDrive using the SkyDrive app and file picker, and Windows Store apps will still be able to access SkyDrive using the WinRT API.

If you disable or do not configure this policy setting, users with a connected account will save files to SkyDrive by default.

Learn more

You can learn more about the new Group Policy features and enhancements in Windows Server 2012 R2 by checking out the following topics on Microsoft TechNet:

- "What's New in Group Policy in Windows Server 2012 R2" at *http://technet.microsoft .com/en-us/library/dn265973.aspx*.

CHAPTER 8

IIS

The Web Server (IIS) role in Windows Server 2012 R2 provides a modular and extensible platform for reliably hosting websites, services, and applications. IIS enables businesses to share information with users on the Internet, a corporate intranet, or a company extranet. IIS is a secure and easy-to-manage unified web platform that integrates IIS, ASP.NET, FTP services, PHP, and Windows Communication Foundation (WCF).

Previous enhancements to IIS

IIS 8.0 in Windows Server 2012 introduced a number of new capabilities that made the Microsoft web server a highly scalable and elastic platform for cloud computing. The results were beneficial to a wide spectrum of customers ranging from an enterprise hosting line of business (LOB) applications or a cloud-hosting provider managing a multitenant public cloud. Some of the significant improvements made to IIS 8 in Windows Server 2012 included:

- **NUMA-aware scalability**   Non-Uniform Memory Architecture (NUMA) was designed to overcome the scalability limits of the traditional symmetric multiprocessing (SMP) architecture, where all memory access happens on the same shared memory bus. SMP works well when you have a small number of CPUs, but it doesn't when you have dozens of them competing for access to the shared bus. NUMA alleviated such bottlenecks by limiting how many CPUs could be on any one memory bus and connecting them with a high-speed interconnection. To utilize these capabilities, IIS in Windows Server 2012 introduced NUMA-aware scalability, which worked by intelligently affinitizing worker processes to NUMA nodes. On NUMA-aware hardware, IIS will try to assign each worker process in a web garden to a different NUMA node to achieve optimal performance.

- **Server Name Indication**   Before Windows Server 2012, you could use host headers in IIS to support hosting multiple HTTP websites using only a single shared IP address. Moreover, if you wanted these websites to use HTTPS, then you had a problem because you couldn't use host headers with HTTPS since IIS didn't support that. Instead, you had to assign multiple IP addresses to your web server and bind a different IP address to each HTTPS site, which incurred a lot of management overhead for IIS administrators. However, IIS 8 in Windows Server 2012 supported Server Name Indication (SNI), which allowed a virtual domain name to be used to identify the network end point of an SSL/TSL connection. This meant IIS could host multiple HTTPS websites, each with their own SSL certificate, bound to the same shared IP address. SNI thus provided increased scalability for web servers hosting multiple SSL sites, and it helped cloud hosting providers to better conserve the dwindling resources of their pool of available IP addresses.

- **SSL central store**   Before Windows Server 2012, managing SSL certificates on servers in IIS web farms was time consuming because the certificates had to be imported into every server in the farm, which made scaling out a farm by deploying additional servers a complex task. Replicating certificates across IIS servers in a farm was further complicated by the need to manually ensure that certificate versions were in sync with each another. IIS in Windows Server 2012 solved this problem by introducing a central store for storing SSL certificates on a file share on the network instead of in the certificate store of each host.

- **CPU throttling**   IIS in Windows Server 2012 allowed you to configure an application pool to throttle the CPU usage so that it could not consume more CPU cycles than a user-specified threshold. You could also configure IIS to throttle an application pool when the system was under load, and this allowed your application pool to consume more resources than your specified level when the system was idle because the Windows kernel would only throttle the worker process and all child processes when the system came under load.

- **Application Initialization**   When users try to open a website in their web browser, and then have to wait for several seconds or longer for the site to respond, they get frustrated. Before Windows Server 2012, the delay that occurred when a web application was first accessed was because the application needed to be loaded into memory before IIS could process the user's request and return a response. With the introduction of Application Initialization in IIS 8, however, application pools could now be prestarted instead of having to wait for a first request to arrive for a web application in the pool. Administrators could choose which applications should be preloaded on their IIS servers, and IIS could even be configured to return a static "splash page" while the application was being initialized so the user felt the website being accessed was responding instead of failing to respond.

- **Dynamic IP address filtering**   Before Windows Server 2012, IIS could use static IP filtering to block requests from specific clients. This functionality was of limited usefulness, however, since it meant that you had to first discover the IP address of the offending client, and then manually configure IIS to block that address. Also, IIS offered no choice as to what action it would take when it blocked a client—an HTTP 403.6 status message was always returned to the offending client. IIS 8, however, introduced a new capability called dynamic IP address filtering, which allowed you to configure an IIS server to block access for any IP address that exceeded a specified number of concurrent requests or exceeded a specified number of requests within a given period of time. You could also configure how IIS responded when it blocked an IP address—for example, by aborting the request instead of returning HTTP 403.6 responses to the client.

By contrast, the improvements made to IIS 8.5 in Windows Server 2012 R2 are targeted at a different audience, namely, website administrators who are highly focused on scalability and manageability. Such improvements are increasingly important in today's world. In fact, both Microsoft's public website and the Windows Azure platform are deeply tied to IIS.

Dynamic Site Activation

One of the key scalability goals Microsoft has for IIS 8.5 is enabling cloud-hosting providers to host more sites on a single IIS server. In Windows Server 2012 and earlier, when IIS starts up on a host, the Windows Activation Service (WAS) loads the entire configuration for IIS. This configuration can be very large if several thousand sites are being hosted on the server, which is typical in many hoster environments. Because of this, loading the IIS configuration can consume a lot of memory on the server, which can impact the performance of other options, such as initializing worker processes for web applications.

To address this issue, the WAS component has been redesigned in IIS to better handle large configurations and improve the memory efficiency of the IIS startup process. In addition, the HTTP protocol stack (Http.sys) now uses a single catch-all request queue and binding to be used by WAS for initializing the worker processes associated with each of the sites running on the IIS server. The result of this change is that when WAS starts up, it no longer has to create thousands of request queues and bindings in Http.sys—one for each of the thousands of worker processes associated with each of the thousands of sites running on the server. The WAS component can now examine a client request in this queue and determine which site and worker process should handle that request. WAS then creates a queue for the request, registers the binding, and spins up the worker process for the site to start the site.

This new functionality is called Dynamic Site Activation, and it addresses the issue of being "config-bound" which hosters who run large numbers of sites on IIS servers can experience. By default, if an IIS 8.5 server is hosting 100 or more sites, this new WAS functionality is used. If the server is hosting fewer than 100 sites, however, the old method of creating separate queues and bindings for each site is still used since such a scenario has only a relatively small configuration that can load quite easily without undue memory being needed. This functionality can be tuned by modifying the *dynamicRegistrationThreshold* parameter using the IIS Configuration Editor, as shown in Figure 8-1. Note that you must restart WAS after changing this parameter for the change to take effect.

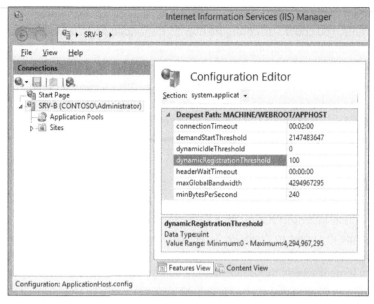

FIGURE 8-1 The Configuration Editor configures Dynamic Site Activation.

Idle Worker Process Page-out

A second scalability issue that can be experienced on IIS servers hosting large numbers of sites has to do with cold requests. A cold request is a request that comes for a worker process that has not yet been started. The cold request has to wait for IIS to initialize, for the appropriate framework (for example, .NET or PHP) to initialize, for the associated site to initialize, and so on. As a result, the response time to cold requests with previous versions of IIS sometimes left something to be desired.

This issue was partly addressed with IIS 8 in Windows Server 2012 where static sites responded much more quickly (typically a few hundred milliseconds) to cold requests than for IIS 7 in Windows Server 2008 R2. However, there was only a small performance improvement in IIS 8 for dynamic sites with managed code, with such sites typically taking several seconds to start in response to cold requests, largely because of the time needed to load the application framework needed by the site. From the perspective of the hoster's customers, however, taking several seconds to launch their LOB web application can be viewed negatively as unacceptable and poor performance.

To improve the start time for dynamic sites in response to cold requests, a module called Application Initialization, was included in IIS 8 in Windows Server 2012 that allowed the administrator to preload the application framework needed for a dynamic site so that the site could respond to a cold request in a few hundred milliseconds instead of several seconds. However, this module is not useful for hosters because such preloaded application frameworks consume additional memory for each site configured to use them. Since the IIS servers of a hoster are typically hosting thousands of sites and are usually memory-bound (assume at least 100 MB needed per dynamic site), such preloading application frameworks for all sites hosted on a server just wasn't feasible. IIS can partly address this problem by killing idle worker processes after a default of 20 minutes of inactivity, and WAS can halve this time interval if it determines that memory pressure has reached 80 percent on the server.

IIS 8.5 in Windows Server 2012 R2 now takes a different perspective on how to address the problem of cold request delays for dynamic sites. A new feature called Idle Worker Process Page-out, saves memory by allowing an idle worker process to be paged to disk so that the worker process is removed from memory. The page-out feature can be made to perform even better by utilizing a solid state disk (SSD) for the paging file of an IIS server. The result is that memory pressure can now be greatly reduced for servers hosting thousands of dynamic sites and the response time to cold requests for these sites can be significantly improved.

Idle Worker Process Page-out is not enabled by default in IIS 8.5. Instead, worker processes simply terminate idle worker processes. You can enable Idle Worker Process Page-out by opening the Advanced Settings dialog for an application pool in IIS Manager and changing the value of the Idle Time-out Action setting from Terminate to Suspend, as shown in Figure 8-2. You can also enable Idle Worker Process Page-out at the server level, and although doing this won't affect the configuration of existing sites, any new sites that are created will inherit this setting.

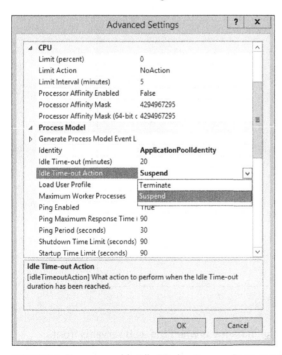

FIGURE 8-2 You can enable Idle Worker Process Page-out through Advanced Settings.

Custom IIS logging fields

Another set of enhancements made in IIS 8.5 is in the area of logging. IIS logging can be used for monitoring and tracking IIS activity and for troubleshooting and debugging IIS when problems occur. One frequent request from customers who use IIS is for the ability to log more kinds of IIS activities.

To address such requests, IIS 8.5 now allows administrators to specify that additional custom fields be logged by IIS in addition to the standard W3C logging fields. This is illustrated by Figure 8-3, which shows the list of additional sources that can be logged for Request Header. Additional custom fields can also be added for Response Header and for Server Variables. In addition to the prepopulated fields for the variables and headers, the administrator can manually specify custom sources.

FIGURE 8-3 You can add custom fields for IIS logging.

A common scenario where this could come in handy is when the web server is front-ended by networking equipment such as a proxy or load balancer. In such a situation, the IIS logs can not accurately track client IP addresses because the IP captured by Http.sys is the proxy or load balancer's IP. Network hardware that proxy HTTP requests usually have the ability to store the original client IP in the custom header X-FORWARDED-FOR, and so the administrator can record it as a custom Response Header and thus record the original IP of the clients.

Note that the custom logging is limited to a total of 64 KB, and if the administrator defines custom fields which exceed that, they will be truncated. This means that care must be taken when deciding which fields to collect. Note also that when enhanced logging is enabled, IIS creates log files with _x appended to their name to indicate that these files are enhanced logging fields.

IIS ETW logging

Another useful enhancement to logging in IIS 8.5 is the ability of the IIS logging mechanism to send data through Event Tracing for Windows (ETW). ETW is a tracing and logging mechanism that is part of the operating system, and many Windows components and applications take advantage of it to standardize their output for the purpose of debugging or troubleshooting. If an application or component uses ETW, administrators can use it to collect the info using a multitude of techniques and tools that are publicly available. This way, administrators, application developers, and support personnel can collect traces or logs in real time, and without complicated setup requirements or specific tools. This can be particularly useful for servers that are very busy, because as you'll see soon, the real-time data can be easily filtered.

Let's now hear from one of our Microsoft insiders about how to configure ETW logging in IIS 8.5.

Configuring IIS ETW Logging

To facilitate ETW logging, IIS has a new service—W3C Logging Service (w3logsvc), which was created to handle both the enhanced logging of custom fields we discussed earlier and ETW. As part of this new design, the logging service can send data to either ETW or the text-based log files, or both. Once the logging service sends the data to ETW, the administrator can hook into the same ETW provider and collect the data.

Enabling ETW logging

By default, IIS doesn't use ETW, so to enable it, follow these steps:

1. Open the IIS management console.

2. Click the server you wish to manage.

3. Navigate down to the site that you want to configure.

4. Open the Logging configuration item in the Feature View pane.

5. Configure IIS for either ETW Event Only or Both Log File And ETW Event.

Once you configure this and initiate traffic to the appropriate website, you should be able to see that the w3logsvc service has started.

The ETW provider for IIS's logging is named Microsoft-Windows-IIS-Logging, and any application that is designed to interact with ETW providers can retrieve the data. One specific application that was designed for system administrators is Message Analyzer. Message Analyzer was developed by Microsoft as a next-generation replacement for Network Monitor, and it provides similar functionality, with the addition of several functions, one of which is the ability to connect to ETW providers.

At the time of writing, Message Analyzer is available in Beta 3, and by the time this book is published, a final version should be available. Head over to *http://blogs.technet.com/b/messageanalyzer/* to find out the current release and for a download link.

Collecting ETW events

Once you have installed Message Analyzer on your IIS server, follow these steps to collect the ETW events from IIS:

1. Launch Message Analyzer.

2. Click the Capture / Trace button.

3. In the top-right corner, in the Search And Add Providers input box, type in Microsoft-windows-IIS-logging

4. Click start-with to start the capture.

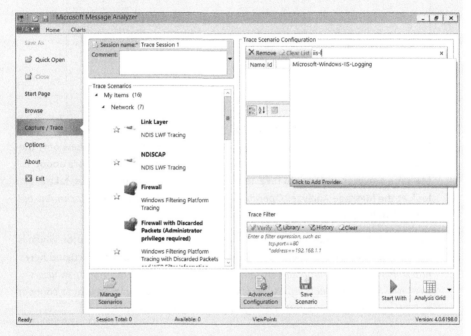

Once the capture is running, it will show an event for every request received by IIS, and the event details will show the data collected by the logging service. For example, in the screenshot below you can see that the field C_ip contains the connecting client's IP address. This means that if you need to troubleshoot a specific client that's connecting to a busy server, you can simply filter the output to show only data from that specific IP or a group of IPs.

Message Analyzer is a very advanced tool, and it allows you to easily configure filters. It even includes an easy to use time-slider, which allows you to view only the requests that were received during a particular time frame. To learn more about Message Analyzer and how to take advantage of its plethora of features, take a look at the Message Analyzer Operating Guide: *http://technet.microsoft.com/en-us/library/jj649776.aspx*.

Another tool that can connect to an ETW provider is Performance Monitor, which is included with Windows Server. Additional tools and techniques are discussed here: *http://blogs.msdn.com/b/oanapl/archive/2009/08/05/etw-event-tracing-for-windows-what-it-is-and-useful-tools.aspx*. In fact, you can even write your own tool to connect to ETW providers, although this is beyond the scope of this book.

Erez Benari
Program Manager for IIS from the Windows Azure team at Microsoft

Learn more

You can learn more about the new features and enhancements in IIS 8.5 by checking out the following resources on IIS.NET:

- "Dynamic Website Activation in IIS 8.5" at *http://www.iis.net/learn/get-started/whats-new-in-iis-85/dynamic-site-activation-in-iis85*.

- "Idle Worker Process Page-Out in IIS 8.5" at *http://www.iis.net/learn/get-started/whats-new-in-iis-85/idle-worker-process-page-out-in-iis85.*

- "Enhanced Logging for IIS 8.5" at *http://www.iis.net/learn/get-started/whats-new-in-iis-85/enhanced-logging-for-iis85.*

- "Logging to Event Tracing for Windows in IIS 8.5" at *http://www.iis.net/learn/get-started/whats-new-in-iis-85/logging-to-etw-in-iis-85.*

- "Fine-tuning Dynamic Worker-Process Page-out on IIS 8.5" at *https://blogs.iis.net/erez/archive/2013/08/28/fine-tuning-dynamic-worker-process-page-out-on-iis-8-5.aspx.*

Be sure also to check out the following video from TechEd 2013 on Channel 9:

- "Internet Information Services: What's New in Window Server 2012 R2" *http://channel9.msdn.com/Events/TechEd/NorthAmerica/2013/MDC-B303.*

CHAPTER 9

Remote Desktop Services

Way back in the mainframe age of computers, dumb terminals ruled the roost. Users keyed their data into a "green screen" terminal and it was sent over the wire to the mainframe. Once the user's commands had been processed, the results were then transmitted back over the wire to the terminal, where they were displayed in bright green on black background. This client/server architecture of dumb terminals and terminal servers can still be seen in operation when you watch classic movies like *Billion Dollar Brain* by Michael Caine.

Terminal servers have come a long way since then. Microsoft first introduced its own version of this architecture way back in 1996 with Windows NT 4.0 Terminal Server edition, and it provided users with session-based desktops they could access remotely as if they were logged on interactively. Then, as successive versions of Windows Server were released, Terminal Services was enhanced in many ways and rebranded as Remote Desktop Services (RDS). Today, RDS is a staple for organizations that want to deploy a wide range of remote work solutions including virtual desktops, RemoteApp programs, and session-based desktops. In fact, RDS can even enable users to securely run business applications over the Internet as if they were sitting at a computer on the company LAN.

Previous RDS enhancements

A big change introduced in Windows Server 2012 was how RDS could be easily deployed in different kinds of scenarios. When you added the RDS role in Windows Server 2012, you first had a choice of choosing two deployment options:

- **Standard**   This option provides you with more flexibility concerning how you deploy different RDS role services to different servers and is intended for production environments.
- **Quick Start**   This option deploys all the RDS role services required on a single computer using mostly the default options and is intended mainly for test environments.

Once you've selected the appropriate deployment option for your environment, you're next choice is which type of RDS scenario you want to implement:

- **Virtual machine-based desktop deployment**   Lets remote users connect to virtual desktops running on a Remote Desktop Virtualization Host to access applications installed on these virtual desktops (and also RemoteApp programs if session virtualization is also deployed).

- **Session-based desktop deployment**   Lets remote users connect to sessions running on a Remote Desktop Session Host to access session-based desktop and RemoteApp programs.

That's not all, though, because there were a number of other significant enhancements to RDS in Windows Server 2012, such as:

- **RemoteFX enhancements**   RemoteFX was first introduced in Windows Server 2008 R2 as a way of delivering a full Windows experience using Remote Desktop Protocol (RDP) across a wide variety of client devices. RemoteFX uses host-side rendering to enable graphics to be rendered on the host instead of the client by utilizing the capabilities of a RemoteFX-capable graphics processing unit (GPU) on the host. RemoteFX vGPU uses GPU virtualization to expose a virtual graphics device to a virtual machine running on a RemoteFX-capable host so that multiple virtual desktops could share the single GPU on the host. RemoteFX functionality was enhanced for RDS in Windows Server in a lot of ways with support included for multitouch gestures and manipulations in remote sessions; improved multimonitor support; dynamic adaptation to changing network conditions by using multiple codecs to optimize how content is delivered; optimization of performance when sending traffic over a wide area network (WAN) by choosing between TCP or UDP (called RemoteFX for WAN); integration throughout the RDS role services instead of being installed as its own separate role service; and more.

- **Enhanced USB Redirect**   USB redirection from within RDS was first introduced in Windows 7 Service Pack 1 and Windows Server 2008 R2 Service Pack 1 to support VDI scenarios. USB Redirect occurs at the port protocol level and enables redirection of a wide variety of different types of universal serial bus (USB) devices, including printers, scanners, webcams, Voice over Internet Protocol (VoIP) headsets, and biometric devices. RDS in Windows Server 2012 enhanced this capability with support for USB Redirect for Remote Desktop Session Host (RD Session Host) to enable new kinds of scenarios for businesses that implement session virtualization solutions. In addition, USB Redirect for Remote Desktop Virtualization Host (RD Virtualization Host) no longer requires installing the RemoteFX 3D Video Adapter on the virtual machine in order to work.

- **User Profile Disks**   Before Windows Server 2012, preserving user state information for sessions and virtual desktops required using Windows roaming technologies like roaming user profiles (RUP) and Folder Redirection (FR). But implementing RUP and FR added more complexity to deployments. RDS in Windows Server 2012 simplifies session-based and VDI deployments with the introduction of User Profile Disks, which store user data and settings for sessions and virtual desktops in a separate VHD file that can be stored on a network share.

RDS in Windows Server 2012 R2 isn't a radical change from what it was in Windows Server 2012, but it does have some exciting new features and enhancements that can make managing remote sessions easier, provide a richer user experience, and allow you to get the best possible value from VDI.

Improved RemoteApp experience

In previous versions of RDS, when you opened a RemoteApp program and dragged it around on the desktop, only an outline of the program's window was displayed. And if you hovered the mouse pointer over the taskbar icon of a RemoteApp program, no thumbnail preview was displayed—only the generic icon associated with the program.

In Windows Server 2012 R2, however, the RemoteFX graphics capability has been enhanced in several ways. For example, dragging around a RemoteApp program now drags the entire contents of the program's window. And as Figure 9-1 shows, hovering over the taskbar icon of the RemoteApp program displays a live thumbnail preview of the program.

FIGURE 9-1 Hovering over the taskbar icon of a RemoteApp program now displays a live thumbnail preview of the program.

As Figure 9-2 shows, these advanced graphics capabilities of RemoteFX in Windows Server 2012 R2 can be configured using Group Policy. RemoteFX advanced graphics functionality is enabled by default, but you can use this policy setting or disable it if some of your published applications don't support them.

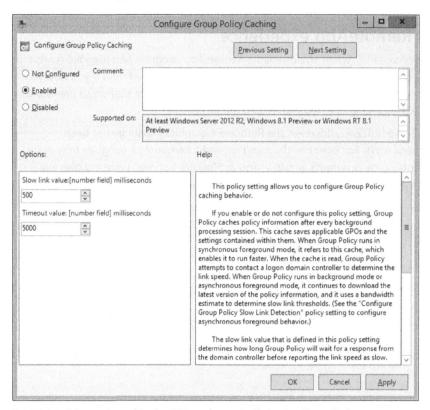

FIGURE 9-2 Advanced graphics for RDS can be controlled using Group Policy.

DX11.1 support

RemoteFX virtual graphics processing unit (vGPU) in Windows Server 2012 R2 also now supports DX11.1 enhanced graphics display capabilities. This means that graphics intensive applications relying on DX11.1 features can now be run in virtualized environments. The requirements for doing this are as follows:

- The system must have DX11.1 capable graphics processing unit (GPU) card.
- The host must be running on Windows 8.1 or Windows Server 2012 R2.
- The virtual machines must be Generation 1 not Generation 2.

In addition, RemoteFX running on Non-Uniform Memory Access (NUMA) based systems will also experience improved scaling capabilities.

Improved video experience

Delivering a quality video experience over RDP has traditionally been a challenge because of the large amount of bandwidth utilized. This is especially true when RDS is being used to stream video content over a WAN connection.

One way of boosting performance in such situations is to compress the video content before streaming it to remote clients. RDS in Windows Server 2012 R2 now has improved codecs that can deliver significantly better video performance especially in WAN scenarios. You can now achieve bandwidth savings of up to 50 percent compared with using RDS in the previous version Windows Server 2012.

Seamless display handling

Improvements made in both Windows 8.1 and Windows Server 2012 R2 now allow RDS to handle a wide variety of display-handling operations. These include:

- Adding or removing monitors
- Adding or removing projectors
- Adding or removing docking stations
- Rotating devices or monitors

RDS can handle these operations for both remote sessions and RemoteApp programs. For example, on tablet devices a remote desktop session will now automatically rotate as you rotate the device.

RDS also allows you to change the display resolution in a remote desktop session and have the session window resize itself properly so you won't have to use the scroll bars to get to the taskbar and charms. This also works in multimonitor scenarios.

The result of all these enhancements is to bring RDS user experience even closer to being on par with that of local devices.

Quick Reconnect

Another new feature of RDS in Windows Server 2012 R2 is called Quick Reconnect. In previous versions of Windows Server, reconnecting to a remote desktop session over a slow or unreliable network connection could sometimes take up to a minute. With RDS in Windows Server 2012 R2, however, reconnecting to disconnected sessions will typically take no more than five seconds even over slow connections. The user will also no longer be stuck seeing that uninformative grey screen when the remote desktop client is trying to reconnect to a previously disconnected session, and instead, will see a more informative message.

Session Shadowing

A frequent request from Microsoft customers who use RDS is to add the ability for administrators to shadow the sessions of remote users. The good news is that this kind of shadowing capability is now an in-box feature of RDS in Windows Server 2012 R2.

To see how Session Shadowing works, Figure 9-3 shows the connections in Server Manager to a Remote Desktop Session Host running Windows Server 2012 R2. In previous versions of RDS, if you right-clicked a remote session, you only got three options: Disconnect, Send Message, and Log Off. But in RDS in Windows Server 2012 R2 there is now a fourth context menu option called Shadow, which enables administrators to shadow the session of a connected remote user.

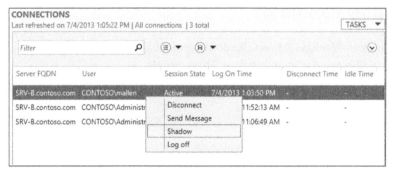

FIGURE 9-3 The new Shadow option provides administrators with the ability to shadow a remote session.

Selecting the Shadow option opens the Shadow dialog shown in Figure 9-4. This dialog offers administrators two options for shadowing the remote session:

- **View** This option allows the administrator only to view what the user is doing in his session.

- **Control** This option allows the administrator to view the user's session and also take control of the session and perform actions on the user's desktop.

FIGURE 9-4 You can view or control remote sessions.

By default, the Prompt For User Consent check box is selected in the Shadow dialog. This means that when the administrator clicks OK to close the dialog, the user's screen dims and a message bar is displayed across his or her screen, as shown in Figure 9-5.

FIGURE 9-5 The user must accept the prompt to allow shadowing of his session.

Let's pause for a few notes at this point:

- By default, Group Policy is configured to require user consent to shadow requests. In many organizations, this might be the correct approach to ensure the privacy of employees. Be sure to consult your legal and human resources departments before changing this policy setting.

- To shadow a remote user, the user doesn't need to be connected to a full remote desktop session. Administrators can even shadow individual RemoteApp programs as remote users work with them.

- Shadowing functionality is also built into the Remote Desktop Client client (Mstsc.exe). By including the /shadow parameter and specifying the remote session when you use mstsc to launch the Remote Desktop Client from the command line, an administrator can use the client to view or control the remote user's session.

To continue now with our walkthrough of shadowing, if the user clicks No in the message bar on her screen, the administrator will not be able to shadow the user's session. If she clicks Yes, the message bar disappears and the user's screen is no longer dimmed, and she can continue with her work as usual. Meanwhile, a new window appears on the RDS administrator's desktop showing the appearance of the shadowed user's desktop in real time, as shown in Figure 9-6.

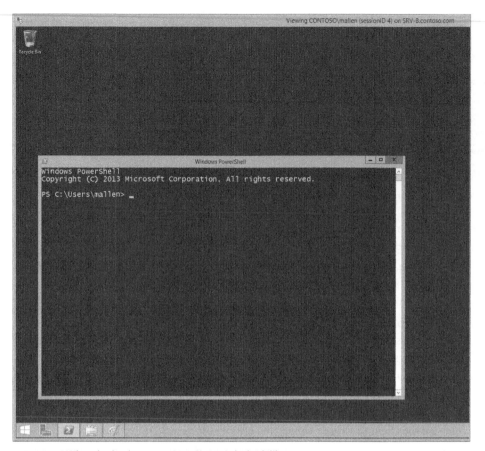

FIGURE 9-6 What shadowing a user's session might look like.

Once the administrator is finished shadowing the session, he can simply close the shadow window.

VDI and data deduplication

Windows Server 2012 previously introduced a feature called data deduplication that allowed more data to be stored in less physical disk space. Data deduplication is highly scalable and is designed to safeguard the reliability and integrity of your data.

New in RDS in Windows Server 2012 R2 is the ability to use data deduplication with actively running personal desktop collections in virtual desktop interface (VDI) environments. To implement this feature, the desktop virtual hard disks (VHDs) must be stored on a file server running Windows Server 2012 R2 and accessed by using Server Message Block (SMB) version 3.0. The benefit provided by this new capability is that you are able to dramatically reduce the storage requirements for personal VDI scenarios.

Restricted Admin mode

Restricted Admin mode is a new optional mode you can use when launching the Remote Desktop Connection client (mstsc.exe) from the command line. When you specify the Restricted Admin switch with mstsc.exe in order to connect to a remote desktop host running Windows Server 2012 R2, your credentials are not sent to the host. If the RDS server verifies that your user account has administrator rights and supports Restricted Admin mode, the connection attempt succeeds. Otherwise, the connection attempt fails.

Restricted Admin mode does not send your credentials to the RDS server as plaintext or any other reusable forms. It works only if the client and server are running either Windows Server 2012 R2 or Windows 8.1.

Learn more

You can learn more about the new Remote Desktop Services features and enhancements in Windows Server 2012 R2 by checking out the following topics on Microsoft TechNet:

- "What's New in Remote Desktop Services in Windows Server 2012 R2" at *http://technet.microsoft.com/en-us/library/dn283323.aspx*.

The following Microsoft TechNet and MSDN blog posts also have lots of information about the new Remote Desktop Services features and enhancements in Windows Server 2012 R2:

- "What's New in Remote Desktop Services for Windows Server 2012 R2" at *http://blogs.msdn.com/b/rds/archive/2013/07/09/what-s-new-in-remote-desktop-services-for-windows-server-2012-r2.aspx*.

- "Lowering the Cost of Storage for VDI Using Windows Server 2012 R2 with Data Deduplication" at *http://blogs.msdn.com/b/rds/archive/2013/08/07/lowering-the-cost-of-storage-for-vdi-using-windows-server-2012-r2-with-data-deduplication.aspx*.

Be sure also to check out the following videos from TechEd 2013 on Channel 9:

- "What's New in Windows Server 2012 Virtual Desktop Infrastructure and Remote Desktop Services?" at *http://channel9.msdn.com/Events/TechEd/NorthAmerica/2013/WCA-B350#fbid=_9VugRgK7SS*.

- "Designing a Virtual Desktop Infrastructure Architecture for Scale and Performance on Windows Server 2012" at *http://channel9.msdn.com/Events/TechEd/NorthAmerica/2013/WCA-B314#fbid=Wp7AXxNqBsG*.

- "VDI Smackdown 2013 Edition" at *http://channel9.msdn.com/Events/TechEd/NorthAmerica/2013/WCA-B345#fbid=80k1afViSd5*.

- "Optimizing Windows 8 for Virtual Desktop Infrastructure" at *http://channel9.msdn.com/Events/TechEd/NorthAmerica/2013/WCA-B330#fbid=Wp7AXxNqBsG*.

- "Windows Server 2012 Desktop Virtualization (VDI) on Dell Active Infrastructure" at *http://channel9.msdn.com/Events/TechEd/NorthAmerica/2013/WCA-B393#fbid=Wp7AXxNqBsG*.

CHAPTER 10

Windows PowerShell

Windows PowerShell has become the de facto platform for automating the administration of Windows-based environments. Built on top of the common language runtime (CLR) and the Microsoft .NET Framework, Windows PowerShell has brought a whole new paradigm for configuring and managing Windows servers in enterprise environments. Windows Server 2012 R2 introduces the latest iteration of the platform, Windows PowerShell 4.0, and it has some exciting new capabilities we'll look at. But first let's begin by briefly reviewing what was introduced in Windows PowerShell 3.0 in Windows Server 2012.

Previous enhancements in Windows PowerShell 3.0

Windows PowerShell 3.0 in Windows Server 2012 previously introduced numerous new capabilities that helped bring added flexibility and power for managing cloud and multiserver environments to the platform. Some of the key enhancements that were added to Windows PowerShell 3.0 included the following:

- **New architecture** Windows PowerShell 3.0 was built upon the Windows Management Framework 3.0, which introduced a new Windows Management Instrumentation (WMI) provider model that reduces dependency on COM, a new application programming interface (API) for performing standard Common Information Model (CIM) operations, and the capability of writing new Windows PowerShell cmdlets in native code. Windows Management Framework 3.0 also introduced improvements that made WinRM connections more robust to support long-running tasks and be more resilient against transient network failure.

- **Disconnected sessions** Windows PowerShell 3.0 introduced persistent user-managed sessions (PSSessions) that are not dependent upon the session in which they were created. By using the New-PSSession cmdlet, you can create and save a session on a remote server and then disconnect from the session. The Windows PowerShell commands in the session on the remote server will then continue to execute, even though you are no longer connected to the session. If desired, you can reconnect later to the session from the same or a different computer.

- **Windows PowerShell Workflow** Windows PowerShell Workflow lets you create workflows using Windows PowerShell or the Extensible Application Markup Language (XAML) and run the workflows as if they were Windows PowerShell cmdlets. This enables Windows PowerShell to use the capabilities of the Windows Workflow Foundation to create long-running management activities that can be interrupted, suspended, restarted, repeated, and executed in parallel. Windows PowerShell workflows are especially valuable in cloud computing environments because they help you automate administrative operations by building in repeatability and by increasing robustness and reliability. They also help increase your servers-to-administrators ratio by enabling a single administrator to execute a workflow that runs simultaneously on hundreds of servers.

- **Scheduled jobs** Windows PowerShell 2.0 previously had the concept of background jobs, which can be scheduled to run asynchronously in the background. Windows PowerShell 3.0 introduced cmdlets such as Start-Job and Get-Job that can be used to manage these jobs. You can also easily schedule jobs using the Windows Task Scheduler. This means that you, as the administrator, can now have full control over when Windows PowerShell scripts execute in your environment.

- **Windows PowerShell Web Access** Windows PowerShell Web Access lets you manage the servers in your private cloud from anywhere, at any time, by running Windows PowerShell commands within a web-based console. Windows PowerShell Web Access acts as a gateway to provide a web-based Windows PowerShell console that you can use to manage remote computers. This lets you run Windows PowerShell scripts and commands even on computers that don't have Windows PowerShell installed. All your computer needs is an Internet connection and a web browser that supports JavaScript and accepts cookies.

- **Show-Command** Windows PowerShell 3.0 includes a new cmdlet called Show-Command that displays a GUI for a command with a simpler overview of any Windows PowerShell cmdlet. This capability can make it much easier to understand the syntax of a cmdlet, as opposed to using the Get-Help cmdlet.

- **More cmdlets** Windows Server 2012 introduced hundreds of new Windows PowerShell cmdlets that help you manage almost every aspect of your private cloud environment. Note that some of these cmdlets are available only when a particular server role or feature is installed on the system.

Now let's examine some of the key enhancements that Windows Server 2012 R2 brings with version 4.0 of Windows PowerShell.

Windows PowerShell Desired State Configuration

Probably the most exciting improvement in version 4.0 of Windows PowerShell is Windows PowerShell Desired State Configuration (DSC), a powerful new management paradigm you can use to deploy and manage the configuration data for software services and also the environment in which these services will be running. The best way we can learn about this new feature is by sitting back and listening to one of our Microsoft insiders explain it and demonstrate how it works.

Managing the data center using Desired State Configuration

IT professionals worldwide are advancing to the cloud with a goal of delivering IT as a service much like that of a utility company. The intent is that delivered services are uniform and easy to use and work with the flip of a switch. In the world of Infrastructure as a Service (IaaS), the challenge is not always how to get there. It is how to stay there.

Today, the world embraces cloud services. The tools and technologies allow us to deploy to private, service provider, and public clouds. But once the systems are deployed there, how do we ensure that they function as expected? How do we ensure that someone does not inadvertently modify a critical setting that renders the service unusable or impaired?

In the past, one solution was to implement an IT Service Management framework to provide process management. For example, in the healthcare industry, a system would be put into production only after it was "validated." The validation process stated that the system would perform an action in repeatable fashion given the same input. The result should never have a deviation. Computer systems would be rigorously documented and tested to ensure they met the appropriate compliance measurements. Once deployed, the systems would be periodically tested by using a series of test protocols. If a system failed, IT professionals were left to evaluating change control documentation and traditional troubleshooting methods to identify what changed.

Some IT organizations began to leverage early automation capabilities (in the form of various scripting languages) to provide a post-execution check after a system was installed. If the organization was fortunate enough to have Microsoft System Center Configuration Manager, they could leverage Desired Configuration Manager (DCM). Similar to the early automation scripts, early versions of DCM could only report on the configuration of a system. The output of the report would tell you that a configuration item (CI) did not match the source template. Although this was greatly beneficial, it did not resolve issues when the configuration did drift from the source template.

In today's data center, this means that you may have gotten to the cloud, but with configuration drift, you may not be able to stay there. To address this, Microsoft updated the Desired Configuration Manager feature of System Center Configuration Manager to become Compliance Settings.

Compliance settings can now apply remediation to configuration drift. See "SCCM 2012 Settings Management – the M in DCM Truly Becomes Management" at *http://technet.microsoft.com/en-us/video/sccm-2012-settings-management-the-m-in-dcm-truly-becomes-management.aspx* and "Compliance Settings in Configuration Manager" at *http://technet.microsoft.com/library/gg681958.aspx*.

This is great, but what if you do not have Configuration Manager in your environment? There are many scenarios where you have the need for monitoring and remediation but Configuration Manager 2012 is not an available option.

Fortunately a solution exists! Windows PowerShell 4.0 now includes Desired State Configuration (DSC). DSC is a new management platform that consists of a suite of language extensions and providers in the form of Windows PowerShell cmdlets along with a host service that is capable of providing the ability to retrieve a configuration, test a configuration, and apply a configuration to a single or set of systems.

Web server example

For this example, you manage a commerce application where the front-end web servers reside in a DMZ or provider cloud. The consistent configuration state of the front-end web servers is key to having a healthy system. Let's face it; the transactions executed on the servers directly impact your company revenue. The health and functionality of the servers have a lot of impact on your company brand. To monitor and maintain the state of the servers, you implement DSC. As the following diagram shows, DSC has four main pieces:

1. **Configuration Instance Document**   The Windows PowerShell script that generates the definition of the desired state.

2. **MOF file**   The Managed Object Format (MOF) file that contains the compiled definition of the desired state.

3. **Local Configuration Manager**   The DSC engine on the client system that executes against the MOF to retrieve the current configuration, compare the current configuration to the MOF, and/or apply the settings defined in the MOF.

4. **Desired State Configuration Pull Server (optional)**   The repository for the definition of the desired state. If clients are configured to execute a PULL instead of receiving a PUSH, the DSC Pull Server hosts the configuration and client data required to remediate.

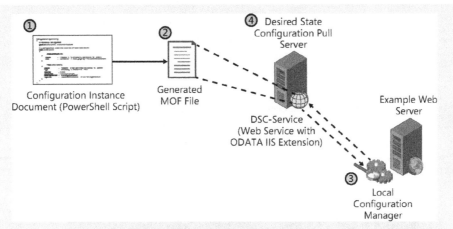

① Configuration Instance Document (PowerShell Script)

② Generated MOF File

④ Desired State Configuration Pull Server

DSC-Service (Web Service with ODATA IIS Extension)

Example Web Server

③ Local Configuration Manager

To begin, you need to ensure Windows PowerShell Remoting is enabled on all involved systems (Enable-PSRemoting). I highly recommend leveraging group policy to put this in place. Group policy has been helping IT professionals enforce policy for more than a decade. It is a perfect complement to your DSC implementation.

> **NOTE** In addition to requiring PSRemoting, DSC applies only to x64 bit system with Windows PowerShell 4.0.

Next, generate the Configuration Instance Document. This Windows PowerShell script contains the definition and execution order of what should exist on the target machine. In this example, your front-end web server requires IIS installed, a set of files (content), an application installed (setup file such as an MSI) as well as specific registry keys. The Configuration Instance Document is a script that contains a configuration block of code. That configuration block contains:

- **Node(s)** A specific target system; defined as "localhost"; or any targeted node system (defined in a hash table).

- **Resource(s)** The actual configuration items that you are looking for as well as their dependencies. For example, the application that must be present has a prerequisite of IIS. Two resources would be specified: a resource name that contains Web-Server and the resource name that contains the application MSI. The application resource would have a dependency set for the resource that defines Web-Server (see *http://technet.microsoft.com/en-us/library/dn249921.aspx*).

DSC is extremely extensible and modular. Your script can be very simple or be scaled out. In Windows PowerShell, you create functions and modules for tasks that you call frequently or leverage from multiple scripts. In DSC you can separate configuration data and your logic as well to make it more modular.

You can control the actions of the Local Configuration Manager. Windows PowerShell DSC cmdlets Get-DscLocalConfigurationManager and Set-DscLocalConfigurationManager are used to call the Local Configuration Manager engine. Using the Windows PowerShell DesiredStateConfigurationSettings keyword in a script, you can generate a separate MOF file that contains an instruction set for the Local Configuration Manager engine. The MOF-generating script can change the functionality of the engine from receiving configuration information via a PUSH to executing a PULL from a DSC server. You can change frequency so that it refreshes its configuration data:

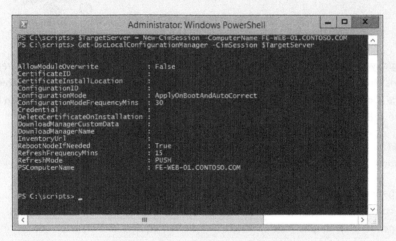

Once the script is built, review it to ensure you have the external dependencies set up:

```
Configuration CommerceConfig
{
    # A Configuration block can have zero or more Node blocks
    Node "FE-WEB-01"
    {
        # Next, specify one or more resource blocks

        # WindowsFeature is one of the built-in resources you can use in a
Node block
        # This example ensures the Web Server (IIS) role is installed
        WindowsFeature CommerceSite
        {
            Ensure = "Present" # To uninstall the role, set Ensure to
"Absent"
            Name = "Web-Server"
        }
```

```
    # File is a built-in resource you can use to manage files and
directories
    # This example ensures files from the source directory are present
in the destination directory
    File CommerceSite
    {
        Ensure = "Present"  # You can also set Ensure to "Absent"
        Type = "Directory" # Default is "File"
        Recurse = $true
        SourcePath = $WebsiteFilePath # This is a path that has web
files
        DestinationPath = "C:\inetpub\wwwroot" # The path where we want
to ensure the web files are present
        Requires = "[WindowsFeature]CommerceSite"  # This ensures that
MyRoleExample completes successfully before this block runs
    }
  }
}

$WebsiteFilePath = "\\2012R2PREVIEW\CommerceSiteSource\SiteData"
CommerceConfig
```

Does your web server require file content? If so, did you set up a share for that content to be pulled from? Your DSC Pull Server might make a good repository for these items. In the example above, the share is \\2012R2PREVIEW\CommerceSiteSource; however, the data is located in \SiteData. The path specified for files cannot be the root of a share, but must be a folder underneath that share.

Execute the Configuration Instance Document (your Windows PowerShell script) to generate the MOF file containing the configuration instructions:

Now comes the really cool part—deploying the DSC job to the client system. The −Path switch points to the directory where the MOF file exists (on the system where the script is being executed from):

```
Administrator: Windows PowerShell
PS C:\scripts> Start-DscConfiguration -ComputerName FE-WEB-01 -Path C:\Scripts\CommerceConfig

Id   Name   PSJobTypeName   State     HasMoreData   Location    Command
--   ----   -------------   -----     -----------   --------    -------
18   Job18  Configuratio... Running   True          FE-WEB-01   Start-DscConfiguration...

PS C:\scripts>
```

If you include the −Wait and −Verbose switches, you can see the progress of the job (and any errors if they occur):

```
DSCEngine
   Applying Configuration
   [ooooooooooooooooooooooooooooooooooooooooooooooooooooooooooooo       ]
   00:00:02 remaining.

   Set
```

Check the Operational and Debug event logs for DSC. You can find these logs in Event Viewer under Applications And Services Logs | Microsoft | Windows | Desired State Configuration or Applications And Services Logs | Microsoft | Windows | DSC.

You can then test the applied configuration. The test compares the desired state configuration to the target system and returns a "True" or "False" result:

```
Select Administrator: Windows PowerShell
PS C:\scripts> $TargetServer = New-CimSession -ComputerName FE-WEB-01
PS C:\scripts> Test-DscConfiguration -CimSession $TargetServer
True
PS C:\scripts>
```

As a verification test, delete a few files from the web server content directory C:\inetpub\wwwroot and perform the test. Note that the returned result is "False." Execute the same DscConfiguration job run previously. Complete the test and now you can see the returned result is again "True" because the issues were remediated:

```
Administrator: Windows PowerShell
PS C:\scripts> Test-DscConfiguration -CimSession $TargetServer
False
PS C:\scripts> Start-DscConfiguration -ComputerName FE-WEB-01 -Path C:\Scripts\CommerceConfig

Id   Name   PSJobTypeName   State     HasMoreData   Location    Command
--   ----   -------------   -----     -----------   --------    -------
57   Job57  Configuratio... Running   True          FE-WEB-01   Start-DscConfiguration...

PS C:\scripts> Test-DscConfiguration -CimSession $TargetServer
True
PS C:\scripts>
```

Your environment and requirements define how far you extend DSC. For example, if you have Microsoft System Center Orchestrator or an existing automation tool within your environment, you may choose to leverage that to manage checking state and performing remediation if necessary.

If that is not an available option, you may choose to switch the client from receiving a PUSH to now autoremediating via a PULL to extract its MOF file from a Desired State Configuration Pull Server. This is a web service utilizing the ODATA IIS extension. The DSC Pull Server can be set up on Windows Server 2008 R2, 2012, or 2012 R2. For Windows Server 2008 R2 and 2012, you can install the role through a set of Windows PowerShell commands that essentially install all of the necessary components. In Windows Server 2012 R2, the DSC Pull Server is a feature:

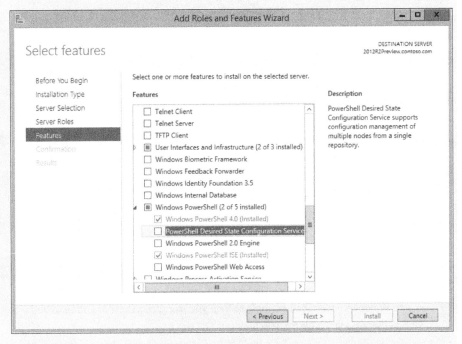

Advancements in Windows PowerShell continue to transform the data center landscape. Features like DSC demonstrate how the push toward IaaS is not only achievable, but is here to stay.

Jeff Butte
Senior Consultant, US Public Sector

Save-Help

One small but potentially very useful improvement in Windows PowerShell 4.0 is a new cmdlet that allows you to save help for Windows PowerShell modules installed on remote computers. Once again, let's hear from an expert inside Microsoft about how this works and why it can be useful.

Save-Help for the disconnected Windows PowerShell world

We live in an increasingly connected world. You can now get almost everything online. However, what if you are not online . . . ever? While the world continues to weave more connectivity, there are networks that will never connect to the Internet. Organizations have determined that for reasons of risk and/or security, physical separation from the Internet is a key requirement.

Cyber-crime has risen to a level that our countries are developing national strategies to combat it. Companies operate isolated networks to protect their most critical or valuable resources from data exfiltration by Advanced Persistent Threats. Governments operate isolated networks for the purpose of protecting their nation's secrets. Manufacturing or transportation systems may be isolated to ensure that neither intentional nor accidental connectivity risks human life or the financial well-being of a company. Then again, the reason for isolation may be as simple as protecting production networks from development networks.

Regardless of the reason, disconnected networks exist and they continue down the path toward a private cloud. Organizations are realizing the benefits gained from simple data center automation to advanced IaaS. They are extending those gains through their environments, including their disconnected ones.

If you are one of the lucky ones performing data center automation in a high-security, disconnected network, you have undoubtedly experienced the scenario where you need a Windows PowerShell example to help you along and there are none to be found—because you have no help files.

Save-Help was introduced in Windows PowerShell 3.0. It downloads and saves the newest help files to a directory or path you specify. These help files can be copied to the isolated network and then be imported (Update-Help) to Windows PowerShell on the isolated systems.

This was a fantastic way to keep the help files current, but it does have limitations. Fortunately, the Windows Management Framework 4 with Windows PowerShell 4.0 solves several of those.

Previously, Save-Help worked only for modules that were installed locally. To obtain the help files you required, a common method involved building a reference machine where you loaded all of the software stacks on the machine so that you could export out all of the Windows PowerShell module's help files. This was time consuming, wasted resources, and was frequently fraught with errors.

With Windows PowerShell 4.0, you can now avoid all of that extra work effort. From a single machine, you can remotely connect to other systems that have those modules you are looking for loaded and download the help. There are three remote connectivity options: Invoke-Command, New-PSSession, and the new CimSession.

The method utilizing Invoke-Command is very effective. Before you save the help files, you can utilize Invoke-Command to Update-Help, ensuring that you have the most current version.

In the example that follows, the Windows PowerShell is executed from a workstation. The commands are invoked against the remote server CM2012SP1PRI. The files are then saved to a directory on the workstation. Here are the commands:

```
Invoke-Command -ComputerName CM2012SP1PRI -ScriptBlock { Update-Help
-Module ActiveDirectory -Force }
$varModule = Invoke-Command -ComputerName CM2012SP1PRI -ScriptBlock {
Get-Module -Name ActiveDirectory -ListAvailable }
Save-Help -Module $varModule -DestinationPath C:\SavedHelp
```

And here are the commands being executed:

The saved help files are then located in the specified directory:

The files can then be copied to the disconnected network using removable media.

Windows PowerShell 4.0 also supports a "pull" method. The method requires you to start on the isolated network. Connect to a system that has the module that requires a help file update. Using Export-CliXml, you can deserialize the PSModuleInfo object of that module to disk. That object can be transported on removable media to an Internet-connected system. Save-Help can be run on the Internet-connected system against the deserialized PSModuleInfo to download the most current help. The help files can then be transported back to the isolated network. This method, however, is not recommended for use on high-security networks where there is concern of data exfiltration on removable media.

If you are a serious Windows PowerShell user who authors your own module, you can also author updatable help. For more information, see "Updatable Help Authoring: Step-by-Step" at *http://msdn.microsoft.com/en-us/library/windows/desktop/hh852735(v=vs.85).aspx*.

Jeff Butte
Senior Consultant, US Public Sector

Yet more new cmdlets

As you might expect, Windows PowerShell 4.0 introduces yet more new cmdlets you can use for configuring and managing various aspects of client and server, especially those running Windows Server 2012 R2 and Windows 8.1. The sections that follow include descriptions of some of the new cmdlets you might find useful for your environment along with some usage examples.

DISM cmdlets

Deployment Image Servicing and Management (DISM) is a command-line platform you can use to mount and service Windows images for purposes of deployment. Windows Server 2012 introduced a DISM PowerShell module that contained 22 different cmdlets. Windows Server 2012 R2 expands the DISM module with more cmdlets including the following ones for managing various aspects of Windows image (.wim) files.

Add-WindowsImage

The Add-WindowsImage cmdlet adds an additional image to an existing image (.wim) file. Add-WindowsImage compares new files to the resources in the existing .wim file, specified by the Name parameter and the ImagePath parameter, and stores only a single copy of each unique file so that each file is only captured once. The .wim file can have only one assigned compression type. Therefore, you can only append files with the same compression type.

The Add-WindowsImage cmdlet does not apply to virtual hard disk (VHD) files.

> **IMPORTANT** It's important to note that you'll need to ensure you have enough disk space before you run Add-WindowsImage. If you run out of disk space while the image is being appended, you might corrupt the .wim file.

Here is an example:

```
PS C:\>Add-WindowsImage -ImagePath c:\imagestore\custom.wim -CapturePath d:\ -Name
"Drive D"
```

This command adds files from d:\"Drive D" to the existing image at c:\imagestore\custom.wim.

Expand-WindowsImage

The Expand-WindowsImage cmdlet applies an image to a specified location. This cmdlet does not apply to VHD files.

Here is an example:

```
PS C:\>Expand-WindowsImage -ImagePath c:\imagestore\custom.wim -ApplyPath d:\ -Index 1
```

This command adds files from d:\"Drive D" to the existing image at c:\imagestore\custom.wim.

Export-WindowsImage

The Export-WindowsImage cmdlet exports a copy of the specified image to another image file. The source and destination files must use the same compression type.

You can also optimize an image by exporting to a new image file with Export-WindowsImage. When you modify an image, DISM stores additional resource files that increase the overall size of the image. Exporting the image will remove unnecessary resource files.

This cmdlet does not apply to VHD files.

Here is an example:

```
PS C:\>Export-WindowsImage -SourceImagePath C:\imagestore\custom.wim -SourceIndex 1
-DestinationImagePath c:\imagestore\export.wim -DestinationName "Exported Image"
```

This command exports the image at Index 1 of the file C:\imagestore\custom.wim to the file c:\imagestore\export.wim with the name Exported Image.

Get-WindowsImageContent

The Get-WindowsImageContent cmdlet displays a list of the files and folders in a specified image. This cmdlet does not apply to VHD files.

Here is an example:

```
PS C:\>Get-WindowsImageContent -ImagePath c:\imagestore\install.wim -Index 1
```

This command lists the files and folders in the first image in c:\imagestore\install.wim.

New-WindowsImage

The New-WindowsImage cmdlet captures an image of a drive to a new WIM file. Captured directories include all subfolders and data. You cannot capture an empty directory. A directory must contain at least one file. This cmdlet does not apply to VHD files.

Here is an example:

```
PS C:\>New-WindowsImage -ImagePath c:\imagestore\custom.wim -CapturePath d:\ -Name
"Drive D"
```

This command captures the Drive D image in the WIM file located on d:\ and saves to the file c:\imagestore\custom.wim.

Remove-WindowsImage

The Remove-WindowsImage cmdlet deletes the specified volume image from a WIM file that has multiple volume images. This cmdlet deletes only the metadata entries and XML entries. It does not delete the stream data and does not optimize the WIM file. This command-line option does not apply to VHD files.

Here is an example:

```
PS C:\>Remove-WindowsImage -ImagePath c:\imagestore\custom.wim -Index 1 -CheckIntegrity
```

This command removes the first image in c:\imagestore\custom.wim.

Split-WindowsImage

This option creates the .swm files in the specified directory, naming each file the same as the specified path_to_swm, but with an appended number. For example, if you set path_to_swm as c:\Data.swm, this option creates a Data.swm file, a Data2.swm file, a Data3.swm file, and so on, defining each portion of the split .wim file and saving it to the C:\ directory.

If a single file is larger than the value specified in the -FileSize parameter, one of the split .swm files that results will be larger than the value specified in the -FileSize parameter, in order to accommodate the large file.

This cmdlet does not apply to VHD files.

Here is an example:

```
PS C:\>Split-WindowsImage -ImagePath c:\imagestore\install.wim -SplitImagePath c:\
imagestore\splitfiles\split.swm -FileSize 1024 -CheckIntegrity
```

This command uses the image from c:\imagestore\install.wim to create a split.swm file, a split2.swm file, a split3.swm file, and so on, defining each portion of the split .wim file with a maximum size of 1024 MB and saving it to the C:\imagestore\splitfiles\ directory.

DHCP server cmdlets

Windows Server 2012 introduced the ability to configure and manage your Dynamic Host Configuration Protocol (DHCP) servers using Windows PowerShell. This capability has been enhanced in several ways in Windows Server 2012 R2.

Multicast support

New cmdlets have been added that allow you to configure and manage multicast scopes, exclusions, leases, and statistics for DHCP servers running Windows Server 2012 R2. The new cmdlets for this functionality include:

- Add-DhcpServerv4MulticastExclusionRange
- Add-DhcpServerv4MulticastScope
- Get-DhcpServerv4MulticastExclusionRange
- Get-DhcpServerv4MulticastLease
- Get-DhcpServerv4MulticastScope
- Get-DhcpServerv4MulticastScopeStatistics
- Remove-DhcpServerv4MulticastExclusionRange
- Remove-DhcpServerv4MulticastLease
- Remove-DhcpServerv4MulticastScope
- Set-DhcpServerv4MulticastScope

You can use the Get-Help cmdlet on Windows Server 2012 R2 to display additional information about these new cmdlets.

DNS credentials management

New cmdlets have been added that allow you to configure and manage the credentials a DHCP server uses to register or deregister client records on a DNS server. The new cmdlets for this functionality are:

- Get-DhcpServerDnsCredential
- Remove-DhcpServerDnsCredential
- Set-DhcpServerDnsCredential

You can use the Get-Help cmdlet on Windows Server 2012 R2 to display additional information about these new cmdlets.

Add-DhcpServerSecurityGroup

The Add-DhcpServerSecurityGroup cmdlet adds security groups to the DHCP server. The cmdlet adds the DHCP Users and DHCP Administrators security groups.

Here is an example:

```
PS C:\> Add-DhcpServerSecurityGroup -ComputerName "DhcpServer03.Contoso.com"
```

This command adds the security groups DHCP Users and DHCP Administrators to the DHCP server named DhcpServer03.Contoso.com.

Repair-DhcpServerv4IPRecord

The Repair-DhcpServerv4IPRecord cmdlet reconciles inconsistent DHCP lease records in the database for the DHCP Server service for the specified DHCP scopes. Specify the ReportOnly parameter to view the inconsistent records without repairs.

Here is an example:

```
PS C:\> Repair-DhcpServerv4IPRecord -ScopeId 10.10.10.0 -ReportOnly
```

This command gets inconsistent DHCP client records for the scope 10.10.10.0. The command specifies the ReportOnly parameter. Unlike the previous example, this command makes no changes to inconsistent records.

DNS server cmdlets

Windows Server 2012 added extensive Windows PowerShell support for configuring and managing DNS servers. Several new cmdlets have been added to the DNS Server module in Windows Server 2012 R2. These new cmdlets are designed to help you configure and manage DNSSEC in your DNS server environment. The new cmdlets for this functionality include:

- Add-DnsServerSigningKey
- Disable-DnsServerSigningKeyRollover
- Enable-DnsServerSigningKeyRollover
- Get-DnsServerSigningKey
- Invoke-DnsServerSigningKeyRollover
- Remove-DnsServerSigningKey
- Set-DnsServerSigningKey
- Step-DnsServerSigningKeyRollover

You can use the Get-Help cmdlet on Windows Server 2012 R2 to display additional information about these new cmdlets.

Hardware certification cmdlets

New in Windows PowerShell 4.0 are cmdlets relating to the Windows Hardware Certification Kit (HCK). These cmdlets can be used to create HCK project definition files and test collection files, create test summary reports, merge test results in different ways, and export/import test collections in XML format. The new cmdlets for this functionality include:

- Export-HwCertTestCollectionToXml
- Import-HwCertTestCollectionFromXml
- Merge-HwCertTestCollectionFromHckx
- Merge-HwCertTestCollectionFromXml
- New-HwCertProjectDefinitionFile
- New-HwCertTestCollection
- New-HwCertTestCollectionExcelReport

You can search Microsoft TechNet if you need more information about these cmdlets.

Hyper-V cmdlets

There are several new cmdlets you can use for managing various aspects of a Hyper-V environment running on Windows Server 2012 R2. The sections that follow include descriptions of some of the new cmdlets you might find useful for your environment along with some usage examples.

Test-VMNetworkAdapter

The Test-VMNetworkAdapter cmdlet tests connectivity between virtual machines by using Internet Control Message Protocol (ICMP) Ping packets. Ping verifies IP-level connectivity to another TCP/IP computer by sending ICMP Echo Request messages.

Here is an example:

```
PS C:\> Test-VMNetworkAdapter –VMName "ContosoVM01" –Receiver –SenderIPAddress
"10.20.20.5" –ReceiverIPAddress "10.20.20.6" –VMNetworkAdapterName "ContosoNic01"
```

This command tests connectivity by using the virtual network adapter named ContosoNic01. The command targets the receiver virtual machine.

Virtual machine firmware cmdlets

The following cmdlets can be used to view or modify the firmware configuration of virtual machines:

- Get-VMFirmware
- Set-VMFirmware

Virtual network adapter isolation cmdlets

The following cmdlets can be used to view or modify the isolation settings for virtual network adapters:

- Get-VmNetworkAdapterIsolation
- Set-VmNetworkAdapterIsolation

Virtual network adapter routing domains

The following cmdlets can be used to configure and manage routing domains and virtual subnets for virtual network adapters:

- Add-VmNetworkAdapterRoutingDomainMapping
- Get-VMNetworkAdapterRoutingDomainMapping
- Remove-VMNetworkAdapterRoutingDomainMapping
- Set-VmNetworkAdapterRoutingDomainMapping

Copy-VMFile

The Copy-VMFile cmdlet can be used to copy files to virtual machines.

Debug-VM

The Debug-VM cmdlet debugs a virtual machine. This deserves more explanation, so let's hear now from another one of our insiders at Microsoft concerning this cmdlet.

Windows Server 2012 R2 Hyper-V and debugging virtual machines

Debugging operating systems and applications running on them is always an important part of software development lifecycle management, particularly when dealing with operating system or kernel mode driver issues. There also could be situations during troubleshooting when a snapshot of a system's state and the contents of its memory in the form of a full or kernel memory dump of the operating system might be required.

On a Windows Server operating system running directly on hardware, administrators and developers have used hardware NMI (Non-Maskable Interrupt), Keyboard "Right Ctrl+Scroll+Scroll," or Live Debug using Remote Null Mode and 1394 (Firewire) cable techniques to freeze the operating system in time and generate a Kernel or Full System Memory dump. NMI is usually a useful troubleshooting method when a system is completely unresponsive and software crash dump or other methods could not be leveraged at all. This is particularly useful for diagnosing systems that have deadlocked due to kernel or user mode components.

When running workloads in Hyper-V virtual machines, the same need for generating memory dumps arises from time to time and administrators might need to initiate some sort of memory dump during troubleshooting, Kernel mode application, or driver development process.

Using windbg

One method that has been available in Hyper-V since the first release has been the use of windbg (Debugging Tools for Windows) over virtual COM port name pipe and using the ".dump /f" to generate a full memory dump. This method is very similar to Remote Debugging using Null Mode or Firewire cable in the physical environment, and there are requirements to have the debug settings configured in the virtual machine's BCD (Boot Configuration Data) store and to attach the debugger during the boot. This also could incur an extended outage to the services running on the virtual machine while the debug session is active. Capturing memory dump also fully freezes the operating system and it might take a while (depends on the size of RAM in the virtual machine and if this is a Kernel memory dump or full memory dump) to transfer the memory dump over the cable to the remote debugger PC.

Please see the following blog post for more information: "Configuring a Hyper-V VM for Kernel Debugging" at *http://blogs.msdn.com/b/ntdebugging/archive/ 2011/12/30/configuring-a-hyper-v-vm-for-kernel-debugging.aspx*.

Using VM2DMP

Another utility that was published on MSDN and that has been used in the field is VM2DMP.exe (Hyper-V VM State to Memory Dump Converter), a command-line tool that converts the saved state of a Hyper-V virtual machine to a full memory dump file compatible with Debugging Tools for Windows. This utility that is compatible with Windows Server 2008 R2 could be used to convert the memory contents of a virtual machine at a point of time to a full memory dump file.

You can find the VM2DMP.exe tool at *http://archive.msdn.microsoft.com/vm2dmp*.

Using Debug-VM

With the release of Windows Server 2012 R2 Hyper-V and its extensive Windows PowerShell integration, there's a new Windows PowerShell cmdlet called Debug-VM that can inject NMI to the virtual machine from the local or remote PC, given the user has been granted local Hyper-V administrator privilege on the Windows Server 2012 R2 Hyper-V hosting that virtual machine.

The following examples are two different syntaxes that can be used;

```
Debug-VM -Name VMName [-ComputerName HostName] [-Force]
-InjectNonMaskableInterrupt
```

```
Debug-VM -VM VMName [-ComputerName HostName>] [-Force]
-InjectNonMaskableInterrupt
```

Here are three examples of using this command:

```
PS C:\> debug-vm -VM WS2012R2 -InjectNonMaskableInterrupt

PS C:\> debug-vm -Name WS2012R2 -InjectNonMaskableInterrupt

PS C:\> debug-vm -VM WS2012R2 -ComputerName HV-Dev-2630.contoso.com
-InjectNonMaskableInterrupt -Force
```

Executing this cmdlet against a virtual machine or set of virtual machines will initiate a memory dump of the system and, depending on the debug settings of the operating system, a respective memory dump could be collected upon the virtual machine restart. The following is an example of the Windows Server 2012 R2 Virtual Machine console after sending the NMI command via Debug-VM cmdlet:

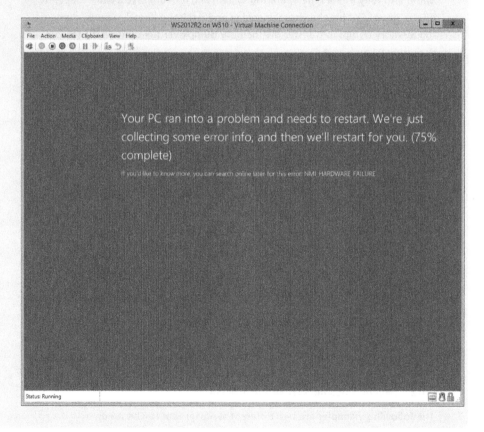

NMI support and Linux virtual machines on Hyper-V

With the wide range of Linux virtual machine support on Windows Server 2012 R2 Hyper-V, if a Linux system enters a complete unresponsive state, administrators and developers can panic the system by using the Debug-VM cmdlet. The syntax is exactly the same as mentioned above for Linux virtual machines.

In order to check successful execution within the Linux virtual machine, you may run the following command inside the terminal:

```
Localhost:~ # cat /proc/interrupts|grep NMI
                1        Non-maskable interrupts
```

For more information, see the blog post "Enabling Linux Support on Windows Server 2012 R2 Hyper-V" at *http://blogs.technet.com/b/virtualization/archive/2013/07/24/enabling-linux-support-on-windows-server-2012-r2-hyper-v.aspx*.

Ideally, kernel or complete memory dump file debugging should be the last resort after all the standard troubleshooting methods have been exhausted. Instantiating this process on a production server could be harmful and extreme care must be used. Since you do not have to make any registry changes or reboots to enable this behavior inside Windows Server 2012 R2, please make sure to try these commands only on test and exposable virtual machines unless you've been instructed by Microsoft Support and you are aware of its consequences.

Mark Gehazi
Data Center Specialist, US-SLG STU Infrastructure

iSCSI target cmdlets

Several new cmdlets have been added in Windows Server 2012 R2 to make configuring and managing Internet Small Computer System Interface (iSCSI) target servers and iSCSI virtual disks easier. The new cmdlets for this functionality include:

- Export-IscsiTargetServerConfiguration
- Import-IscsiTargetServerConfiguration
- Resize-IscsiVirtualDisk
- Stop-IscsiVirtualDiskOperation

You can use the Get-Help cmdlet on Windows Server 2012 R2 to display additional information about these new cmdlets.

Net TCP/IP cmdlets

Three new cmdlets have been added in Windows Server 2012 R2 for performing various Net TCP/IP-specific tasks:

- Get-NetCompartment
- Test-NetConnection
- Find-NetRoute

You can use the Get-Help cmdlet on Windows Server 2012 R2 to display additional information about these new cmdlets.

Network Address Translation cmdlets

Windows Server 2012 R2 has some new cmdlets you can use for managing various aspects of a Network Address Translation (NAT) environment. The cmdlets for this functionality are:

- Add-NetNatExternalAddress
- Add-NetNatStaticMapping
- Disable-NetNatTransitionConfiguration
- Enable-NetNatTransitionConfiguration
- Get-NetNat
- Get-NetNatExternalAddress
- Get-NetNatGlobal
- Get-NetNatSession
- Get-NetNatStaticMapping
- Get-NetNatTransitionConfiguration
- Get-NetNatTransitionMonitoring
- New-NetNat
- New-NetNatTransitionConfiguration
- Remove-NetNat
- Remove-NetNatExternalAddress
- Remove-NetNatStaticMapping
- Remove-NetNatTransitionConfiguration
- Set-NetNat
- Set-NetNatGlobal
- Set-NetNatTransitionConfiguration

Network event packet capture cmdlets

Windows Server 2012 R2 has a number of new cmdlets you can use for managing network packet filtering. For a list of the cmdlets available, type the following command:

```
Get-Command *NetEvent*
```

Network Virtualization cmdlets

Windows Server 2012 R2 adds Windows PowerShell support for configuring and managing a Network Virtualization environment. The cmdlets for this functionality are:

- Get-NetVirtualizationCustomerRoute
- Get-NetVirtualizationGlobal
- Get-NetVirtualizationLookupRecord
- Get-NetVirtualizationProviderAddress
- Get-NetVirtualizationProviderRoute
- New-NetVirtualizationCustomerRoute
- New-NetVirtualizationLookupRecord
- New-NetVirtualizationProviderAddress
- New-NetVirtualizationProviderRoute
- Remove-NetVirtualizationCustomerRoute
- Remove-NetVirtualizationLookupRecord
- Remove-NetVirtualizationProviderAddress
- Remove-NetVirtualizationProviderRoute
- Select-NetVirtualizationNextHop
- Set-NetVirtualizationCustomerRoute
- Set-NetVirtualizationGlobal
- Set-NetVirtualizationLookupRecord
- Set-NetVirtualizationProviderAddress
- Set-NetVirtualizationProviderRoute

You can use the Get-Help cmdlet on Windows Server 2012 R2 to display additional information about these new cmdlets.

Physical Computer System View (PCSV) cmdlets

New in Windows Server 2012 R2 are some cmdlets you can use for remotely managing certain aspects of Intelligent Platform Management Interface (IPMI) and Web Services-Management (WSMAN) devices. The cmdlets for this functionality are:

- Get-PcsvDevice
- Restart-PcsvDevice
- Set-PcsvDeviceBootConfiguration
- Start-PcsvDevice
- Stop-PcsvDevice

You can use the Get-Help cmdlet on Windows Server 2012 R2 to display additional information about these new cmdlets.

Software Inventory Logging cmdlets

Windows Server 2012 R2 adds some cmdlets you can use for managing Software Inventory Logging. The cmdlets for this functionality are:

- Get-SilComputer
- Get-SilData
- Get-SilLogging
- Get-SilSoftware
- Get-SilUalAccess
- Get-SilWindowsUpdate
- Publish-SilData
- Set-SilLogging
- Start-SilLogging
- Stop-SilLogging

Start screen cmdlets

Administrators who need to be able to customize the Start screen on Windows 8.1 and Windows Server 2012 R2 will be glad to learn about the following new cmdlets.

Export-StartLayout

The Export-StartLayout cmdlet exports the layout of the Start screen of the current user. You can export layout as an .xml file to verify the layout, or you can export layout as a .bin file to modify the layout of an existing Windows image. Specify the appropriate file name extension, .bin or .xml, in the name of the file. To modify the layout of a Windows image, export the layout as a .bin file, and then import it into a Windows image by using the Import-StartLayout cmdlet.

Here is an example:

```
PS C:\> Export-StartLayout -Path "C:\Layouts\Marketing.bin" -As BIN
```

This command exports the layout of the Start screen to a file named Marketing.bin in the C:\Layouts folder. The command specifies a value of BIN for the As parameter, so the cmdlet creates a .bin file.

Import-StartLayout

The Import-StartLayout cmdlet imports the layout of the Start screen into a mounted Windows image. When you import a layout, it replaces the existing layout of the Start screen. Before you use this cmdlet, mount the Windows image file to import the layout into.

Use the Export-StartLayout cmdlet to create a .bin file, and then use this cmdlet to import that file. You must have administrator rights to import a layout.

The Export-StartLayout cmdlet also exports layouts as .xml files, but this cmdlet imports only .bin files.

Here is an example:

```
PS C:\> Import-StartLayout -LayoutPath "Layout.bin" -MountPath "E:\MountedImage" -WhatIf
```

This command validates the layout file and the Windows image by using the WhatIf parameter. Besides that parameter, the command is the same as the previous example, but this command makes no changes.

Get-StartApps

The Get-StartApps cmdlet gets the names and AppIDs of apps in the Start screen of the current user. An AppID is an AppUserModelID. You can specify a particular app by using its name, or you can specify a name that includes the wildcard character (*). If you do not specify a name, the cmdlet displays all the apps from the Start screen.

Here is an example:

```
PS C:\> Get-StartApps
Name AppID
---- -----

A. Datum Pro Center Datum.ProCenter
Proseware Studio Proseware.Studio.5
A. Datum 2010 prog..tion_0000000000000000_ebec13db489e8ef9
Fabrikam Initializer Fabrikam.Initializer.1
A. Datum Connector Contoso.Datum.Connector
Proseware Design Pro Proseware.Design.3
```

This command gets all the names and IDs of apps in the Start screen for the current user.

Windows Deployment Services cmdlets

Windows Server 2012 R2 now has cmdlets you can use for managing Windows Deployment Services. This improvement will definitely help administrators who deploy Windows images using Windows Deployment Services. The cmdlets for this functionality are:

- Add-WdsDriverPackage
- Approve-WdsClient
- Copy-WdsInstallImage
- Deny-WdsClient
- Disable-WdsBootImage
- Disable-WdsDriverPackage
- Disable-WdsInstallImage
- Disconnect-WdsMulticastClient
- Enable-WdsBootImage
- Enable-WdsDriverPackage
- Enable-WdsInstallImage
- Export-WdsBootImage
- Export-WdsInstallImage
- Get-WdsBootImage
- Get-WdsClient
- Get-WdsDriverPackage
- Get-WdsInstallImage
- Get-WdsInstallImageGroup
- Get-WdsMulticastClient
- Import-WdsBootImage
- Import-WdsDriverPackage
- Import-WdsInstallImage
- New-WdsClient
- New-WdsInstallImageGroup
- Remove-WdsBootImage
- Remove-WdsClient
- Remove-WdsDriverPackage
- Remove-WdsInstallImage
- Remove-WdsInstallImageGroup
- Set-WdsBootImage
- Set-WdsClient

- Set-WdsInstallImage
- Set-WdsInstallImageGroup

You can use the Get-Help cmdlet on Windows Server 2012 R2 to display additional information about these new cmdlets.

Windows PowerShell Web Access cmdlets

If you use Windows PowerShell Web Access so you can manage the servers in your private cloud from anywhere, at any time, by running Windows PowerShell commands within a web-based console, you'll probably be glad to learn about the following new cmdlets in Windows Server 2012 R2:

- Add-PswaAuthorizationRule
- Get-PswaAuthorizationRule
- Install-PswaWebApplication
- Remove-PswaAuthorizationRule
- Test-PswaAuthorizationRule
- Uninstall-PswaWebApplication

Windows Search cmdlets

Windows Search is a powerful feature you can use for searching for the attributes and contents of documents, email messages, and much more. You can now use the following Windows PowerShell cmdlets to view or modify how Windows Search works.

Get-WindowsSearchSetting

This cmdlet gets the values of settings for Windows Search. Here is an example:

```
PS C:\> Get-WindowsSearchSetting
Setting                                       Value
-------                                       -----
EnableWebResultsSetting                       True
EnableMeteredWebResultsSetting                True
SearchExperience                              PersonalizedAndLocation
WindowsSafeSearchSetting                      Moderate
```

Set-WindowsSearchSetting

This cmdlet modifies values that control Windows Search. Here is an example:

```
Set-WindowsSearchSetting -SearchExperienceSetting "Personalized"
```

This command allows Windows Search to use search history, but not specific location of the user, to personalize results.

Learn more

You can learn more about the new capabilities in Windows PowerShell 4.0 on Windows Server 2012 R2 by checking out the following topics on Microsoft TechNet:

- "What's New in Windows PowerShell" at *http://technet.microsoft.com/library/ hh857339.aspx*.

- "Scripting with Windows PowerShell" at *http://technet.microsoft.com/en-us/library/ bb978526.aspx*.

- "Windows and Windows Server Automation with Windows PowerShell" at *http://technet.microsoft.com/en-us/library/dn249523.aspx*.

The following Microsoft TechNet and MSDN blog posts also have lots of information about the new Windows PowerShell features and enhancements in Windows Server 2012 R2:

- "DAL in Action: Introducing PCSV Cmdlets for Out-of-Band Management of Server Hardware" at *http://blogs.msdn.com/b/powershell/archive/2013/07/31/dal-in-action-introducing-pcsv-cmdlets-for-out-of-band-management-of-server-hardware.aspx*.

- "DAL in Action: Managing Network Switches Using PowerShell and CIM" at *http://blogs.msdn.com/b/powershell/archive/2013/07/31/dal-in-action-managing-network-switches-using-powershell-and-cim.aspx*.

Be sure also to check out the following videos from TechEd 2013 on Channel 9:

- "Desired State Configuration in Windows Server 2012 R2 PowerShell" at *http://channel9.msdn.com/Events/TechEd/NorthAmerica/2013/MDC-B302*.

- "Advanced Automation Using Windows PowerShell" at *http://channel9.msdn.com/ Events/TechEd/NorthAmerica/2013/MDC-B400*.

- "Windows PowerShell Unplugged" at *http://channel9.msdn.com/Events/TechEd/ NorthAmerica/2013/MDC-B340*.

CHAPTER 11

Windows Server Essentials

M icrosoft has strived to serve the computing needs of small business users over the years with a variety of offerings. Windows Small Business Server (SBS) was a popular product that went through several versions including 2003, 2008, and 2011. When Windows Server 2012 was released, Microsoft repositioned its small business offering by rebranding it as Windows Server 2012 Essentials and marketing it as an ideal first server for small businesses with up to 25 users. Windows Server 2012 Essentials was a cost-effective and easy-to-use solution to help protect data, organize and access business information from virtually anywhere, support the applications needed to run a business, and quickly connect to online services for email and backup.

The new version of this offering is Windows Server 2012 R2 Essentials and it's designed as a flexible, affordable, and easy-to-use server solution for small businesses and medium-sized businesses. It's also priced affordably in order to help businesses reduce costs and increase their productivity. And it can even be deployed as the primary server in a multiserver environment for small businesses.

Specifically, Windows Server Essentials is now available in two ways:

- As an Edition for Small Businesses that have up to 25 users and 50 devices
- As a server role in Windows Server 2012 R2 Standard edition for medium-sized businesses that have up to 100 users and 200 devices

In addition, both forms of Windows Server Essentials can be deployed in either a physical or virtual environment.

To learn more about this latest version of Windows Server Essentials, let's go to the source now and hear directly from the Windows Server Essentials team at Microsoft.

Introducing Windows Server 2012 R2 Essentials

L ess than a year ago we introduced Windows Server 2012 Essentials to the market. Since then, the team has been working really hard to put forward a great release for Windows Server 2012 R2 Essentials that further builds on the value that Windows Server Essentials brings to small businesses. In addition to being a great primary server for small businesses, we've made some major investments in Windows Server 2012 R2 Essentials that allows the experience that Windows Server Essentials offers to scale to larger, more diverse topologies. We've also made investments to help our small and medium businesses (SMB customers) to more easily virtualize their environments, as well as provide super simple access to the cloud through deep integration with Microsoft Office 365 and Windows Azure. This sidebar describes some of the many improvements introduced in Windows Server 2012 R2 Essentials.

Virtualization made easy

Virtualization continues to be a popular trend in enterprise computing; however, adoption by SMBs is not as aggressive. One of the reasons SMBs are hesitant to move to virtualization has to do with the complexity of properly configuring and managing virtual instances of the operating system.

With Windows Server 2012 R2 Essentials, we have addressed the problem by enabling the virtualization of a Windows Server Essentials guest VM on a Windows Server Essentials host server. This can be set up manually by the administrator or, depending on your OEM configuration, a simple wizard will guide you through the process of setting up the guest VM during the installation process of the server. All of the setup, configuration, and connection to your Essentials server from client PCs is made to the guest virtual machine.

Running Windows Server 2012 R2 Essentials in the cloud

With the availability of Windows Azure Virtual Machines, you can deploy your own customized Windows Server 2012 R2 Essentials image into a **commercially backed SLA** production environment in minutes.

Although this ability has been available previously, with the introduction of Windows Server 2012 R2 Essentials, configuration options are available to deliver an optimized experience in a hosted deployment. Specifically, features such as client backup and storage spaces are turned off by default because moving large amounts of data across the Internet may be slow and costly.

These configuration settings are not only for Windows Azure–hosted deployments, but also for private hosted deployments. Windows Server 2012 R2 Essentials is designed to work with the Windows Azure Pack, enabling service providers to provide hosted solutions that are easy to deploy and maintain.

In addition, when you are running Windows Server Essentials in the cloud, you can use BranchCache to cache files locally to reduce traffic between the cloud and your local office. Enabling this BranchCache functionality in Windows Server Essentials is as easy as flipping a switch.

Integration with cloud services

In Windows Server 2012 Essentials, we did deep integration with cloud services to provide seamless access for daily administrative tasks. Our goal was to keep a consistent user experience for the administrator and avoid the jarring experience of switching from one administration console (the Dashboard) to a completely different one—typically a separate web portal. By keeping the experience within the Dashboard as much as possible, we not only provide ease of use for the administrator, but also save time by surfacing only the key tasks needed for the service as shown here:

In many cases, SMB customers are not even aware of the cloud services that are offered by Microsoft that can help them simplify their businesses. In Windows Server 2012 R2 Essentials, we have added a services integration status page that shows you not only what services are available, but also whether your server is attached to these services.

One of the things you'll notice in the screenshot above is that in addition to services previously available, some new services are integrated as well. The following are some of the new services and key features available with Windows Server 2012 R2 Essentials.

WINDOWS AZURE ACTIVE DIRECTORY

Windows Azure Active Directory is a service that provides identity and access capabilities for on-premises and cloud applications. Integrating Windows Azure Active Directory with Essentials enables SMBs to have single sign-on and password synchronization between the local Active Directory and cloud services such as Office 365.

Additionally, we have enabled user group management directly from the Dashboard, and by using Windows Azure Active Directory integration, these groups are synchronized as well as the user accounts.

MICROSOFT OFFICE 365

Whereas the integration of Office 365 in Windows Server 2012 Essentials was a great step forward, with Windows Server 2012 R2 Essentials we wanted to continue to enhance the experience by providing even deeper integration. As I mentioned earlier, a key goal for the new release was to expand beyond small business to SMB. When you move from an environment of fewer than 25 users to potentially hundreds of users, new challenges surface that need to be addressed.

To help make these management challenges easier, we have integrated the following Office 365 features in the Dashboard:

- **Distribution Groups**   The ability to create and manage email distribution groups

- **Mobile Device Management**   The ability to manage mobile devices connected to the Office 365 service, enabling remote wipe, policy enforcement, and access management (see the screenshot below)

- **SharePoint Online Library Management**   The ability to create and manage SharePoint libraries

WINDOWS INTUNE

Windows Intune is a cloud-based solution for managing your organization's PCs, including device management for multiple operating system platform devices, security management for software patch distribution and endpoint protection, and management of application distribution for bring your own devices (BYOD).

In Windows Server 2012 R2 Essentials, integration with Windows Intune enables the administrator to manage users, security groups, and licenses for Windows Intune services right from within the Dashboard.

WINDOWS AZURE BACKUP

Previously known as Windows Azure Online Backup, the ability to back up your server's key data to Windows Azure cloud storage was made available as an add-in in Windows Server 2012 Essentials. In Windows Server 2012 R2 Essentials, the Windows Azure Backup add-in is now surfaced on the services integration tab of the Dashboard as shown here:

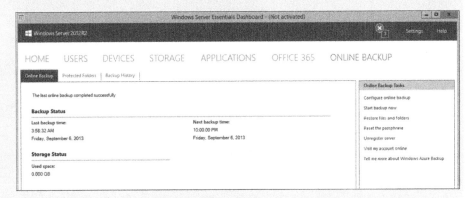

The Windows Server Essentials Experience server role

Consistent feedback we heard from customers and partners was why some of the features unique to Windows Server Essentials were, in fact, unique. Why not make these features available in the Windows Server Standard and Datacenter editions?

It's a great question and one that we took seriously. One of the challenges of doing this, however, was the fact that some of our specific features require dependent roles and services in Windows Server that take additional overhead on the system. Enabling these by default on every server running Windows Server was not the right thing to do out of the box. We have solved this dilemma in Windows Server 2012 R2 with the addition of the Windows Server Essentials Experience server role shown here:

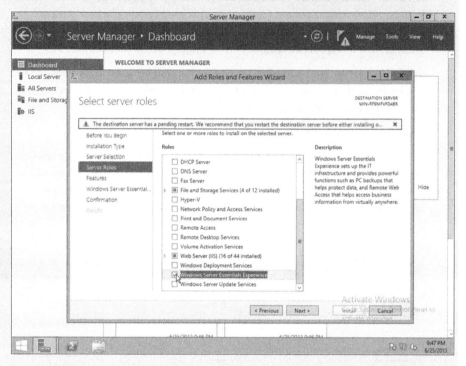

In the Standard and Datacenter editions of Windows Server 2012 R2, administrators who want the full features and functionality of Windows Server Essentials will be able to add a new server role to the system called the Windows Server Essentials Experience.

The Windows Server Essentials Experience server role enables all the features and dependent services and roles of the Windows Server 2012 R2 Essentials edition, without the locks and limits that are in place for the edition. Enabling or disabling the Windows Server Essentials Experience role is as simple as turning it on or off in Server Manager.

This change enables not only an easy upgrade path for small businesses that want more flexibility, but also offers the following benefits:

- The flexibility to implement a Standard or Datacenter edition server running the Windows Server Essentials Experience role as a domain member rather than as the root domain controller.

- The ability to add the Windows Server Essentials Experience to an existing domain environment that already has multiple servers running Windows Server.

- Running the Standard or Datacenter edition gives you all the features and licensing rights of the operating system (such as expanded virtualization rights and larger hardware configurations).

Empowering remote workers and BYOD

With the continuing trend of mobile PCs outselling desktop PCs, as well as double-digit tablet and smartphone growth, ensuring that multiple devices can easily connect to the Windows Server 2012 R2 Essentials server regardless of location is key.

In addition, touch as a primary input mechanism while on the go is becoming a requirement rather than a luxury. As such, we have made significant new investments in two key areas that are already available today with Windows Server 2012 Essentials: My Server apps for Windows Phone and Windows 8, and Remote Web Access.

MY SERVER APPS FOR WINDOWS PHONE AND WINDOWS

With Windows Small Business Server 2011 Essentials, we introduced the My Server application for Windows Phone 7. With Windows Server 2012 Essentials, we added the My Server app for Windows 8 and Windows RT. We've seen a tremendous number of downloads of these great applications and will continue to update them both for the next release to support key new features such as Microsoft SharePoint Online libraries.

For example, you can access files and folders on your server by using the My Server
Windows Phone application:

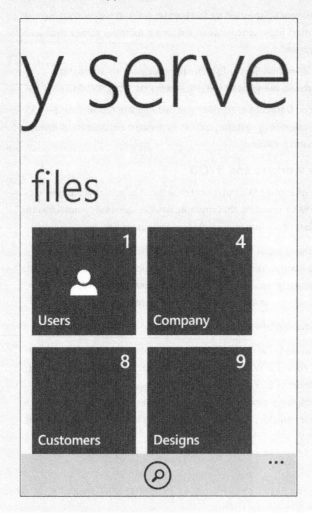

You can manage users, devices, and alerts by using the My Server Windows Phone application:

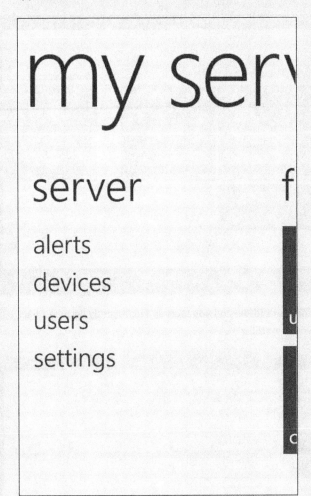

You can also manage alerts and access shared folders on the server by using the My Server Windows Store application:

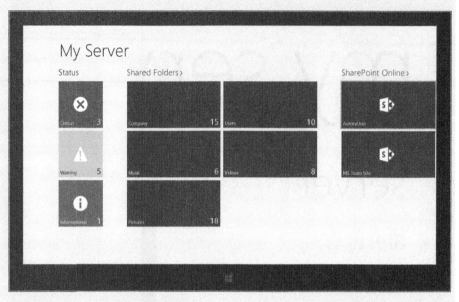

And you can even access files and folders on your server. The recently accessed files are available even when you are offline:

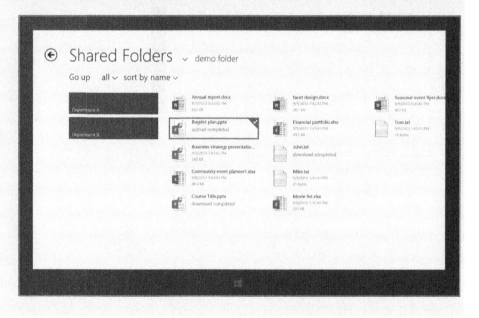

MODERNIZED REMOTE WEB ACCESS

Remote Web Access (RWA) enables users and administrators to access data and connect to computers running in their office network from any Internet browser. The RWA interface that ships with Windows Server 2012 Essentials, although very functional, is not optimized for touch devices. With Windows Server 2012 R2 Essentials, we have completely overhauled the interface to be touch-optimized, as well as leveraging HTML5 rather than Silverlight, enabling a consistent experience across any HTML5-compliant browser.

Improved Connector software

The Connector software connects the client PCs on your network to your Windows Server Essentials server in order to automatically back up the PCs and monitor their health. The Connector also allows you to configure and remotely administer your Windows Server Essentials server. In Windows Server 2012 R2 Essentials, the Connector has been improved in the following ways:

- Its performance has been significantly improved by reducing memory and CPU usage.
- It can be installed and configured on a client PC regardless of where it is located.
- It provides auto-dial virtual private network (VPN) connectivity to domain-joined PCs in order to provide a seamless remote working experience just as if the user is in the office.

Protecting data on the client

In the previous release of Windows Server 2012 Essentials, we centralized the File History management to better protect the important data on the client PCs. In Windows Server 2012 R2 Essentials, we further improved this by providing a quick restore feature to help you more easily replace a PC and restore all the profile data to a new PC.

We also made client full system restore easier. With more and more PCs now selling without a DVD drive, restoring a PC with a DVD is not possible on some models. The new Client Full System Restore capability supported by Windows Deployment Services now allows you to boot a client PC to the network and quickly perform a full system restore on it. This means that you no longer need to maintain hard copies of your restore environment on a DVD or a USB bootable drive.

Conclusion

This sidebar has described a few of the many improvements introduced in Windows Server 2012 R2 Essentials. But there are lots of other enhancements we unfortunately don't have space to describe in detail here, such as the new BranchCache integration functionality, the improved File History feature, support for deploying Windows Server Essentials on a member server in a domain, support for creating user groups (and Office 365 distribution groups if your server is integrated with Office 365), improved client deployment options, and much more. For a full list of new features and enhancements, see the TechNet article "What's New in Windows Server 2012 R2 Essentials" referenced in the Learn More section below.

Jason Anderson
Group Program Manager with the Windows Server Essentials team

Learn more

You can learn more about the new Windows Server Essentials features and enhancements in Windows Server 2012 R2 by checking out the following topics on Microsoft TechNet:

- "What's New in Windows Server 2012 R2 Essentials" at *http://technet.microsoft.com/en-us/library/dn303448.aspx.*

- "Windows Server Essentials" at *http://technet.microsoft.com/en-us/sbs/jj159331.aspx.*

The following Microsoft TechNet and MSDN blog posts also have lots of information about the new Windows Server Essentials features and enhancements in Windows Server 2012 R2:

- "Understanding Licensing for Windows Server 2012 R2 Essentials and the Windows Server Essentials Experience role" at *http://blogs.technet.com/b/sbs/archive/2013/09/03/understanding-licensing-for-windows-server-2012-r2-essentials-and-the-windows-server-essentials-experience-role.aspx.*

Additional resources

The following additional resources can be used to learn more about Windows Server 2012 R2:

- Download Windows Server 2012 R2 from the TechNet Evaluation Center at *http://technet.microsoft.com/en-us/evalcenter/bb291020.aspx*

- Windows Server 2012 R2 on the Microsoft Server and Cloud Platform at *http://www.microsoft.com/en-us/server-cloud/windows-server/windows-server-2012-r2.aspx*

- What's New in Windows Server 2012 R2 in the TechNet Library at *http://technet.microsoft.com/en-us/library/dn250019.aspx*

- See also the Windows Server Blog on TechNet at *http://blogs.technet.com/b/windowsserver/*

- You can find videos and slide decks about Windows Server 2012 R2 from Microsoft TechEd North America 2013 on Channel 9 at *http://channel9.msdn.com/Events/TechEd/NorthAmerica/2013*

- Post your questions about Windows Server 2012 R2 to the Windows Server forums on TechNet at *http://social.technet.microsoft.com/Forums/windowsserver/en-US/home?category=windowsserver*

Index

Symbols and Numbers

.wim files, 186–187

A

access control
    multi-factor, 127
    role-based, 108–110
activation
    dynamic site, 155–156
activation, virtual machine, 11–12
Active Directory
    detached clustering, 82
    enhancements in Windows Server 2012, 124
    Kerberos authentication, 146–148
    LDAP search performance, 131–135
    multi-factor access control, 127
    Web Application Proxy, 127–131
    Windows Azure, 206
    Work Folders in, 53
    Workplace Join, 125–126
Active Directory Administrative Center (ADAC), 124
Active Directory Certificate Services (AD CS), 123
Active Directory Domain Services (AD DS),
    112, 123, 131–135
Active Directory Federation Services (AD FS),
    123, 127, 130
Active Directory Lightweight Directory Services
    (AD LDS), 123
Active Directory Rights Management Services
    (AD RMS), 123
AD CS (Active Directory Certificate Services), 123
AD DS (Active Directory Domain Services),
    112, 123, 131–135

AD FS (Active Directory Federation Services),
    123, 127, 130
AD LDS (Active Directory Lightweight Directory
    Services), 123
AD RMS (Active Directory Rights Management
    Services), 123
ADAC (Active Directory Administrative Center), 124
Add-DhcpServerSecurityGroup cmdlet, 190
address assignment, 114
address filtering, 154
Address Hash, 93, 95–96
address management. *See* IP Address
    Management (IPAM)
address translation, 196
Add-WindowsImage cmdlet, 186–187
administrators
    access to user files, 57
    use of Work Folders, 51
aliases, 55
Anderson, Jason, 214
Application Initialization, 154, 156
application pools, 154, 157
apps
    group policy settings, 144–145, 150
    My Server, 209–212
    publishing, 130–131
    Start Screen view, 143
    Window Store, 150
architecture
    extensible switch, 119–120
    Hyper-V extensible switch, 115–117
    IP Address Management (IPAM), 109
    private cloud solution, 30–31
authentication. *See also* preauthentication
    compound, 146–147
    device, 125, 127
    multi-factor, 127

M

N

O

P

About the author

MITCH TULLOCH is a well-known expert on Windows Server administration and virtualization. He has published hundreds of articles on a wide variety of technology sites and has written or contributed to over two dozen books, including the *Windows 7 Resource Kit* (Microsoft Press, 2009), for which he was lead author; *Understanding Microsoft Virtualization Solutions: From the Desktop to the Datacenter* (Microsoft Press, 2010); and *Introducing Windows Server 2012* (Microsoft Press, 2012), a free e-book that has been downloaded almost three quarters of a million times.

Mitch has been repeatedly awarded Most Valuable Professional (MVP) status by Microsoft for his outstanding contributions to supporting the global IT community. He is a nine-time MVP in the technology area of Windows Server Software Packaging, Deployment & Servicing. You can find his MVP Profile page at *http://mvp.microsoft.com/en-us/mvp/Mitch%20Tulloch-21182*.

Mitch is also Senior Editor of WServerNews (*http://www.wservernews. com*), a weekly newsletter focused on system admin and security issues for the Windows Servers platform. With more than 100,000 IT Pro subscribers worldwide, WServerNews is the largest Windows Server–focused newsletter in the world.

Mitch runs an IT content development business based in Winnipeg, Canada that produces white papers and other collateral for the business decision maker (BDM) and technical decision maker (TDM) audiences. His published content ranges from white papers about Microsoft cloud technologies to reviews of third-party products designed for the Windows Server platform. Before starting his own business in 1998. Mitch worked as a Microsoft Certified Trainer (MCT) for Productivity Point.

For more information about Mitch, visit his website at *http://www.mtit.com*.

You can also follow Mitch on Twitter at *http://twitter.com/mitchtulloch* or like him on Facebook at *http://www.facebook.com/mitchtulloch*

Now that you've read the book...

Tell us what you think!

Was it useful?
Did it teach you what you wanted to learn?
Was there room for improvement?

Let us know at http://aka.ms/tellpress

Your feedback goes directly to the staff at Microsoft Press,
and we read every one of your responses. Thanks in advance!

 Microsoft

Lightning Source UK Ltd.
Milton Keynes UK
UKOW06f0831081113

220548UK00002B/6/P